SHAKESPEARE'S CLOWN

Actor and text in
the Elizabethan playhouse

DAVID WILES

Lecturer in drama and theatre studies,
Royal Holloway and Bedford New College, University of London

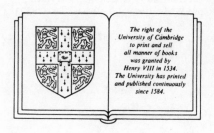

The right of the
University of Cambridge
to print and sell
all manner of books
was granted by
Henry VIII in 1534.
The University has printed
and published continuously
since 1584.

CAMBRIDGE UNIVERSITY PRESS

Cambridge
New York   New Rochelle
Melbourne   Sydney

Published by the Press Syndicate of the University of Cambridge
The Pitt Building, Trumpington Street, Cambridge CB2 1RP
32 East 57th Street, New York, NY 10022, USA
10 Stamford Road, Oakleigh, Melbourne 3166, Australia

First published 1987
Reprinted 1988 (twice)

Printed in Great Britain by the
Athenaeum Press Ltd, Newcastle upon Tyne

British Library cataloguing in publication data
Wiles, David
Shakespeare's clown: actor and text in
the Elizabethan playhouse.
1. Shakespeare, William - Characters -
Fools   2. Fools and jesters in literature
I. Title
822.3'3   PR2992.F6

Library of Congress cataloguing in publication data
Wiles, David
Shakespeare's clown.
Bibliography.
Includes index.
1. Shakespeare, William, 1564 — Stage history —
To 1625.   2. Clowns — England — History — 16th century.
3. Kemp, William, fl. 1600.   4. Authors and the
theatre — England — History — 16th century.   5. Actors —
Great Britain — Biography.   I. Title.
PR3095.W55   1987   792'.0941   86–28393

ISBN 0 521 32840 3

Shakespeare's clown
Actor and text in the Elizabethan playhouse

Contents

Illustrations

Preface

IN THE CONTEMPORARY THEATRE, the dominant figure is of course the director. Before the twentieth century, artistic decision-making lay in other hands. What sort of play should be staged? How should it be staged? These were not decisions for a 'director' but (chiefly) for the actor and for the writer. The historical relationship between the actor and the writer is inevitably elusive. The writer's work survives, the actor's work can only be inferred. It is all too easy to assume, in retrospect, that the actor was the servant or interpreter of the writer: to forget that the writer was, in no less real a sense, the servant or interpreter of the actor. This is the paradox that I shall explore in this book, in relation to the Elizabethan theatre. My subject is the role of the clown, and my particular focus is the relationship between two particular artists – the clown William Kemp and the writer William Shakespeare.

The actor's view of the writer is, as usual, lost. The writer's view of the actor is, or seems, easier to excavate. Shakespeare's commentary upon the clown's art in *Hamlet* is an obvious point at which to begin:

And let those that play your clowns speak no more than is set down for them, for there be of them that will themselves laugh to set on some quantity of barren spectators to laugh too, though in the mean time some necessary question of the play be then to be considered; that's villainous, and shows a most pitiful ambition in the fool that uses it.   (*Hamlet* III.ii)

It is impossible to resist the conclusion that the passage is topical. The Elizabethan audience knew that a company of adult actors from the city (unlike an 'aery of children' such as the Paul's or Chapel boys) would include a specialist player of the clown's part. Since Hamlet is arranging for the presentation of a tragedy in which no part whatsoever is set down for the clown, his strictures must seem otiose, until we allow that Shakespeare was deliberately reminding his audience of their own situation as theatre-goers. In 1600, the Chamberlain's Men, the performers of Shakespeare's tragedy *Hamlet*, had recently lost the services of the most famous clown of his

generation, William Kemp, and the audience are being invited to notice the loss.

In the 'bad' First Quarto of 1603, Hamlet's speech is extended in order to give Hamlet the opportunity of mimicking the mannerisms and intonations of a clown. The punctuation is mine:

And then you have some again that keeps one suit of jests, as a man is known by one suit of apparel, and gentlemen quotes his jests down in their tables, before they come to the play, as thus:
'Cannot you stay till I eat my porridge?'
and:
'You owe me a quarter's wages!'
and:
'Your beer is sour!'
and blabbering with his lips:
'. . .'
and thus:
'. . .'
– keeping in his cinque-pace of jests, when, God knows, the warm clown cannot make a jest unless by chance, as the blind man catcheth a hare. Masters, tell him of it. (III.ii)

Hamlet touches on many conventional aspects of the clown's role. The clown-actor plays a character of servant status. The character is not historicized, but earns the standard pay and wears the standard uniform of an Elizabethan serving-man. His needs and aspirations are material, not spiritual. To draw laughter, the clown relies both on verbal gags and on non-verbal techniques. The image of hare-chasing evokes the clown's speed of delivery. The *cinque-pace* metaphor is a reminder that dancing was also part of the clown's repertoire.

The 1603 Quarto is specific in its reference to a single clown: 'let not your clown . . .' Although Hamlet in the 1603 text draws the audience's attention to Kemp's departure, he does not offer them a simple caricature of Kemp. It is the idea of the clown that is at stake. The style of clowning which Hamlet conjures up left its imprint upon the theatre of the 1590s, but belongs properly to an earlier generation. The players at Elsinore perform in an outmoded Marlovian style. The charge of improvisation and anarchic up-staging could fairly be levelled at Tarlton, the famous clown of the 70s and 80s, but there is no evidence that Kemp wreaked havoc with writers' scripts in this way.[1]

Preface

Hamlet's discussion of the clown in the 'bad' Quarto may be an actor's interpolation. There is no firm evidence, and the question is not of great importance. Far more important is the widely held assumption that Hamlet in the canonical text of III.ii serves as his author's mouthpiece. He is, of course, no such thing. Hamlet is a prince, a scholar from the university, a man who dismisses most of the groundlings as 'capable of nothing but inexplicable dumb-shows and noise'. Shakespeare himself catered not only for Hamlet's 'judicious' spectators, but also for 'a whole theatre of others'. The men who stood in the yard of the Globe would not have tolerated Shakespeare's play had they not been able to make the obvious distinction between 'Hamlet' and Shakespeare. Once obvious, this distinction is less easy for a modern audience to perceive – partly because the topicality has vanished, and partly because modern performances of Shakespeare observe an aesthetic code not dissimilar to that which Hamlet propounds.

Hamlet wants to cast his audience as passive voyeurs, peeping in at a mimesis of the sordid reality of Gertrude and Claudius's crime. Shakespeare's pointed reference to Kemp makes it clear that he has no intention of isolating his own audience from the world of the play. Shakespeare never shows much inclination to copy the attempts of Jonson and Chapman to reproduce social reality. He was a commercially minded actor-manager rather than a classically trained man of letters, and his art always retained its roots in the popular tradition. The clown was a major link with this tradition.

The neo-classical aesthetic necessarily involved a new realist approach to acting. Hamlet applauds the player's rendering of a role that had proved a disaster in public performance. He approves this player on the grounds that he 'in a dream of passion / Could force his soul so to his own conceit'. The traditional actor in the role of Herod is scorned because his acting is conscious artifice, because the actor's *soul* is not transformed. We must not forget that Shakespeare's dramatic theorist is on the brink of lunacy. When given 'the motive and the cue for passion', he tries to become the role, and fails. The discussion of acting is introduced because of its bearing upon Hamlet's state of mind. There is no evidence that Shakespeare shared Hamlet's scorn for volume, projection and large gestures – or Hamlet's implicit preference for theatre performed in intimate spaces, spaces where the psychological self-transformation of the actor

could be accurately gauged by the spectator – one who was of necessity an elite spectator.

The clown is an important figure to study because he stands at the heart of the Elizabethan debate about acting. Sir Philip Sidney represents the neo-classicist point of view. He criticizes those who 'thrust in clowns by head and shoulder to play a part in majestical matters, with neither decency nor discretion'. He wishes spectators to see their own world mirrored in the play, and he approves of theatre when 'we get, as it were, an experience of what is to be looked for of a niggardly Demea, of a crafty Davus, of a flattering Gnatho, of a vain-glorious Thraso'.[2] By such means, the spectator learns to recognize and to reject evil. Hamlet espouses the same theory. His theatre will 'show Virtue her own feature, Scorn her own image'. It follows that the clown must be banished from such a theatre. For the clown's brief is not to 'imitate humanity' but, in the first instance, to 'make those laugh whose lungs are tickle a th' sear'.

When we consider the matter from the opposite viewpoint, it is clear that the clown needs to appear the product of 'nature's journeymen', for only thus can he be grotesque, eccentric, unique. His task is to make his audience love him, not to reject him as an exemplar of sin. The servant-clown whom Hamlet mimics is not trying to assume the inner reality of a real-life serving-man. His mannerisms exploit the fact that he is a known theatrical performer dressed up in a servant's livery. The audience are actively involved, egging on the clown to repeat conventional formulae, and to disrupt the orderly progress of the narrative. The neo-classical argument proposed that the theatre audience look passively into a mirror containing an image of their society – but the Elizabethan clown's performance rested on the assumption, or illusion, that the audience are active participants, necessary helpers in the creation of theatre.

Shakespeare's position was of course more complex than I have so far implied. The Elizabethan theatre was always in flux, but its underlying history was one of a drift towards characterization/acting based on notions of mimesis, and away from acting based on iconography or non-representational signalling. The replacement of Kemp by Robert Armin was part of a broad drift towards a new type of theatre. The play had to depict a coherent social milieu. Characterization had to be based on careful observation. The actor had to be responsible to the author, and to realize a character possessing an anterior existence in the author's imagination. The rift which took

Preface

place in 1599 between Kemp and the Chamberlain's company is a moment which I view in this book as a significant jolt on the graph of theatrical change.

My project in the chapters that follow is to trace the history of the role of the Elizabethan clown with a particular focus upon the writing career of Shakespeare. There is a factual core to the book: I argue that specific lines were written to be spoken by a specific individual. But any presentation of factual data becomes at once an interpretation of the facts. A value-neutral positivist historiography must be seen as an impossibility. Positivist theatre historians like E. K. Chambers and C. R. Baskervill did much valuable work on the clown, but they always refrained from moral and aesthetic judgements on texts, seeing such work as the province of a different type of scholar. My own view is that any historical study, like any literary study, is necessarily interpretative. I see it as desirable, therefore, to marry an interpretative historiography to a historically based mode of textual criticism. I shall make it clear in the final chapter of this book why any assessment we made of the clown's significance is an interpretation shaped by premises about the art and theatre available to us in the present.

I begin the book by looking at the clown or 'Vice' in medieval tradition. We can begin to shed modern naturalistic assumptions only when we have grasped the complexity and power of medieval dramaturgy. The centrality of the clown or Vice in medieval theatre warns us against underestimating the Elizabethan clown.

Actors, like most visual and literary artists, learn by imitating predecessors, and only slowly develop an innovative style. In Chapter 2, therefore, I examine the work of Richard Tarlton, the great comic actor of the 1570s and 1580s, and a seminal influence upon later clowns.

Chapter 3 is an exercise in biography. I piece together all that is known about Kemp's career in order to show that writers had an obligation to cater for his distinctive talents. Chapter 4 deals with a single aspect of Kemp's art, the jig. This was probably the acme of his accomplishment in terms of skill, originality and impact. I place the jig within the structure of the play-goer's experience.

In Chapter 5 I analyse playhouse conventions and terminology in order to establish what Elizabethan writers mean when they script a role for 'the clown'. I show that this refers always to a known individual. On this basis, I analyse in Chapter 6 the roles which

Kemp played as a company 'clown'. In Chapter 7 I consider the process by which the Elizabethan text (and thence the modern text) is generated.

In Chapter 8 I try to disentangle the idiosyncrasies of one actor, Kemp, from the broader workings of a theatrical convention. I argue that Kemp's particular background and abilities helped to shape theatrical convention.

I postpone discussion of Falstaff until Chapter 9 because the character is the focus of so much critical controversy. I argue that Kemp played the part of Falstaff, and that the part could not have been written without him. The role developed logically from Kemp's previous roles, yet at the same time threatened to undermine the very idea of a 'clown'.

In Chapter 10 I analyse Armin's clowning, using the same methodology that I applied to Kemp. When the Chamberlain's company acquired a new clown in Armin, they discovered a new possibility of blending popular and intellectual modes of clowning. I examine the marked readjustment which writers had to make.

The Elizabethan theatre stood at a point of transition between the modern concept of theatre as part of a leisure industry and the medieval or pre-urban concept of drama as part of an inversionary or carnivalesque mode of living life. Kemp's clowning was intimately related to this older understanding of drama. That is why I have chosen to focus this book upon Kemp, even though Armin's career offers significantly better documentation. In my final chapter I develop a theoretical line of argument. I argue for a social/anthropological approach towards theatre, an approach which sees a performance as a historical process. I look at some modern analyses of carnivalesque enactments in order to suggest the kind of intellectual perspectives that are necessary if we wish to further our understanding of a phenomenon like William Kemp.

Acknowledgements

Ian Bell, John Edmunds, Richard Southern and Elan Closs Stephens
commented on early drafts of some individual chapters. My principal debt is to Michael Smith of The University College of Wales,
Aberystwyth, who read the whole book in draft. The book owes
much to his acute criticisms and constructive suggestions. Anonymous readers at Cambridge University Press helped me to clarify my
logical processes and keep to the straight and narrow of my theme.
My doctoral thesis included a chapter on Kemp and Armin, and I
have a long-standing debt of gratitude to my supervisor, Michael
Anderson. Chris Harris, twentieth-century begetter of 'Kemp's jig',
gave me lessons in clowning. Audiences at Brixton, Holloway,
Kneesworth, Leyhill, Wandsworth and elsewhere saw to my under-
graduate education in popular theatre.

D.W.

Note

For line references to Shakespeare's plays, I have used the New Arden edition. For old books without numerical pagination, I have given the printer's signature (abbreviated to 'Sig.', with 'v.' for verso). Thus for example 'Sig. C2v.' would be the reverse side of the second leaf of the third quire of the book as originally bound.

CHAPTER I

The Vice: from *Mankind* to *Merchant of Venice*

T HE CLOWN'S ANCESTRY in the Tudor 'Vice' is a generally accepted fact of theatre history. The precise nature of the Tudor 'Vice' is less clear. An examination of the Vice tradition helps us to understand the centrality of the clown's role on the Elizabethan stage.

It seems appropriate to begin with one of the earliest professional English plays to have survived, *Mankind*. Theatre history tends to be Shakespeare-centric, and to present us with a crude medieval tradition evolving into the sophisticated late Elizabethan theatre. The *Quem Quaeretis* trope or the *psychomachia* can be enlisted as the convenient *fons et origo*. It is easy to paint such a picture because so much medieval drama was written for amateurs with a limited range of performance skills. The complexity of *Mankind* is an important corrective to the evolutionary perspective, and the play therefore requires examination.

The play was written in *c.* 1470 for a troupe of six East Anglian actors. It shows how Mischief and three subordinate rogues bring about the fall of Mankind, who can be saved only by the priestly Mercy. Mischief opens the play by interrupting Mercy's sermon. He presents himself as an itinerant *winter* corn-thresher, and seems to be riding a hobby-horse. His actions are governed at every stage by his statement in the opening scene:

> I am come hither to make you game.

And he keeps inventing new games for his companions, and the audience, to play: a miraculous healing in the manner of a mumming play, a mock manorial law court, a reenactment of Christ's sending out of his disciples, and ceaseless parody of ecclesiastical speech. He is at once the villain, whom the audience learn to shun, and the

welcome game-maker who makes the play possible. The idea that Mischief is a game-maker and master of ceremonies is central to the dramatist's conception. Modern editors seem to me to have overlooked an important element in the dramatist's strategy.

Half-way through the play, the audience are told that the devil will be called up. They will be shown 'a man with a head of great omnipotence' – but only on condition that they pay. Once the collection has been taken, the promised 'Titivillus' appears. 'Titivillus' extracts the takings from Mischief's three accomplices, and sends them off to steal horses from identified individuals known to the audience. Mischief has nothing to say in this scene, and his exit is unmarked. Editors have assumed, wrongly in my view, that the player of Mercy doubles as Titivillus. It is more appropriate if Mischief, the showman *par excellence*, doubles the part. He can slip behind the screens to deliver Titivillus's off-stage bellow: 'I come with my legs under me', and return as himself, before leaving again to don the devil's mask, the 'head of great omnipotence'. Stage directions in the manuscript – 'Loquitur ad New Guise' etc. – signal moments when Mischief drops the melodramatic role of Titivillus in order to bicker with his associates. Titivillus's exit line is equally an exit line for *Mischief*:

> Farewell, everyone! for I have done my game;
> For I have brought Mankind to mischief and to shame.[1]

Mischief, in this reading of the text, does not 'double' Titivillus so much as play him in a play-within-a-play. Two important dramaturgical principles are at stake here. First, the Vice, the principal comedian, dominates the play whenever he is physically present. Secondly, the Vice has power to juggle layers of reality. He plays at one and the same time the devil, the allegorical person of Mischief, and a crooked actor organizing robberies from houses that are empty because everyone has come to see the play. At the same time, the player is himself, gathering real money to fund the itinerant troupe in which he is the principal. There is no fixed boundary between actor and role – for to perform a play is in a sense necessarily to create 'mischief'.

Bernard Spivack's argument that the Vice originates as a *radix malorum* finds no support in this play. Mischief's name indicates a dual function. Though Mischief is the personification of a particular sin, this sin is hardly the 'root' of all the evils represented. Mischief's function is equally to be a carnivalesque celebrant. Like a Lord of

The Vice

Misrule, a boy bishop, or a *prince des sots*, he inverts the established order. He offers, in Glynne Wickham's terms, 'life in play' rather than 'life in earnest'. The play-within-a-play device forces the audience to be aware of their own dual status as sinners (through being alive) and celebrants (through being at a play). When Spivack writes of morality drama that 'such a stage was fundamentally a pulpit and its audience fundamentally a congregation',[2] he ignores the fact that early interludes generally used an unbounded *platea* rather than a raised stage. There was no physical line of demarcation to set apart the fictive world of the play from the real world of the audience.

Mischief has a central and controlling function. The play's existence is contingent upon his. He can shift the boundaries of the action at will, physically implicating the spectators in Mankind's downfall – as for example when he makes them pay for the pleasure of meeting the devil. The audience's stance is always being renegotiated, for the audience is composed of 'Mankind', but it is also composed of 'Mischief'. Steered by the Vice, the principal game-maker, the audience is always on the move between the polar positions of observer and participant.

We can accept the views of scholars who trace an important part of the Vice's ancestry to the fool of folk festivals.[3] In other early interludes written for professional troupes we find that the Vices are venial rather than deadly sins. They offer man a life of holiday pleasures. Pride is paired with Riot in *Youth*. Lust-and-liking and Folly in *Mundus et Infans* set up carnivalesque freedom as an alternative to ecclesiastical discipline. In *Hickscorner*, the fantastic illogicality of Hickscorner, Freewill and Imagination is not in any obvious sense the product of an allegorical imagination. As a last example: in that most elaborate of interludes, *Magnificence*, the part of Fancy, the most conspicuous of the Vices, is given to a dwarf. In the course of the play Fancy emerges in his true colours when he dons a fool's coat and proves brother to Folly. Fancy is simultaneously the key to the protagonist's ruin and the creator of entertainment at court.

An important convention seems to be initiated in *Magnificence*. The Vices enter the service of 'Magnificence', the protagonist, and become household servants. The Vices become servants again in such plays as *Mundus et Infans*, *Youth*, *Horestes*, *Cambises* and *Three Ladies of London*. The Vice/servant proved a useful figure when writers tried to weld the indigenous comic tradition onto

3

neo-classical plots which gave a pivotal role to the comic slave. The Vice/servant in *Magnificence* is also a social climber, and social mobility was another theme which Elizabethan dramatists proved keen to explore. The linked motif of the Vice who is revealed as a fool also stood the test of time. Parolles is a striking Shakespearean example. The upstart Parolles incites his master to vice/sport, and his scarves are the emblem of his pride, pride being his master's cardinal fault. Once his master has been reformed, Parolles emerges at last in his true colours and becomes Lafeu's retained fool.

The word 'vice' is first used as a technical theatrical term by John Heywood in 1532. In his experimental courtly interludes *Love* and *Weather*, the characters of Neither-lover-nor-loved and Merry-report are labelled as the Vices of their respective plays. Spivack is clearly right in his etymolgy here.[4] The characters are so labelled because the characters are no longer personifications of one particular vice, yet the actor fulfils the same dramatic function as Mischief, Fancy and the rest. Neither-lover-nor-loved is both comedian and deceiver, and in his disputation proves that the successful lover is no less a fool than himself. Merryreport is taken on as Jupiter's servant, despite the 'lightness' of his apparel, and he functions as a wisecracking compère and interviewer; he mediates between the god and his suitors, and by extension between actors and audience. Heywood has here taken the first step in detaching the stage clown from the morality tradition.

The word 'vice' is often used as a synonym for fool in the sixteenth century. We can trace, however, a fine distinction between the Vice who *acts* the fool's part and the born or natural fool. Thus in an Oxfordshire may-game we find the Whitsun lord being attended by 'the vices that played the fools'.[5] In contrast to the Whitsun lord, a humble nobody elected to high office, the Vice of the may-game had to be something of a specialist. He was therefore paid a fee for his services: sixpence was normal, but five shillings was paid to the Vice in a Surrey may-game in 1611.[6] The subtle distinction – or lack of it – between the artful Vice and the natural fool was the concern of moral interludes from *Magnificence* to William Wager's *The Longer Thou Livest The More Fool Thou Art*. It became, eventually, the obsession of the clown/fool Robert Armin.

When we look at the activities of the Tudor Vice, two features demand our attention. First was his skill in improvisation. Puttenham mentions that lascivious poems are often uttered by 'vices in

The Vice

plays', and in a pseudo-historical description of the classical world he describes how 'counterfeit vices' fill out the acts between plays, while the players are changing, by giving a ridiculous cross-construction of the action. A Vice provided 'pastime' before and after a miracle play at Bungay, and a fool accompanied the criers of the banns before a passion play at New Romney. We hear that it was the part of 'a Vice in a play to prate what is prompted or suggested to him'. Just as the fool in a morris dance broke formation and danced where he pleased, so the Vice swept aside the confines of a script.[7] The Vice's costume justified his function as an improvisator. It is clear from the profusion of references that no useful distinction can be made between the costume of the 'vice' and the costume of the 'fool'. In Armada year, English Catholics in Rome dressed a Protestant traveller in 'a fool's coat . . . half blue, half yellow, and a cockscomb with three bells'. And in the court of Queen Mary we find a gown of yellow and blue fabric being chopped up to make 'two vices' coats for a play'.[8] The Revels documents of Edward VI use the terms 'vice', 'fool' and 'dizard' interchangeably for a man who wears a suit of many colours and carried as his props a ladle with a bauble pendant and a dagger.[9] A Tudor Vice/fool, therefore, would play a scripted part in an interlude as long as the script required, but he would wear his fool's coat and play the fool's part as long as the occasion required.

We must beware of imposing upon the Tudor world our own conceptual separation of a 'play' from a festival. The Vice who makes pastime within an interlude cannot be dissociated from the Vice who is given a function within the festival. The boundary between interlude and festival was never rigidly defined. A Lord of Misrule would often set up plays in the course of his carnivalesque reign: at Christ's College, Cambridge, for instance, a stage was set up in 1553 'when the Xmas lords came at Candlemas to the College with shows'. The summer lord of South Kyme in 1601 participated in a libellous 'stage play' on the village green.[10] We must not forget also that Elizabethan professional players were normally called to court to play in the context of inversionary festivals. Until such time as the 'play' was isolated and redefined as a work of *art*, the Vice had the task of ensuring that no boundary emerged between the play and the playful context of its performance.

Inevitably the function of the Vice changed in the formal circumstances of performance before a public audience in London. Audience

and actors ceased to be co-celebrants in a festival, and the relationship became a broadly commercial one. Troupes and audience alike became larger, and the stage constituted a physical barrier between them. *Cambises* is a good example of the kind of play that the first purpose-built theatres were designed to accommodate.

The Vice acts as a link between the exotic and remote world of the play and the immediate world of the audience. In his first speech he sets himself up as a fool by making elaborate preparations to joust with a snail. And having created an illusion, he revels in dissolving it, and bursts into laughter as he explains the significance of his name. The name, Ambidexter, signifies duplicity; it also suggests the shifting relationship between actor and audience, actor and role. In a sequence of monologues Ambidexter gives a running commentary on the state of the action. Confidentially he describes his feelings in the scene that has passed and lets his listeners into the secret of what is to come. After Ambidexter has betrayed Cambises' brother, the actor's eyes alight on one of the spectators:

> Marry, sir, I told him a notable lie.
> If I were to do it again, I durst not do it, I.[11]

We are unsure whether the actor or the character is speaking. Similarly, in the course of describing the royal wedding, 'Ambidexter' imagines a proposal of marriage from a maid in the audience. And again it seems to be the *actor* who regularly directs remarks to his 'cousin', a cut-purse supposedly operating amongst the audience. In his emotional reactions, 'Ambidexter' is always doing a double-take on himself. An example is his reaction to the death of Smirdis, addressed as ever to 'ye' the audience:

> I cannot forbear weeping, ye may me believe.
> *Weep.*
> Oh my heart! How my pulses do beat,
> With sorrowful lamentations I am in such a heat!
> Ah, my heart, how for him it doth sorrow!
> Nay, I have done, in good faith, now. And God give ye good morrow!
> Ha, ha! Weep? Nay, laugh, with both hands to play![12]

The actor detaches himself from the character's emotions and responses, and presents his grief for the sheer pleasure of demonstrating his skill as a performer. At the end of the play, Ambidexter brings

The Vice

back the action from Persia to London, as he hurries off to catch a barge before he misses the tide. The Vice never allows the audience to forget that the play is a game which requires their active involvement. The actor's technique lies in his ambidexterous juggling with two worlds.

The Vice's language sets him apart from the rest of the play. His diction is that of the common man. The sentences twist about as they follow his thought. There are no boorish malapropisms or affected conceits. The heavy rhythm of the fourteener, characteristic of the play and parodied in Shakespeare's 'Pyramus and Thisbe', vanishes in Ambidexter's monologues. The pattern is an irregular four-beat line, broken in the middle and held in shape by the rhyme. For the improvisator, it would be an easy verse form to sustain. The illusion is set up that the Vice is inventing his part, and the play, as he proceeds. There is an obvious continuity forwards to the prose of Shakespeare's clowns and backwards to the earthy Anglo-Saxon diction of the vices in *Mankind*.

Like the vices in *Magnificence*, Ambidexter elevates himself to the position of retainer at court. He claims that 'the king doth me a gentleman allow', and forces his fellow servant to address him as 'your mastership'. Since other characters throughout tend to address him as 'Master Ambidexter', a fanciful and socially imprecise outfit seems appropriate. In practice and by law, a main function of Elizabethan costume was to signal publicly where people stood on the social scale. Clearly some kind of fool costume allows Ambidexter to sidestep the normal conventions of dress.

Ambidexter remains a Vice in the moral sense. He sets the peasants fighting for no reason, sends Smirdis to his death, hobnobs with the corrupt judge, kisses the whore at length, and bullies his way to the royal table. Yet within the framework of a historical/melodramatic/romantic narrative, the moral ambiguity of the audience's response cannot so easily be pointed up. The equilibrium once set up by Mischief and Mercy has vanished. The Vice is on the verge of becoming the Clown.

The Vice tradition left its imprint upon late Elizabethan theatre. *The Merchant of Venice* provides a good example of how Shakespeare continued to work within the Vice convention. The conventions governing the role of clown/Vice can be summed up under three headings as set out below.

Shakespeare's clown

The personification of a moral Vice

'Launcelot Gobbo' is noted for his greed, laziness and lechery: he is a 'huge feeder' who 'sleeps by day' and gets the mooress with child. He creates mischief for the fun of it when he tries confusions with his father. It is appropriate that in his opening speech he presents himself as the servant of the devil.

Since the nature of a Vice was encapsulated in his name, it was common for a Vice to expound the meaning of his name.[13] Shakespeare follows convention to the extent of using a name that is emblematic and contrasts with the Italian nomenclature of the other characters. Putting centuries of tradition aside, we return to the First Quarto and Folio to find – to our surprise – that the clown's correct name throughout is Launcelet Jobbe. The 'Gobbo' is borrowed from his father and from the unreliable Roberts Quarto. The father may be a 'gobbo' or hunchback, but the son is different. The *OED* tells us that a 'launcelet' is a small lance or lancet, and 'jobbe' is the regular Elizabethan spelling of our 'jab'. The name has phallic overtones, and links him to fellow clowns 'Launce' and 'Falstaff'. The clown's jest: 'Do I took like a cudgel or a hovel post, a staff or a prop?', though pointed up by a stick he or his father carries, turns upon the clown's name, so carefully enunciated in his first speech. The clown's later reference to his rib-cage comically belies the fact that his eating has rendered him fat. The name 'Launcelet Jobbe' therefore signifies both the lecher and the overeater. It suggests that he is a moral Vice who jabs those who toy with him. And it associates him with the physical instrument of Shylock's viciousnes, the lancet that is to cut into Antonio's flesh. Dramatic tradition has accepted the name 'Gobbo' for so long because of a neo-classical desire for internal plausibility, for a realistic Italian context. In order to rediscover the Elizabethan clown buried in the text, we have to take a more medieval perspective.

Boundaries of the action

The clown establishes a rapport with the audience when he opens and closes his first scene with monologues. (Though his father is on stage for the second, the clown reads his own palm for the audience's benefit, not for his blind father.) The deceit of the father is set up for the audience's entertainment: Launcelet explains clearly to the audi-

ence who his father is and what he intends to do to him. In his fooling at Belmont, Launcelet is again no servant of the plot but a self-conscious entertainer.

The linguistic demarcation of Launcelet's role is an important feature. The fact that the clown speaks in prose when most of the play is in verse creates the illusion of spontaneity, of an actor who is speaking to the audience *in propria persona*. Launcelet's jigging rhyme:

> There will come a Christian by
> Will be worth a Jewes eye

has the clumsiness of an improvisation. The patterning of the mono-logues gives the supposed improvisator a framework for his performance.

Actor begins to separate out from role when the audience are forced to wonder whether stupidity or cleverness lies behind the clown's jests. When Launcelet tells Bassanio that 'the suit is imperti-nent to myself', laments that 'tears exhibit my tongue', or complains that his father 'may tell every finger I have with my ribs', he hides truth beneath a veneer of idiocy. There is no way of telling what Launcelet 'really' thinks and feels. No central locus of 'character' can be identified. Launcelet's language allows the audience to sense that the character is stupid but the actor is clever – clever enough to mock the character he plays. The dichotomy of actor and role is reinforced if the part of slender 'Launcelet' is given to an actor who is fat, if the part of a young apprentice is given to a middle-aged master actor.

Costume

The clown initially is in rags. Shylock complains of how he has managed to 'rend apparel out'. When the clown enters Bassanio's service, he is promised 'a livery more guarded than his fellows' ' – and there is no reason to doubt that this costume materializes. The stage direction which reclassifies Launcelet as Shylock's 'man that was the Clowne' points to the change. Lorenzo puns on the new livery coat after the clown's exit with the comment: 'how his words are suited' – and he adds that he knows 'many fools that stand in better place / Garnished like him'.[14] There is an iconographic signifi-cance in the clown's change of costume. Vices such as Ignorance in *Wit and Science* and Moros in *The Longer Thou Livest The More*

Shakespeare's clown

Fool Thou Art were given a fool's costume in the course of the
interlude, and the same technique is used here.[15] Bassanio's extrava-
gance is plainly foolish, and he fritters away money dressing up the
embodiment of folly. When he places his own livery badge upon the
Vice, he identifies the Vice as one of his party, and himself as one of
the Vice's party. At the same time, paradoxically, Bassanio is the
hero, who plays the game of romantic love and wins. It is fitting that
he saves the principal game-maker from destitution, and admits him
to the Utopian world of Belmont, where all the values of Venice are
inverted. Shakespeare thus successfully exploits the dual significance
of the medieval Vice convention.

So much for continuities. There is also an obvious change. Launcelet
is modelled on two observed social types: the country boy turned
apprentice, faced with a moral dilemma over his indentures, and the
threatened species of 'idle servingman', whose prosperity depends
upon his master's economic suicide. In the longer term, social realism
proved a limiting factor. The stage became a mirror of society, but
only part of society was reflected in the mirror, only one angle of
vision was possible. In the course of the seventeenth century the stage
servant became a mere cipher, unable to make any impact upon the
decisions and life-chances of the gentleman. When the carnivalesque
model of the Vice/clown was finally obliterated, the clown/servant
fell victim to decorum and verisimilitude.

CHAPTER 2

Tarlton: the first 'clown'

IN ORDER TO APPRECIATE the clowns who performed in Shakespeare's plays, we have to understand how they learnt their art. In the present century, the great clown Grock sums up his own experience:

Your clown, just as much as any other artist, is the product of tradition. Just as a painter knows how to use the experience of countless forerunners, just as an author who *is* an author largely owes his existence to the pioneer work of those who have gone before and influenced him, so every clown that is worth his salt is but carrying on the torch handed to him by all the eminent clowns who preceded him or who work with him still. Your painter will swear by Raphael, or Calame, or Stuck as the case may be, your author by Paul de Kock, Goethe, or Edgar Wallace, while your clown will acknowledge his debt to Bébé and Serillo, or Pippo and Toniloff, or Toto, or Willi and Adolf Olschonski, or La Water Lee, or Gobert Belling, or Les Briators, or Rico and Alex, or Seiffer, or Carlo and Mariano, or Little Walter, or Averino Antonio, or the three Fratellini, or Antonet.

Umberto Guilleaume, who goes by the name of Antonet, a leading clown of the Cirque de Paris, was my teacher.[1]

In the history of Elizabethan clowning, one figure exerted a seminal influence: Richard Tarlton. John Singer, the clown of the Admiral's company, worked alongside Tarlton in the Queen's Men. In the volume entitled *Tarlton's Jests*, first printed in 1600,[2] we find the story of how Robert Armin first came to the master's attention, and was promised Tarlton's 'clown's suit' after him. Kemp's name also was linked with Tarlton's. Nashe described Kemp as 'jest-monger and Vice-gerent general to the ghost of Dick Tarlton', and Heywood states that Kemp 'succeeded' Tarlton in the favour both of Queen and general public.[3]

We seem to have an echo of Hamlet's Yorick in the following epitaph:

Shakespeare's clown

Here within this sullen earth
Lies Dick Tarlton, lord of mirth,
Who in his grave – still laughing – gapes,
Sith all clowns since have been his apes.
Erst he of clowns to learn still sought,
But now they learn of him they taught.
By art far past the principal,
The counterfeit is now worth all.[4]

There is a quibble here on 'clowns' as both rustics and stage entertainers. Tarlton studied real rustic simpletons to create his own
clown character, the poet claims; but now the stage rustic seems
more real than the original, and modern clowns prefer to copy
Tarlton's counterfeit rather than the reality.

The word clown is ambiguous in Elizabethan usage, meaning both
'countryman' and 'principal comedian'. In *Cambises* the functions of
rustic and Vice were distinct: Hob and Lob, the 'country patches',
are given a risible Mummerset accent, and are the objects of the
Vice's mockery. In Tarlton, the Vice and the rustic are fused. The role
of Derick in *The Famous Victories of Henry V*, which Tarlton played
towards the end of his life,[5] illustrates the fully realized clown type.
Though the extant text is too corrupt to yield precise information
about Tarlton's technique, the gist is clear enough. In his opening
scene, Tarlton/Derick jests upon the fact that he is only a 'plain
clown' despite the eccentric finery in which he makes his entry.
During the play, Derick abandons his Kentish employer and becomes a London cobbler's apprentice. The rustic transposed to an
urban setting was the type that Tarlton made his own. It was to be the
inspiration for such later clown parts as Launcelet in *The Merchant
of Venice*.

Tarlton's Jests gives us a vivid picture of the man, a picture which
is corroborated by snippets of information from other sources. The
problem lies in separating the man from the projected public image.
No information about his drunkenness and his marriage can be
taken at face value. The comedian might bewail his poverty, but
after his death his mother claimed in Chancery that £700 had been
wrongly assigned in the will.[6] Though the early drawing (Fig. 1)
depicts him in the stage costume of a peasant, we have to remember
that he also became a Groom of the Chamber and a Master of
Fence. The *Jests* confirms that he walked the streets with a rapier
at his side, not a slapstick. Tarlton's stage career brought him, like

Fig. 1 A drawing of Richard Tarlton. Reproduced with permission of the British Library, from Harley MS 3885, fol. 19.

Shakespeare and Alleyn a few years later, both social and financial elevation.

The *Jests* was published in three sections, 'court', 'city' and 'country' jests. But for present purposes it is more helpful to analyse the material in relation to the three spaces in which Tarlton practised his craft: the stage, the tavern, and the banqueting hall.

Tarlton was named as one of the Queen's Men when the company was formed in 1583. On the stage we see him in action at the Curtain and at the two tavern theatres where the Queen's Men were licensed to play – the Bell and the Bull. He also tours with the company. The author of the *Jests* is not interested in Tarlton's scripted stage role but in his improvisation. These are given free rein at the end of a play, when members of the audience throw up clever rhymes with the aim of outwitting the comedian, whose task it is to give an instant riposte. The battle of wits is competitive and aggressive. Tarlton is also given to improvising in the course of a play. In one play he is kneeling to ask his father's blessing before a journey when a man in the gallery throws an apple at him. A devastating rhyme is required to quash the trouble-maker, and the actor has no trouble coming out of role to deliver it (Sig. B2). Probably such moments were more often of the actor's choosing. Another anecdote tells of how Tarlton picked on a man who was pointing him out to a friend. A verbal battle built up, so embarrassing the luckless spectator that he was obliged to leave (B2v). In the role of 'Derick', Tarlton caused chaos when at short notice he doubled for a missing actor.

Tarlton's improvisations were of doubtful legality. There was always a danger to the peace when 2,000 people gathered together. The Mayor and Common Council of London tried to make improvisation illegal when in 1574 they forbade innkeepers to:

suffer to be interlaced, added, mingled or uttered in any such play, interlude, comedy, tragedy or show any other matter than such as shall be first perused and allowed.[7]

Although this regulation could not apply to players with a royal patent, the patent granted to Leicester's Men in the same year did specify likewise that the Master of the Revels had first to see and allow their plays. The licensing system grew progressively tighter. Tilney's patent of commission in 1581 allowed him to amend scripts – which implies a more detailed surveillance of the text.[8] No doubt Tarlton's personal reputation, and his status as a royal favourite,

gave him special latitude. His successors were compelled to work in a different style.

Tarlton's second sphere of activity was the tavern. We are told that he kept an ordinary in Paternoster Row and a tavern in Gracechurch Street. Tarlton must have owned the latter, as he let it out to a tenant. We are led to picture Tarlton as a genial mine host, given to 'sitting with gentlemen to make them merry' (C3). The links between the tavern and the theatre are close. The Bell also stood in Gracechurch Street, and the Bull stood further up the same road. If Tarlton was not licensed to present stage plays in his own premises, no doubt he pushed the regulations as far as he could in presenting less formal entertainments to draw in custom. The inns were used for performances in winter, and, as Glynne Wickham has shown, these performances usually took place indoors, not in the yard.[9] Once we dispense with the old notion that the inn-yard was the main forerunner of the Elizabethan playhouse, we can see why there was a necessary continuum between the activities of the stage clown and the activities of the tavern fool or table-side jester.

At court and in private houses, Tarlton's function was to appear at banquets. No common guest, 'he was there of purpose to jest amongst them' (A2v), and he usually stayed until the small hours. When Burleigh entertained the Queen at his house in the Strand, Tarlton appeared 'in his clown's apparel' (A3) – so his role as a jester was clearly formalized. Yorick's repertoire of 'gibes . . . gambols . . . songs . . . and flashes of merriment' gives some idea of Tarlton's range on these occasions. Crushing personal attacks were interspersed with other types of verbal wit. Singing was central to Tarlton's act: two of his ballads survive – a mock-tragic narrative about flood damage, and some antifeminist advice from a crow[10] – and the rhymes which men gave him to cap were often sung rather than spoken. Tarlton's dancing is not directly attested, however. It was Kemp rather than Tarlton who made dancing the centrepiece of his clowning.

When Tarlton appeared at banquets, the borderline between theatre and extempore jesting remained fluid. In this eyewitness account, the setting is still the supper table:

Tarlton, who was then the best comedian in England, had made a pleasant play, and when it was acting before the Queen, he pointed at Sir Walter Rawleigh and said: 'See, the knave commands the Queen' – for which he was corrected by a frown from the Queen.[11]

This is a dramatic performance, yet it is at least partially unscripted. Tarlton moved easily between the theatre and the dining table. Indeed the basis of his theatrical technique was to recreate in the theatre the intimate atmosphere of the table-side, making spectators feel like participants.

It is clear, then, that no absolute distinction can be made between Tarlton the man and the roles which he played in different environments. Again, we may compare the views of Grock:

My attitude has always been that if I am a clown in the ring I can and should be a clown out of it. Either you should be a thing or *not* be it.[12]

This merging of man and role is a quality that Tarlton's successors were to retain.

Deduction is required if we are to understand from the *Jests* why Tarlton was so popular. Clever verbal humour is conspicuous by its absence. A sample of his word-play is the crudity of the following: a lady threatens to punish him with a 'cuff', and he invites her to but reverse the spelling of the word and carry out her wishes (A3). As always, Tarlton's opponent becomes the shame-faced victim of general laughter. In the end Tarlton always has the last laugh, but his genius lay in setting up situations in which he himself would first be humiliated. Many of the tales in the *Jests* are anecdotes which Tarlton told against himself – tales of how he is apprehended by the watch, deceived by women, or left penniless. Tarlton's manifest social and financial success provided these tales with their context.

Tarlton's Jests helps us to reconstruct the comedian's technique. After a performance in Worcester, a gallant sang out a witty couplet that hinted at Tarlton's failure to rule his wife:

> Methinks it is a thing unfit
> To see a gridiron turn the spit.

And Tarlton's reaction is instructive:

The people laughed at this, thinking his wit knew no answer thereunto, which angered Tarlton exceedingly – and presently, with a smile looking about, when they expected wonders, he put it off thus:

> Methinks it is a thing unfit
> To see an ass have any wit.

The people hooted for joy to see the theme-giver dashed, who like a dog with his tail between his legs left the place.   (C4v)

The comedian's skill lies in convincing the audience that he has been outwitted and humiliated. He then judges the timing of his reply carefully, offering a throwaway insult in place of cleverness. He crushes his victim with mimicry, yet continues to present himself as one so stupid that anybody ought to outwit him. In a similar incident, an enquiry is made about his flat nose. Tarlton becomes 'mad at this question, as it was his property sooner to take such a matter ill than well' (c4v). Tarlton's physical ugliness is essential to a comic persona that invites mockery from the audience.

In his scripted theatrical roles, the technique is the same. Jonson describes how finely Tarlton would be robbed by Adams, his fellow actor who played the rogue.[13] As Derick in *The Famous Victories of Henry V* he spends much of the play as the aggrieved victim of a highway robbery. Many years later Henry Peacham recalled a play in which Tarlton played a youngest son at his father's deathbed. His father chastises him at length for a life spent in and out of prison, and bequeathes him nothing but the gallows and a rope. The comedian plays out his humiliation as long as possible before delivering the punchline which gives him the final laugh:

Tarlton weeping and sobbing upon his knees, as his brothers, said: 'Oh father, I do not desire it. I trust in God you shall live to enjoy it yourself.'[14]

We have clues that help us to visualize Tarlton. With his flat nose and squint, he was remembered as a swine-faced clown, and a sight of his face was enough to set an audience laughing.[15] He projected rustic stupidity both through his face and through costume. One favourite outfit was the idiosyncratic peasant costume depicted in the extant drawing (Fig. 1). But, like later Elizabethan clowns, Tarlton chose to vary his appearance. Peacham remembered him acting 'in a foul shirt without a band, and in a blue coat with one sleeve, his stockings out at heels, and his head full of straw and feathers'.[16] Tarlton's giant slops were even better remembered than his russet-coloured peasant trousers. Slops were a convenient storehouse for props, for we know of one early clown who kept a bottle of beer in one slop and a larder of beef in the other.[17] Tarlton never wore the emblematic costume of the Vice. His clothing always placed him socially, either as a rustic or as a rustic trying to be fashionable.

The professional 'clown' was a new phenomenon. Tarlton's clown can be regarded historically as a synthesis of three different types of

Fig. 2 Tudor minstrel in a seventeenth-century Book of Hours.
Reproduced with permission of the Bodleian Library, from Douce
Portfolio 133, No. 567.

medieval entertainer: the professional minstrel, the amateur lord of misrule, and the Vice examined in the last chapter. Although these three types overlap, it is helpful to consider each separately.

Figure 2 is a seventeenth-century reconstruction of a Tudor minstrel at work. The minstrel is playing the Beggar's Fiddle, and his costume is based on the fool's cockscomb and jerkin hung with bells. The overlap between Vice and minstrel is clearly established.

The term 'minstrel' started to become redundant in Tarlton's time because the type vanished. In Ipswich, for example, from 1556 to 1573, William Martin and four fellow 'minstrels' were retained by the town in order to play at ceremonial functions. Records refer variously to their music, to 'a play at the Moot hall', and to their 'playing the fools in the hall'. By the 1580s the town 'waits' under new leadership are simply identified as a company of musicians.[18] Across the country, acting and music-making were tending to become specialized activities.

Because performances were given extempore, we know little about the art of the solo entertainer in Tudor England. We can only speculate about the career of a predecessor of Tarlton's, Queen Elizabeth's first 'jester'. This was a man by the name of Lockwood who travelled round the country between 1542 and 1572. He is referred to as 'the King's Jester so named' or 'the Queen's jester' or the 'King and Queen's', depending on the reign. His circuit covered Plymouth and Ipswich, Folkestone and Nottingham; he performed with one or two assistants; and his fee was about three times that of a local 'jester', though usually less than that commanded by the royal bearward or royal juggler.[19] Beyond this, we know nothing of the songs, dances, mime, anecdotes and banter that must have made up his act. The simple fact of his career is important, however, for it reveals that the art of the solo entertainer was well established in Elizabeth's reign, and commanded royal patronage.

We get a vivid picture of a minstrel's activities from Laneham's description of a pastiche minstrel's act at Kenilworth in 1575. This minstrel is (supposedly) employed by the small town of Islington, but he behaves as if his master were a great nobleman. A spoof town crest dangles from his neck, and he begins with a solemn exposition of the heraldry. Before playing his harp, he engages in banter with the audience, but the audience prove quicker than the performer:

Hereat everyone laughed agood, save the minstrel; that though the fool were made privy all was but for sport, yet to see himself thus crossed with a country cue that he looked not for, would straight have given over all, waxed

very wayward, eager and sour. How be it, last, by some entreaty and many fair words, with sack and sugar, we sweetened him again, and after he came as merry as a pie.[20]

The technique is broadly that of Tarlton's in the theatre. The minstrel's (or fool's) relationship with the audience is interactive and competitive. The audience are keen to participate.

For an authentic minstrel at the start of Elizabeth's reign we have the evidence of the Sheale manuscript. Richard Sheale was retained by the Earl of Derby, but not supported by him. His collection of ballads contains many sober pieces in addition to the jocular and satirical ones. His role was not only to sing but also to improvise. Sheale describes how, after a traumatic robbery, he could neither 'sing nor talk':

> My audacity was gone, and all my merry talk.
> There is some here have seen me as merry as a hawk;
> But now I am so troubled with fancies in my mind
> That I cannot play the merry knave according to my kind.[21]

Sheale's minstrelsy earned him dinners rather than cash, and he had to rely on the income his wife gained from her embroidery. The manuscript is primary evidence for the decline of the minstrel's profession. Lord Strange, the Earl of Derby's son, was more interested in players of stage plays, as cultural life began to centre on the capital rather than great provincial households. Tarlton's fame in stage plays ensured his continued welcome at the tables of the elite.

Tarlton's clowning did not draw its vitality from professional minstrelsy. Its new energy derived rather from a rediscovery of qualities within the amateur misrule tradition. The rigid social hierarchies of late medieval England relied on inversionary enactments of 'misrule' to create a sense of release, and ultimately a reaffirmation of hierarchy. Whatever the community – city, village, institution or great household – a Lord of Misrule would be elected annually from amongst males of low status. In villages, the maying at Whitsun was the focus; in households and institutions, where warmth and space were available indoors, Christmas was the main inversionary festival. In prosperous towns, both Christmas and summer lords might be appointed. In Tarlton's day, this tradition, no less than minstrelsy, was in decline. The efforts of puritanical clergy and town councils were compounded by the impoverishment of the

countryside and the decline of the feudal household. Tarlton in a sense became a surrogate Lord of Misrule.

Tarlton's licence to play the fool derives from the assumption that, through being the ugliest, poorest and stupidest member of the community, he is entitled to the office of Lord of Misrule. Tarlton assumes a cover of naivety, and represents himself as being penniless. He cultivates a reputation for drunkenness. These aspects of his projected character are the frame which lends form to his anarchy.

Ceremonial combat was the Lord of Misrule's central activity. He had to prove his title to lordship through conquest. Thus, Edward VI's Lord of Misrule engaged in combat with William Somers, the famous congenital fool in the royal household.[22] The extant Tudor may-games of Robin Hood are skeletal texts which allow the Summer Lord to engage in combat with staves or sword and buckler.[23] Lodge describes the competitive dancing of a Lord of Misrule: the Lord leaps over tables or higher than men's heads, and defeats his rivals by tripping their heels.[24] Tarlton worked within this tradition when he jousted against the Queen's little dog with sword and longstaff. It was part of the tradition that the Lord of Misrule should prove himself worthy of office by losing. Just as Friar Tuck had to be allowed to defeat Robin in the may-game, so Elizabeth's foreign 'mastiff' – as Tarlton jestingly termed it – had to be allowed to emerge victorious.[25] When Tarlton engaged in verbal duels with spectators in the theatre, and manoeuvred himself into a losing position, he drew upon a rich vein of folk humour.

The Lord of Misrule used to enlist as many people as he could into his retinue. In the may-game, he sold his livery badges to all and sundry.[26] The paradigm is an important one. In *Mankind*, Mischief functions as a rampant Lord of Misrule when he makes Mankind swear an oath of allegiance and refashion his coat as a livery. In the same scene, the audience are assumed to be part of Mischief's 'fellowship' when they are cast as part of the 'Court of Mischief'. As Derick in *The Famous Victories*, Tarlton remains in this tradition. He summons a law court, chooses himself a master, and goes soldiering only to cull the battlefield for shoes. The text does not give us the measure of Tarlton's relationship with the audience, however, for Tarlton's script existed only in order that he could destroy it. He destroyed it through improvisation, and in the process enlisted the spectators as his accomplices. It was an increasingly hazardous busi-

ness, in the Elizabethan period, to refuse to differentiate between a stage play and a revel, and sometimes Tarlton paid the price. On one occasion he could not make his prologue be heard above the hissing. On another, his opening jest is said to have 'brought the whole company into such vehement laughter, that not able again to make them keep silence, for that present time they were fain to break up'.[27]

The third strand in Tarlton's clowning is the Vice tradition. In a sense, however, Tarlton's originality lay in his ability to escape that tradition.

It is important to understand that the Vice and the Lord of Misrule became separate and distinct figures in Tudor festival. In Oxfordshire, Bedfordshire and Lincolnshire village may-games, we find one or two Vices attending on the Summer Lord. In 1556, we find a Vice in his fool's coat described as the 'minion' of a Christmas Lord. In Shropshire in 1652, and in Edward VI's Christmas revels a century earlier, we find the Vice being cast as the Lord of Misrule's son.[28] In the may-game, the morris was performed in honour of the Summer Lord, and the Vice/fool played a part within the morris. While the lord was an amateur, the Vice/fool was a specialist. The lord served once, the Vice/fool served regularly. A coat was kept for the Vice from year to year, and there are frequent bills for its mending. The lord had no coat to be mended because he wore improvised regalia. Beaumont's May Lord, for instance, simply wears a 'crossed scarf', and he instructs his followers to wear scarfs and garters *as you please*.[29]

These distinctions help us to see how Tarlton distanced himself from the Vice tradition. The apparent crude amateurishness of his recorded jokes is simply part of his act. The contrast between the Vice and the misrule traditions becomes plain when we compare his clowning with that of his fellow comedian and improvisator in the Queen's Men, Robert Wilson. Soon after the formation of the company, Wilson published a script with parts for two principal comics. The character of 'Dissimulation' is marked out as a Vice by his parti-coloured head. 'Simplicity' the miller is marked out as a simple clown by his gaping mouth and mealy white face. While the Vice's art lies in adroit metamorphoses, the clown is a constant, equally vacuous in any situation. There can be little doubt that the part of Simplicity was written for Tarlton, who was so adept at seeming to be outwitted. In a sequel to the play written a few months after

Tarlton: the first 'clown'

Tarlton's death, the role of Simplicity is constructed in the form of an elaborate tribute to the dead comedian.[30]

While the Vice exists in a moral/philosophical dimension, the clown exists in a social dimension. While the Vice represents a negative pole in relation to virtue and wisdom, the clown is a negative pole in relation to urbanity and status. The character of Tarlton's clown emerged in response to post-medieval social conditions. The majority of Tarlton's London audience must have been visitors or first-generation immigrants. Tarlton tapped spectators' anxieties about the rustic boor latent within themselves. Apprentices, servants, students and demobbed soldiers were not of course the only immigrants. The establishment of court in the capital, and the accompanying new ideals of gentlemanly or courtly behaviour, contributed to the force of Tarlton's clowning. While the literary culture generated the pastoral, the oral culture generated Tarlton: the figures of shepherd and clown served alike to define the concepts of gentleman and courtier.

The rustic clown was a response to London. London was some twelve to fifteen times bigger than any other city in the country in the 1580s, and was still swelling. In these conditions, inversionary civic and parochial rituals, which in smaller communities served to give the individual a sense of place, degenerated into spectacle. As a surrogate Lord of Misrule, Tarlton the theatrical clown helped to foster in Londoners a new sense of community, shared values, and active participation in the making of a culture. His comedy cut across barriers of class, proving acceptable both at court and in the tavern, because most people could accept the proposition that beneath every human exterior there lurks a coarse anarchic peasant. By the end of the century, this proposition was less acceptable. Court, theatres, Protestantism and many sometime immigrants had achieved permanence. There was less concern with original sin, more with the innate character of gentility, and with the power of education to change the man. Inversionary anarchy, both at court and in the playhouse, was perceived as a threat to social order. For such reasons as these, stage clowns in the 1590s and 1600s confronted new conditions and adopted new working methods.

CHAPTER 3

Kemp: a biography

KEMP'S ONLY PUBLISHED WRITING, *Kemp's Nine Days' Wonder*, relates the details of his famous morris dance from London to Norwich in 1600, and it is to this that we must turn to get a feel for the man's voice and character.

Let us begin, however, with his physique. As a man of powerful build, he despises 'thin-breeched' ballad singers. Even though he spread his nine days' dancing over a month, the dance testifies to his stamina, especially given the condition of the roads in February. He moved fast, for, as he remarks, 'my pace in dancing is not ordinary'. And he has the traditional morris dancer's prowess in leaping. He can leap ditches when his companions land in the middle. And his leap over the churchyard wall in Norwich was so remarkable that his shoes were nailed to the wall of the Guildhall to mark the height. To this day, a plaque on the wall of St John Maddermarket commemorates the famous leap. To be a morris dancer was to be a species of athlete.

Tarlton's squint marked him out as a clown, and Kemp's 'ill face' served the same purpose. For this reason alone, Kemp could never have played the part of a tragic hero. Kemp's face sits well with his self-image as one who would, 'being a plain man, call a spade a spade'. In his dedication, he asks his mistress to accept his pamphlet

such as it is, rude and plain, for I know your pure judgement looks as soon to see beauty in a blackamoor, or hear smooth speech from a stammerer, as to find anything but blunt mirth in a morris dancer, especially such a one as Will Kemp that hath spent his life in mad jigs and merry jests.

Except in self-mockery, he is never a man to aggrandize himself. Others may address him as 'Master Kemp', but he refers to himself as plain 'Will Kemp'. In this way, he presents himself as the common Englishman, and makes it clear that he is no gentleman, nor would wish to be. He is equally happy dancing alongside a butcher or

accepting hospitality from country gentry. As the common Englishman, he can establish relations of 'fellowship' with everyone he meets. He speaks as an equal to the 'honest fellows' he meets on the road, and his favourite term of approbation – 'honest' – implies a lack of pretension.

Kemp is a traditionalist who looks back to a more stable order when every man knew his place. On the one occasion when 'wit' gives way to 'moral precepts', he condemns gentlemen who sell their lands in order to go into trade. He calls attention to the virtues of the Mayor of Norwich, a rich Merchant Venturer who refuses to buy himself a place among the landed gentry. He is delighted to find exceptional wealth in the widow of one who remained a commoner. His own plebeian tastes are illustrated by his reputation as a lover of bear-baitings. And he admires Thomas Deloney, the writer who – as he points out – celebrates the exploits of shoemakers and clothiers ignored by the official Tudor chroniclers. Kemp's pamphlet as a whole is witness to a consistent middle-class code of values. More accurately, we might say that the inconsistencies are buried beneath the conventional assumptions of populist Protestantism.

Kemp conceived his dance to Norwich as a commercial venture, and he invited spectators to gamble on his failure. As he passed through the countryside, he distributed pledges for a given sum – in the form of points, garters or gloves – in order that if successful he could recoup his stake threefold as he journeyed homewards. He laments in his pamphlet that the majority of those who had pledged themselves subsequently failed to pay up. This outcome can scarcely have surprised him. Nevertheless, one reason for publishing must have been to certify his achievement in the hopes that more would come forward and pay. We do not know how profitable his dance turned out to be.

Kemp complains about ballad-makers whose lies are pasted on every post. It is not clear precisely what lies are supposed to have been told about Kemp. Kemp's prime slanderer is said to be a 'jig-maker', and Kemp's search for him takes him into a playhouse on Bankside, because a leading suspect is an actor. When Kemp addresses his enemies as 'Shakerags', we may infer that Shakespeare's stage was the scene of the ballad-maker's attacks on him. (This correlates, of course, with the evidence of *Hamlet* in the same year.) It is not clear whether Kemp's projected paranoia is real, or a Tarltonesque posture – or a subtle fusion of both. When Kemp

pleads in apparent penitence, 'revive not a poor fellow's fault that is hanged for his offence', we must remember that for a clown all publicity is good publicity. Kemp's emphasis on how little he drank implies that drunkenness was a major point at issue. Kemp's accounting of gifts implies that he had been accused of losing money in the venture, and he denies failure to pay tolls when he denies that 'roads were laid open for me'. Drunkenness and poverty were part of Tarlton's public image, and Kemp's indignant denials must be read as part of a humorous battle waged by jig-makers on rival stages.

Kemp's opponents gave him the mock-heroic title 'Knight of the Red Cross', we learn. Kemp's promised epic journey to the Continent helped sustain the image of knight errant. Spenser's original Red Cross Knight was in the service of the Fairy Queen, and Kemp's relationship with the Queen therefore came into question. Kemp denies that he 'delivered gifts' to her, and complains that her 'sacred name' has been dragged into the dispute.

The lying ballad-maker's name is closely akin to 'Jansonius'. It is probable, therefore, that Kemp has been identified with the hero of Richard Johnson's burlesque narrative *Tom-a-Lincoln, the Red-Rose Knight*, published about the time of Kemp's dance.[1] The hero, bastard son of King Arthur, is elected as a Summer Lord of Misrule. He distributes red roses as his livery badges to young men, who then turn highway robbers and dwell (like Robin Hood) in Barnsdale. The hero becomes a knight errant, journeys with Sir Launcelot, and is seduced by the queen of fairyland. It is easy to see how satirists could link Kemp's journey to the yet more fantastic journey of Johnson's anti-hero. It is also easy to see from Johnson's narrative how Kemp's progress could be construed as a threat to the Queen's peace.

Kemp plays upon the idea that he is a traditional Lord of Misrule. Like Robin Hood, the Tudor Summer Lord, he partners a 'Maid Marian'. He accepts challenges from all comers. The Tudor Summer Lord used to distribute paper livery badges in return for a levy which was then paid into church funds; and in his entrepreneurial version of the game, Kemp distributes his own identifying keepsakes to those who support him. The title-page shows him dressed in the full regalia of a country morris dancer: a plume, scarves waving from his arms, and a special shirt decorated with flowers to symbolize the coming of spring (Fig. 3). Kemp emphasizes his identity as a 'plain man' the better to set off his alternative lordly identity:

Kemps nine daies vvonder.

Performed in a daunce from London to Norwich.

Containing the pleasure, paines and kinde entertainment
of *William Kemp* betweene *London* and that Citty
in his late Morrice.

Wherein is somewhat set downe worth note; to reproove
the slaunders spred of him: many things merry,
nothing hurtfull.

Written by himselfe to satisfie his friends.

LONDON
Printed by *E. A.* for *Nicholas Ling,* and are to be
solde at his shop at the west doore of Saint
Paules Church. 1600.

Fig. 3 Title page of Kemp's *Nine Days' Wonder* (1600). Reproduced with permission of the Bodleian Library, from 4°.L.62 Art.

myself, that's I, otherwise called Cavaliero Kemp, Head-Master of Morris
Dancers, High Headborough of hays, and only tricker of your Trill-lillies
and best bell shangles between Sion and Mount Surrey.

To play such a part was to offer an open invitation to those who
wished to burlesque his exploits. Kemp's sensitivity relates to the
ambiguous status of his exploit. On the one hand, the Summer Lord
was by ancient tradition the lord of the morris dance. Yet, on the
other hand, ceremony has yielded to commerce. Not only did Kemp
collect money for personal profit, he also chose to do his dance
during Lent. The time suited him because the theatres were closed,
but in traditional England the morris never started before Lent was
out.[2]

The misrule tradition provides the clearest link between Kemp and
the medieval past. More tenuously, Kemp's pamphlet also links him
to the Vice/fool tradition. He offers bells and parti-coloured bonnets
to the fools who have libelled him, and when dancing opposite a
retained household fool he describes himself as a second 'fool'.

Kemp does not seem to have succeeded Tarlton as the Queen's
unofficial personal fool. His response is self-deprecating when an
inn-keeper identifies him as one of 'the Queen's Majesty's well-
wishers or friends'. Kemp claims that his 'mirths mean though they
be, have been and ever shall be employed to the delight of my royal
Mistress'. This tallies with Heywood's statement that Kemp succeeded Tarlton 'as well in the favour of her Majesty as in the opinion
and good thoughts of the general audience'.[3] But these remarks
imply only that the Queen enjoyed Kemp's stage roles. If Kemp had
recently abandoned the Queen's favourite Company, and had dis-
appeared into the underworld of unlicensed companies and playhouses, it is altogether likely that he would have been out of favour.

We have seen that some uncertainty surrounds Kemp's relationship with the Queen. Kemp's dedication to Anne Fitton compounds the enigma. Anne Fitton is described as 'true ennobled . . .
Maid of Honour to the . . . Queen', despite the fact that she had
married a country gentleman (not a nobleman) some years before
and gone to live in Warwickshire. She was never Maid of Honour to
the Queen. The obvious dedicatee is not her sister, Mary *Fitton*, but
Anne Russell, whose impending wedding was to be the social event
of the year. Her father had died too early to inherit his earldom, but
marriage to Worcester's heir would truly 'ennoble' her.[4] To *mistake*

the name of a dedicatee is frankly implausible under any circumstances, and the Queen's sensitivity about her Maids of Honour was notorious. Kemp's error must be a deliberate one. Posturing as a man bidding for court patronage, Kemp ironically certificates his true identity as a plain man, a man with no courtly aspirations. It was no accident that he dedicated his pamphlet to a lady who eschewed courtly success.

Kemp's *Nine Days' Wonder* informs us not only about his life and attitudes, but also about his art as a performer. He includes in the pamphlet two set-piece Skeltonesque 'rhymes' written for him by another hand. In one, he impersonates a country lass with swinging hips, in the other, a drunken innkeeper who reenacts battles in which he claims to have fought. Sketches such as these, demanding a fusion of song with mime or dance, would have been Kemp's normal method of presenting his life and adventures to the London public. Publication was a new experiment.

Behind Kemp's prose in the *Nine Days' Wonder*, we can hear the idiom of the professional improvisator. It will be helpful to analyse a sample. I retain the original punctuation.

I rested a while from dancing, but had small rest with those that would have begged me to drinking. But I warrant you *Will Kemp* was wise enough: to their full cups, kind thanks was my return, with Gentlemanlike protestations: as, truly sir, I dare not: it stands not with the congruity of my health. Congruity, said I? how came that strange language into my mouth? I think scarcely that it is any Christen word, and yet it may be a good word for aught I know, though I never made it, nor do very well understand it; yet I am sure I have bought it at the word-mongers, at as dear a rate, as I could have had a whole 100 of Bavins at the wood-mongers. Farewell Congruity, for I mean now to be more concise, and stand upon evener bases: but I must neither stand nor sit, the Tab'rer strikes alarum. Tickle it good Tom, I'll follow thee.

The most striking feature of this writing is the split personality of the narrator. The 'Will Kemp' who uses the gentleman-like word 'congruity' is engaged in a dialogue with the 'I' who uses homely words like 'bavins'. 'Will Kemp' is presumed to visit word-mongers just as the 'I' is used to visiting wood-mongers. While 'Will Kemp' competes in verbal battles, 'I' prefers the physical game of 'base'. The device of two personalities is well suited to provide variety and continuity in a dramatic monologue. It enables Kemp to project two levels simultaneously: the pretentious idiot on the surface, and the plain man beneath who rejects all pretension.

Shakespeare's clown

There are frequent shifts of register in the pamphlet as Kemp forgets that he is meant to be addressing 'Anne Fitton' and speaks instead to 'my masters'. In this passage, the phrase 'I warrant you' points to the assumed mode of address to a live audience. The phrase anticipates the characteristic slide from past tense to present, from a narrative to a dramatic mode. The pompous word which Kemp once uttered to gentlemen at Bow becomes a word that he utters now in the present before his live audience. In this way Kemp conjures up a moment of theatricality as he has to extricate himself from the confusion in which his audience seem to have trapped him. Having extricated himself, he cues in an exit line to remove himself physically from the stage.

A formal analysis of the language reveals elaborate patterning. The phrases fall into balanced pairs in which words and syntax are echoed:

> I rested . . . but had small rest
> from dancing . . . to drinking
> I dare not: it stands not
> Christen word . . . good word
> made it . . . understand it
> at the word-mongers . . . at the wood-mongers
> stand upon . . . neither stand

The rhetorical patterning is reinforced by alliteration, a device which Kemp has inherited from popular balladry:

> cups, kind thanks
> dancing/drinking
> warrant/Will Kemp/wise
> have had a whole hundred
> word/wood
> congruity/concise
> stand/sit
> taborer/tickle it/Tom

The improvisator has internalized rhythms which enable him to sustain his momentum. Through free association of ideas, or association of sounds, each phrase suggests the next. Kemp's skilful verbal embroidery serves to conceal the triteness of the subject matter.

The insistent beat of the drum can be heard behind Kemp's prose. When Kemp rises to his climax in this passage, he falls into the ballad metre of four and three:

Kemp: a biography

But I must neither stand nor sit,
The tab'rer strikes alarum.

Kemp's most original contribution to the history of clowning was musical. His farce jig or *Singspiel*, which I analyse in the next chapter, emerged from the popular morris, and the morris in turn links Kemp back to the world of Tudor festival, and to the lord of misrule who was the focus of the festival.

Let us turn now to the historical records, and reconstruct as much as we can of Kemp's career. When we first meet Kemp, he is a servant of Robert Dudley, Earl of Leicester. It is probable that he first comes to light when Leicester's players visited Ipswich in 1580. After the company had been paid, 6d was also paid for 'carrying a letter to Mr Kempe' – an invitation to come and perform, perhaps.[5]

Kemp was certainly part of the entourage with which the would-be governor of the Low Countries surrounded himself as he made a triumphal progress from Flushing to the Hague in December 1585. The entourage included fifteen actors and twelve musicians, who all helped Leicester to reciprocate the lavish entertainment that he received en route. No independent public performances were given. Once Leicester had entered the Hague, his chosen capital, he was able to send home his players. He paid twelve pounds in reward and expenses to his players, and made a significantly separate payment of one pound to 'William Kemp the player'.[6]

Kemp's relationship with Leicester was a personal one. It was in his bed-chamber that Leicester acted as money-changer for Kemp, using some of his gambling funds to change a gold coin that Kemp had received from the German Count Philip von Hohenlo. Hohenlo was an important new ally, a convivial man with a reputation for heavy drinking, and Leicester evidently used his clown, like his card playing, to cement diplomatic relations.[7]

When Kemp returned to England, he carried with him correspondence from Leicester's nephew, Philip Sidney. Sidney had had difficulty in getting London to respond to the dire state of his underpaid and underfed regiment. To ensure delivery, he enclosed a letter to Walsingham inside a letter to his wife. He also advised Walsingham to restrain Leicester's wife, Lady Dudley, from joining her husband – for it was now common knowledge that Leicester's court was excessively regal. Unfortunately he chose the wrong postman. Kemp

ignored instructions and passed all the correspondence to Lady Dudley, who for obvious reasons suppressed the letter in question. Sidney dubbed Kemp a 'knave' for an act that we may prefer to construe as intelligent loyalty. At all events, it was an ironic act of revenge on the man who complained of how clowns are thrust into plays 'to play a part in majestical matters, with neither decency nor discretion'.[8]

By the spring, Kemp had returned to his master. Obviously he went over to Holland to participate in the old show based on the labours of Hercules which was performed after the St George's Day dinner. He may also have participated in the quasi-dramatic tilting at barriers which followed in the evening. We learn from an account of 1584 that at such events knights would appear in role, and one of their servants, also in role, would deliver an appropriate speech, commonly designed to provoke laughter. In a miniature of Essex dressed for tilting, we have an illustration of such a comic servant. At events such as these, a retained clown proved his value.[9]

Two weeks later, Kemp was involved in some impromptu clowning which anticipates his leaps on the road to Norwich. The occasion was Leicester's excursion out of town to review the troops – who were certainly in need of cheering at this point. Leicester's accounts record payment 'to William Kemp after his leaping into a ditch before your Ex[cellency] and the Prince Elector as you went a-walking at Amersfoort: five shillings'.[10] Kemp may not have functioned as court jester to the Queen as Tarlton had done, but he obviously was able to take up that role in Leicester's notorious alternative court in the Netherlands.

Kemp did not linger in the Netherlands, where serious fighting was about to begin. Leicester was keen at this juncture to woo the King of Denmark as a military ally, so once again Kemp's talent was employed for diplomatic purposes. Armed with letters of commendation, Kemp made his way to London, where a Danish ambassador was engaged in crucial negotiations. In London Kemp had the opportunity of making contact with a group of English musicians who were part of the Danish retinue. When the ambassador's mission ended, Kemp joined his ship, along with five other English actors, and arrived at Elsinore in June 1586. The five were described as 'instrumentalists and tumblers', and included two who were to become actors in Shakespeare's company – Thomas Pope and George Bryan. Kemp himself was described as an 'instrumentalist',

and was accompanied by a boy. The troupe of five later moved on to Saxony. Kemp and his boy left Elsinore a month before they did, but obviously gave satisfaction for they received an extra month's pay as a bonus.[11]

Two facts seem significant here. First, Kemp was a solo comedian. In the Low Countries he accompanied Leicester's players but was not integrated with them, and in Denmark likewise he seems disinclined to work as part of a troupe. Secondly, music is the main ingredient of his act. Kemp's work abroad must have done much to sharpen his non-verbal performance skills. When Kemp's five colleagues went to Saxony, they were required to play at banquets, and in particular to give demonstrations of their leaping. Kemp's duties at Elsinore must have been similar: to play his instruments, to demonstrate his athletic English dancing, and to provide such other forms of table-side entertainment as he had in his repertoire. Although formal stage plays were presented at Elsinore, the stage play was not yet the focus for Kemp's dramatic talents.

We do not know what happened to Kemp after he left Elsinore. Leicester died in 1588, and Kemp, like other of Leicester's actors, duly acquired a new patron in Lord Strange. Around this time, the most famous of Kemp's jigs, *Rowland*, emerged.[12] In 1590 Nashe dedicated a book to him as 'jest-monger and vice-gerent general to the ghost of Dick Tarlton', though there is no reason to trust Nashe's assertion that Kemp's fame had reached Italy by this time.[13] The death of Tarlton in 1588 created a vacancy for a new folk hero, and the success of Kemp's jigs made him a leading contender.

Kemp's period of association with Strange's company appears to mark a transition – from solo comedian to regular company member, from patronage to commercial theatre.

Kemp's name does not appear alongside those of his former companions at Elsinore, Pope and Bryan, in *Seven Deadly Sins* in *c.* 1591. Perhaps he still preferred to maintain a separate identity, dancing and jesting in the intervals between the parts. In June 1592 Strange's Men produced a new play entitled *A Knack to Know A Knave*. The play includes an episode entitled 'Kemp's applauded merriments of the men of Gotham in receiving the King into Gotham'. Kemp's section is completely self-contained. The chief part is that of the mayor of Gotham, Jeffrey the cobbler, who has a petition to present to the king. A crafty smith and a moronic miller vie for the privilege but Jeffrey stands firm. The climax of the merriment is the fact that

the petition, it turns out in the end, is for a patent to brew ale. The striking feature of the scene is the way it is disengaged from the rest of the play, as though Kemp and his two assistants did not choose to merge with their fellow actors. Nashe confirms that the 'merriment' was Kemp's normal mode at this time.[14] An obvious parallel instance of a short clown episode's being inserted into a play of very different texture occurs in *Titus Andronicus*. The 1594 Quarto puts Strange's company first in the list of those that had performed the play, so it is not unlikely that the part was written in for Kemp's benefit.

The history of Strange's Men is a confused one, and no further probing of Kemp's career with them is possible. But after Lord Strange's death, matters become clearer. The company had been successful at court,[15] and when their patron died Kemp and many of his fellows passed into the service of the Lord Chamberlain. At the end of the year, Kemp acted as payee alongside Burbage and Shakespeare for a performance at court – a fact which indicates that these three were the pivotal members of the new company. During this period, Kemp and Burbage became the most famous actors of their generation. Cambridge students in 1601/2 brought the pair on stage to represent the archetypal common players of comedy and tragedy respectively, familiar alike to gentlemen and to country wenches.[16] The five years of Kemp's association with Shakespeare seem to have been an unusually stable period for him.

At the same time as he created his Shakespearean stage roles, Kemp continued to have success with his jigs. He published three in 1595. One satirist parodies John Davies's description of the planets dancing a galliard in order to capture the spinning and leaping that characterized Kemp's dance:

> A hall, a hall!
> Room for the spheres! The orbs celestial
> Will dance Kemp's Jig. They'll revel with neat jumps –
> A worthy poet hath put on their pumps.[17]

Another comments on the moral and social standing of those who enjoyed the entertainment that Kemp offered:

> rotten-throated slaves,
> Engarlanded with coney-catching knaves,
> Whores, beadles, bawds, sergeants filthily
> Chant Kemp's Jig...[18]

Kemp: a biography

There is, as we have seen, no evidence that Kemp had any contact with court except in his capacity as a player in stage plays. With due allowance for Juvenalian exaggeration, we may see here an indication that Kemp's jigs had a broadly plebeian appeal.

Kemp took to working within a theatre company in the 1590s because this, rather than personal patronage, was now the best road to fame and prosperity. We do not know how difficult Kemp found the process of adaptation, and how he coped with the tyranny of a script. The only direct evidence is late: but Brome had been in the theatre all his life and knew the tradition when he wrote the following dialogue in 1636/7:

> – But you, sir, are incorrigible, and
> Take licence to yourself to add unto
> Your parts your own free fancy, and sometimes
> To alter or diminish what the writer
> With care and skill compos'd; and when you are
> To speak to your coactors in the scene,
> You hold interlocutions with the audients.
>
> – That is a way, my lord, has been allow'd
> On elder stages to move mirth and laughter.
>
> – Yes, in the days of Tarlton and Kemp,
> Before the stage was purg'd from barbarism
> And brought to the perfection it now shines with.
> Then fools and jesters spent their wits, because
> The poets were wise enough to save their own
> For profitabler uses.[19]

Brome implies that it was normal for Kemp to add to his scripted part, while cutting or changing it was slightly rarer; clowns, it would seem, were able to interact with the audience so long as the playwright lacked his proper status of 'poet'. On the face of it, it is indeed inconceivable that a man of Kemp's background could have restrained himself from taking some liberties with his scripts. But censorship regulations and the evidence of reported texts must oblige us to treat Brome's evidence as cautiously as we treated Hamlet's. We must be content to observe that there was a historical conflict of interests between clown and poet. In the 1590s the conflict was temporarily resolved – but with what incidental stresses and strains we do not know.

In 1599 the partnership between Kemp and Shakespeare ended abruptly. Kemp acquired a fifth actor's share in the Globe when he

signed the lease in February, but by the autumn he had gone. He does not appear in the actors' list of *Every Man Out of His Humour* late in 1599, and there is no obvious clown part in *Julius Caesar*, which was in performance by September. It is therefore uncertain whether Kemp performed in the new theatre. We have no direct evidence of why he relinquished an obviously profitable investment. The Chamberlain's/King's company was a stable and prestigious organization, so Kemp must have had strong reasons for leaving. We may, I think, reasonably seek the explanation for his sudden departure in professional differences rather than in mere personal whims and antagonisms.

We do not know for certain where Kemp spent the winter of 1599/1600. The Earl of Derby's Men arrived in London at this time, and took over the newly built Boar's Head theatre – so this may have looked like a prestigious venture worth joining.[20] More likely, Kemp returned to the theatre which his colleagues had abandoned, the Curtain. In *Every Man Out Of His Humour*, the tavern fool, told he must remember to attend a celebration at the Mitre, expresses the wish that he 'had one of Kemp's shoes to throw after' his friend, the knight Puntarvolo. This seems to be an allusion to a play which Platter saw at the Curtain in the autumn of 1599. Platter particularly recalled a drunken servant's throwing a shoe at the head of his master, a valiant German soldier.[21] This play at the Curtain was followed by graceful dances 'both in English and in Irish fashion'. While the Curtain had a reputation for obscene jigs in 1598, and was to retain this doubtful renown for some years, the theatres south of the river never acquired such notoriety. Kemp's jigs had probably acquired a local clientele – an audience happy to welcome him back.

In February 1600, when the theatres closed for Lent, Kemp set off on his famous morris dance to Norwich. The success of this venture sparked off the grandiose idea of dancing to Italy. After publicizing his intentions, and committing his pamphlet to the press, he left for Calais.

Kemp crossed the Alps and eventually reached Rome, where in the summer of 1601 he met the famous traveller Sir Anthony Shirley. John Day, with Rowley and Wilkins, dramatized the meeting a few years later. In a wholly fictitious scene, he represents Kemp preparing an extemporal entertainment with an Italian Harlequin. In point of fact, the only Italian known to have played under the name of *Arlecchino* at this period was in Paris at the time.[22] Day also takes

the liberty of transposing the scene to Venice at the time of Shirley's arrest three years later. Day did at least know Kemp well, for he wrote for Worcester's Men in 1602, so the scene is of some value for its impression of Kemp's character. Kemp's introduction of himself is characteristically blunt: 'He calls himself Kemp.' He prefers to improvise, claiming to be 'somewhat hard of study'. His spectators expect nothing too refined:

> We neither look for scholarship nor art
> But harmless mirth, for that's thy usual part.

The 'harmless mirth' consists mainly of sexual innuendo. Kemp makes play of the fact that an Italian female is to act, and argues that since actors are 'fellows' they should hold wives in common. He wants to play the lover's part, but is typecast as the Pantaloon's peasant servant. Day's characterization offers us a man who combines blunt self-deprecation with the overweening ambition of Shakespeare's Bottom.

A popular song tells us that Kemp's motive for making his solitary journey across the Alps was profit:

> ... When Kemp did dance alone-a.
> He did labour
> After the tabour
> For to dance.
> Then into France
> He took pains
> To skip it.
> In hope of gains
> He will trip it.[23]

Evidently his hopes were not realized. A diarist who met him on his return refers to his wanderings and return on account of misfortune.[24] If Kemp conceived his journey as another stunt, he did not achieve the same notoriety as before. Another popular song mentions his return in order to achieve bathos:

> Diana and her darlings dear,
> The Dutchmen, ply the double beer,
> Boys rings the bells and make good cheer –
> When Kemp returns from Rome![25]

The queen, young boys and immigrants, it seems, celebrate Kemp's return, but not the general public.

The Cambridge students who referred to Kemp as 'Emperor of

Germany'[26] probably had in mind the next episode in Kemp's career. Kemp was back in England by 2 September 1601. And twelve weeks later we hear of a group of English actors playing at Münster after a tour of the Low Countries. An older man by the name of 'John Kemp' was in charge. This is surely not a 'relative' as Chambers suggests. The name is readily explained by the fact that an 'English John' was a generic name for a clown – in much the same way as the Italian *Giovanni* became the Italian *zanni*.[27] Kemp's wanderings had taken him through Germany, where his jigs were very much in vogue: four texts of his jig of *Rowland* survive from the period 1599–1603.[28] We must conclude, therefore, that on his homeward trip Kemp established the possibility of making a successful tour. He gathered up ten younger actors in London, and returned to the continent in the new capacity of actor-manager. At Münster his company performed five plays on five nights, but since these were in English the success of the enterprise depended on other ingredients. We are not surprised to learn that the company carried lutes, citherns, fiddles, pipes and such like, and many unfamiliar dances were performed at the beginning and at the end. A clown appeared during the costume changes, and impressed the audience by interspersing his act with quips in German.[29] This would seem to confirm that the clown was the organizer of the tour. During his travels, Kemp had picked up enough of the language in order to jest in it.

Kemp did not linger in Germany, but was back in England by Christmas. We find him in the service of the Earl of Worcester, who seems to have decided at this time that a company of players would enhance his status at court. Kemp and the actor-playwright Thomas Heywood were the leading lights in the new company, serving as payees for a performance at court given on 3 January. The company gathered its members from many quarters. At least two followed Kemp in abandoning Shakespeare. John Duke, though an experienced actor, probably could not afford to become a sharer in the Globe. Christopher Beeston was later to acquire an unpleasant reputation for financial wheeling and dealing. Robert Pallant, who had been with Strange's Men, may also have been hired by the Chamberlain's.[30] All had obviously decided on a new start.

The last two years of the reign were less hungry and more turbulent than the few years preceding. The Privy Council declared in June 1600 that there were to be only two playhouses in London, the Fortune and the Globe, but they had to rely on unwilling or impotent

JPs to enforce this ruling. A year later they virtually admitted that censorship of performed work was impossible when they complained about an unlicensed and libellous play at the Curtain. Some months later, they had to note that plays and playhouses were still on the increase.[31] The anarchic state of the theatrical world is underlined by the impunity with which Shakespeare's company mounted *Richard II* on the eve of Essex's rebellion. Worcester was on the Privy Council, but put personal interest first when he allowed his own company to establish itself in London. The new company had no base, but freebooted in various parts of London. Their patron complained in 1602 that they 'change their place at their own disposition', and tried to confine them to the Boar's Head, the place they 'like best of'. A year later they appear at the Rose, and early in 1604 the Curtain had joined the Boar's Head as 'their now usual housen'.[32]

There is every reason to imagine that Kemp thought working with Worcester's Men a more attractive proposition than working at the Globe. Part-ownership of a magnificent permanent building may not have been the attraction for him that it was for other players. The lack of a fixed venue would have been no disincentive to a lifelong wanderer. Kemp's jigs flourished north of the river – as we shall see in the next chapter – and he was probably reluctant to sever his links with audiences that he knew well. The new company was an energetic one, putting on a new play every fortnight or so.[33] Kemp was not to know that Shakespeare rather than Heywood would monopolize the attention of future residents.

Four plays survive from Worcester's Men's repertoire during this period. The ethos of these four plays is wholly different from the ethos of Shakespeare's writing. Given Kemp's orientation towards city rather than court, it is likely that he found the new company ideologically more acceptable.

How a Man May Choose a Good Wife from a Bad and *A Woman Killed with Kindness* are bourgeois comedies,[34] and deal with the stresses of middle-class marriage. Where Shakespeare glorified romantic love, these plays glorify marital faithfulness. *How a Man May Choose a Good Wife from a Bad* is conceived as a riposte to *Romeo and Juliet*, complete with feast, sleeping potion, tomb scene and accompanying rhetoric, and the play shows the plight of those who marry too young. The other two plays are historical/political in their subject matter. *Sir Thomas Wyatt* idealizes a Protestant rebel against

Mary. *The Royal King and the Loyal Subject* deals with a monarch's delusions about his powerful, admirable, and above all loyal Marshal. The company also revamped *Sir John Oldcastle*, which in a similar way deals with a monarch's delusion about a loyal but deeply Protestant subject. These plays were all performed in the aftermath of Essex's rebllion, and in this context their thrust is markedly un-Shakespearean. While Shakespeare tends to legitimate heredity and the preservation of an aristocratic order, these three plays offer as hero a man of the people at odds with the monarchy. Kemp had been with Essex and Leicester in the Low Countries, and as a personal servant of Leicester he would have learned to identify with the populist Protestantism that drove a wedge between these two earls and the Queen. On the basis of the extant repertoire, it is a reasonable conclusion that one who hopes 'he may, being a plain man, call a spade a spade' would be drawn to the work of Worcester's Men.

It is a less straightforward matter to establish whether Worcester's Men had a different attitude to the art of the clown. In the long term, it became clear that the Jonsonian neo-classicism adopted by the King's Men would leave no place for the clown, while the more romantic material performed at the Red Bull allowed the clown his traditional place. In the immediate period 1601–3, this is not clear at all. There is a more logical place for the clown in Shakespearean dramaturgy than in the emergent mode of domestic realism which culminated in Heywood's *A Woman Killed with Kindness*.

One further play is often attributed to the Worcester's repertoire at this time. The *albere galles* of Henslowe's *Diary* has long been conjectured to be *Archigallo*, and the play therefore an early version of *Nobody and Somebody*, published by the company in a revised text four years later.[35] The day payment was made for *albere galles*, a further entry in the *Diary* reads: 'A suit for Wm Kemp: the sum of 30/-'. A further 8/8^d was paid next day 'for making of Wm Kemps suit and the boys'.[36] If *albere galles* has been correctly identified we can explain what occasioned these payments. While the version of *Nobody and Somebody* performed by English actors in Germany gives the central comic part of the eponymous 'Nobody', the version published by Kemp's company gives equal scope to Nobody's servant, called simply 'the clown'. A small boy would have suited the bodiless Nobody. Kemp would have dressed his apprentice in the disembodied clown's slops illustrated on the title page, and played

his own clown part alongside. These deductions explain why 'Kemp's suit and the boy's' had to be specially made.

It is not certain that Kemp lived to perform in Heywood's masterpiece *A Woman Killed with Kindness*. The play may still have been in rehearsal when Elizabeth's terminal illness intervened, followed by an epidemic of plague. By the time playing began again, Thomas Greene was installed as clown and effective leader of the company.[37] Over 30,000 people died in London in the summer of 1603, and Kemp was probably one of them, buried without trace in the confusion of the time. If he survived the epidemic, then his death would seem to be recorded on 2 November 1603 in the burial entry of 'Kempe, a man' in the Southwark parish where he lived. In his *Nine Days' Wonder* Kemp doubts whether certain jig-mongers will be 'honestly buried' – and it may be that a censorious parish official refused to dignify Kemp's career as a performer of 'mad jigs and merry jests' by styling him 'player'.

At all events, it is clear that Kemp died with nothing. Henslowe in 1602, in a section of the *Diary* used for private debts, records that Kemp had to borrow 20/- 'for his necessary uses'.[38] He left no known will. He had no shares to assign. When we compare his career with his colleagues', we see that he was an exception in an upwardly mobile profession. Of the two actors who were with him in Denmark and went on to join the Chamberlain's Men, George Bryan became a permanent Groom of the Chamber in 1603, and Thomas Pope died a gentleman in 1604, holding shares in both the Globe and the Curtain. Pope and Shakespeare were not the only members of the Chamberlain's to become gentlemen: Robert Armin, Kemp's successor as clown, and Augustine Phillips, who wrote or performed jigs, also acquired coats of arms. John Singer, clown for the Admiral's Men, was another, like Tarlton before him, who became a Groom of the Chamber. Thomas Sackville, who migrated to a German court and played the clown 'John Posset', invested his earnings in a silk business around 1603 and became very rich.[39] Kemp's failure to acquire money or status marks him out. Money was probably something that he sought and squandered. Gentrification was something that he resisted. There is an important parallel between Kemp himself and the low status 'clowns' that he played on stage. The blunt burial entry 'Kempe, a man' makes, in a sense, a fitting epitaph.

It has been important to chart Kemp's career from a biographical standpoint. It becomes obvious at every turn that theatre – as we

now understand the term – was a mode of performance which Kemp adopted only in the last ten years of his life, and even then with a major interruption. His roots as a performer lay elsewhere.

Though Kemp had to adapt himself to the demands of writers, it is no less certain that writers had to adapt themselves to the demands of Kemp. Today, a contemporary dramatist writes in the knowledge that any given group of actors will be trained in building a character, and in playing a range of classic and contemporary roles. Casting can more or less safely be left to the discretion of the director. The Elizabethan dramatist knew that his actors had quite individual backgrounds as performers. There was no director to impose a unifying performance style upon a given cast for a given play. The dramatist was therefore obliged to write to the requirements of his actors. He could mould them only by slow degrees. And many, like Kemp, clung tenaciously to principles of their own. Kemp and Shakespeare in the Chamberlain's company, Kemp and Heywood in Worcester's, carried equal status, both within the company and in the eyes of the public. The plays that the two companies mounted were co-operative enterprises. To analyse an Elizabethan play as the product of a single mind is to impose a selective modern point of view.

CHAPTER 4

Kemp's jigs

I HAVE ARGUED that there was always a potential conflict of interests between the comedian who played 'clown' or 'Vice' and the Elizabethan dramatist who wanted scope and recognition for his own talents as a writer. Marlowe's case is typical. He claimed in his prologue to *Tamburlaine* that he was leading his audience away

> From jigging veins of rhyming mother wits
> And such conceits as clownage keeps in pay.

Yet the printer informs us that in performance the play was contaminated by 'some fond and frivolous jestures, digressing and . . . far unmeet for the matter', which had to be omitted if the text was to be rendered suitable for a 'wise' readership. We do not know whether Marlowe was responsible for this clownage. What we can discern clearly is tension between a neo-classical aesthetic which could not accommodate the clown and a performing tradition in which the clown was central.

This tension resolved itself in the 1590s. Within the authorial script, the clown was generally given a self-contained sub-plot and a smaller proportion of available stage time than the Vice used to receive. But after the scripted play was over, the clown was allowed the freedom of the stage, freedom for improvisation, rhyming and dancing. The old balance between order and carnivalesque inversion was maintained, but in a new way. As plays grew increasingly orderly, in respect of their writing, performance and reception, the traditional enactment of misrule was displaced onto the postlude. Tarlton had established the custom of taking over the stage at the end in order to sing and exchange extemporal verses with the audience. As the relationship between player and spectator grew more impersonal, as a hunger for narrative was stimulated, Tarlton's techniques were superseded. A contained dramatic action, the jig, became the central event in the postlude.

The origins of the jig can be found in folk drama. As the Reformation permeated parish life, elaborate King-games and other seasonal rituals were suppressed. Elements of these games and rituals nevertheless survived through attaching themselves to the morris dance. The morris was a vital enough institution, and sufficiently small-scale, to thrive without organization from above. The early morris men used to dance in honour of an elected Summer King or May Lady, but by the end of the century the ritual framework had vanished, and the fool replaced the Summer King as leader of the dance. Within the dance, older wooing games were subsumed in the fool's wooing of the man-woman, the burlesque descendant of the May Queen known as the 'Maid Marian'. Nashe describes a typical Elizabethan morris when he pictures

the Maid Marian trimly dressed up in a cast gown and a kercher of Dame Lawson's, his face handsomely muffled with a diaper napkin to cover his beard, and a great nosegay in his hand . . . [*The fool*] dances round him in a cotton coat, to court him with a leathern pudding and a wooden ladle.[1]

The fool's wooing gives the stage jig its basic structure.

The morris dance was the centre-piece of Elizabethan folk culture. It symbolized the sense of community that everyone supposed to have existed in some past golden age. It was at the same time associated with anti-authoritarian summer festivals in which the boundary between game and rebellion was ill defined. Shakespeare's comparison of Jack Cade with a morris dancer makes the point.

> I have seen
> Him caper upright, like a wild morisco
> Shaking . . . his bells.   (2 *Henry VI* III.i.364–6)

The author presents this 'morris dancer' as an egalitarian rebel who, in the festive tradition, knights himself, offers feasting and free love to his followers, and commands them to wear his livery. One of his followers points to the Utopian element in the misrule tradition when he refers back to a golden age of equality: 'it was never merry world in England since gentlemen came up' (IV.ii.8). The jig is a product of this folk culture, and occupies an ambiguous terrain somewhere between patriotism and subversion.

C. R. Baskervill, in his invaluable study of the jig, lays great emphasis on the folk element. The stage jig, however, also represents the first flowering of secular farce in England. It is significant that the

Kemp's jigs

finest extant medieval English farce, *Johan Johan*, is a translation from the French. The form had never taken root in England, and the stage jig may therefore be considered a 'renaissance' form – an example of Renaissance sub-culture, one might say. Rambling plots derived from minstrels' anecdotes, jest books and foreign novellas were subjected to a formal discipline which derived both from ceremonial dance forms and from the new theatrical professionalism. Baskervill describes the stage jig as merely 'a fad of the London populace when Elizabethan drama was at its height'.[2] He sees the jig as a residual form, not essentially connected to developments on the London stage. He cannot therefore offer any clue as to why the most celebrated jig-maker of the age teamed up with the most celebrated dramatist.

The emergence of the jig is also related to the history of dance. Baskervill tells us of 'the freest transference of features from one type to another' around 1600, and considers that the jig, the morris and the galliard influenced each other strongly.[3] In the stage jig, the conventional acrobatic leaping or 'capering' of the morris was enriched by the whirling characteristic of the courtly galliard – whence the satirist's comment that the 'orbs celestial/Will dance Kemp's Jig'.[4] When Hamlet scorns the clown's 'cinque-pace of jests', he is referring to the basic step of the galliard – which a more skilful performer would enrich with variants, exaggerations and tumbles. The jig flourished because its performers were able to draw freely on both the morris and the galliard in order to improvise new steps and movements of their own. The jig represents a creative synthesis of a courtly and a popular language of dance, and its development thus correlates with that of mainstream Elizabethan drama.

The word 'jig' was commonly used of social dances between couples, and the stage 'jig' owes its name to the fact that its theme is overtly sexual. In dancing in general, the trend was towards physical freedom in terms both of movement and of touching taboos. Puritans were provoked by the vogue for 'uncleanly handlings, gropings and kissings', and enquired 'what good doth all that dancing of young women, holding upon men's arms that they may leap the higher?'[5] We have to understand the function of the stage jig in relation to the sexual needs of a population which included innumerable men severed from family and parish life. Elizabethan public theatres and brothels tended to be sited in the same localities. Both were products of the new urban environment, yet neither could be

45

dovetailed into the official framework of the Elizabethan commonwealth. For prostitutes, the adjacent theatre was an ideal place in
which to solicit clients.[6] The same satirist who wrote of bawds and
whores chanting Kemp's jig also describes the reactions of an elderly
citizen to a jig at the theatre where Kemp was then playing. The jig
fires his breast and succeeds in

> making him young again –
> Who, coming from the Curtain, sneaketh in
> To some odd garden noted 'house of sin'.[7]

When apprentices went on the rampage, they made no distinction
between brothels and playhouses, and vandalized both in order

> to bring to end
> All that is vile and bawdy –
> All players and whores thrust out a' doors,
> Seductive both and gaudy.[8]

It is reasonable, therefore, though always insufficient as a final analysis, to regard the jig as a form of soft commercial pornography.

In most discussions of Elizabethan theatre the jig is brushed aside
and forgotten. Yet from a sociological standpoint the jig has to be
seen as an essential component in the fragile balance which the
Elizabethan theatre set up between popular and courtly modes. To a
large though far from complete extent, the economically dominant
occupants of the sixpenny gallery and the lords' room, together with
the actors' patrons in the Privy Council, were able to dictate the tone
in the public theatres; but at the end of a day's performance the
balance shifted, and the actors surrendered a degree of control to
those who stood in the yard. Something of the mood of excitement
and danger at the end of a play is given in the account of the Italian
diplomat who stood in the yard of the Curtain around the time when
jigs were suppressed in 1612. In what was obviously normal practice, the groundlings clapped and shouted and called for the play of
their choice to be performed next day. The Italian had the misfortune
to be mistaken for a Spaniard, and was booed from the theatre.[9]

We may safely deduce from the quality of the poetry written for
Elizabethan audiences that those audiences normally listened atten-
tively. After the play was over, two hours of concentration required
some release, and the jig provided this release. The audience were
encouraged to take an active part, clapping time and joining in with
some of the words. We hear that

Kemp's jigs

A jig shall be clapped at, and every rhyme
Praised and applauded by a clamorous chime.[10]

Dekker explains that much of the pleasure of the jig lay in the ritualized anarchy that accompanied its performance: 'The stinkards speaking all things, yet no man understanding anything; a mutiny being amongst them, yet none in danger . . . the swiftness of such a torrent, the more it overwhelms, breeding the more pleasure'.[11]

One cause of this anarchy seems to have been the swelling of the audience by many who could not afford the entry fee for the main play. While some left, others must have entered – the poor apprentices, for instance, who used to hang about at the theatre door.[12] Certainly this was the case at the Fortune by 1612 when jigs had to be suppressed because 'by reason of certain lewd jigs, songs and dances . . . lewd and ill-disposed persons in great multitudes do resort thither *at the end of every play*' (my italics).[13] These people could not have come if they had not been able to enter the theatre – though whether they paid, stampeded their way in, or entered freely is still unclear.

The jig perpetuated the kind of anarchic theatre that flourished under Tarlton. It found no place in the private playhouses, and came mainly to be associated with the Curtain and the Fortune. It was only north of the river that jigs were suppressed in 1612, and the obvious explanation must be that the north and east were the poorest parts of the city.[14] Many complaints stress that theatre drew apprentices and handicraftsmen from their work. Working Londoners would have preferred theatre which did not involve them in a time-consuming journey across the bridge or the expense of a water-man to carry them by boat. Bear-baiting continued on Bankside, but bears had to be shipped to Court upon demand. The Globe was the only playhouse on Bankside to prosper in the seventeenth century, and this must be because it attracted an audience from the prosperous west side of London. The Chamberlain's Men evidently aimed to enhance their status as early as 1596, when the Burbages purchased and refitted the Blackfriars', only to be prevented from using it for over a decade.[15] In the circumstances, it can be no coincidence that the Globe never acquired a reputation for jigs. The jig did nothing to raise the status of the company, and increased the risk of crowd trouble. It is therefore likely that there would have been some difference of opinion between the Chamberlain's company and Kemp in respect of the jig. Kemp would have come to realize that the move to

47

the Globe stood to deprive him of the free hand and the receptive audiences to which he had been accustomed at the Curtain.

Since the jig is a sub-literary form, any study of it is impeded by lack of evidence. Of the extant jigs, many exist only in German or in very late editions; dating is therefore difficult. And it is in the nature of the evidence that an atypical body of jigs should have survived, since the more scandalous never found their way into print. We are even less well informed about the musical and visual aspects of the jig.

Since no illustration of an English jig survives, a German woodcut must serve to communicate the flavour of a jig in performance. The German *Singspiel* was modelled on the English form; Figure 4 illustrates an early example. Though some texts have three or five actors, four is the conventional number for a jig since, as here, it breaks conveniently into two dancing couples. The plot deals with a priest's attempt to seduce some of his flock. The costume is ceremonial rather than representative, and a hat alone serves to signify that the fool on the left plays the priest. The two ladies in farthingales seem to be played by males, and their shovel-shaped head-dresses parody a transient fashion. The bells and ribboned shoes help to pick out the rhythm and movement.

This illustration provokes us to ask what the clown wore in the English jig. Some form of ceremonial costume seems likely. Groups of 'fools' do not appear in English folk drama – unlike the continental *Sottie* or *Fastnachtspiel*. Two English jigs centre on a fool in fool's costume, but these are not representative examples.[16] Stubbes describes how morris men normally wore the colours of the lord of misrule – yellow or green – with improvised trimmings.[17] The problem is whether the clown of the stage jig derives himself from the Lord of Misrule, or from the fool of the morris. Either way, representational costume was unnecessary.

The texts survive of four jigs attributed to Kemp, and these are worth close examination. Two have English texts, two survive only in German versions. One in each language is certainly Kemp's; the other is, at the least, modelled on his style.[18]

The German jig of *Rowland* is an economical piece of dramatic writing. It is to be identified as the first or second part of 'the jig between Rowland and the Sexton', the second part of which was

Elster Aufzug.
Erster Narr.

JA Pfaffe/lieber Pfaffe/
Du rechter Heüchelaffe/
Wilt du noch sein geehrt?
Kanst du die Schäfflein führen/
Kanst du Sie recht regieren/
und bist kaum halb gelehrt?

Fig. 4 An early German *Singspiel*. Reproduced with permission of the Bodleian Library, from Douce Portfolio 142, No. 292.

registered in 1591. The plot is simple, but its development is never predictable. The carnivalesque motif of death and rebirth can be discerned in the background. Rowland acts dead when his Peggy abandons him for the Sexton; Peggy grieves briefly, and then decides she might just as well marry the Sexton; but she declares her love for Rowland when the latter springs indignantly to life. The jig is played by the standard number of four actors, and is constructed so that two dancers dance opposite each other while the second pair remains back or aside. The central comic role is that of Rowland, who keeps up a running commentary to the audience. He is allocated the punchline at the end of ten out of eighteen quatrains, where the break in the music gave space for laughter. Rowland's initial description of the situation, and the asides which he delivers even when acting dead, oblige the audience to look at events from his point of view.

In one sixteenth-century pamphlet, *Rowland* is paired with a companion piece which is a deliberate reversal of its plot. This time it is the wife who acts dead, after three wives have debated which has the most faithful husband. The husband, John, recovers quickly from his grief, and tries to seduce one of the other wives, who is happy to acquiesce. Again the piece is a vehicle for the central comic character. The laugh is constantly turned by John against his wife as he strips her of her keys and wedding ring, and promises to send a wheelbarrow to cart her away. Eventually John is given a thrashing by his wife, and has ruefully to promise that he will from now on obey her as his master.

As in *Rowland*, there is no verbal obscenity, but there is ample opportunity for lascivious dancing. In this piece, each quatrain characteristically culminates in an action, rather than a quip, on the part of the clown. In order to appreciate the jig, we must recall how little physical contact takes place between lovers in Shakespeare's plays. One puritan described actors 'who by their wantonizing stage-gestures can ingle and seduce men to heave up their hearts and affections', and continued: 'by how much more exact these are in their venerean action, by so much more highly are they seated in the monster-headed multitude's estimation'.[19] Kemp's jigs allowed him the option of winning success in this manner.

This is even more obvious in the case of *Rowland's Godson*, a manuscript English jig, the title of which links it to Kemp's 'Rowland' jigs. The refrain of 'love . . . love' tends itself to mimetic adumbration. The action is the successful concealment of adultery

between the servant John and his master's wife. The suspicious master dresses up as his wife, and a thrashing convinces him of the loyalty of both wife and servant. There is considerable sexual ambiguity as the triangle is reconstituted, and the husband, still dressed as a woman, sings of his love for his servant.

The jig of *Singing Simpkin* appears in the Stationers' Register in 1595 as 'a ballad called Kemp's new jig betwixt a soldier and a miser and Sim the clown'. The theme is that of *Rowland's Godson*, the techniques are those of *Rowland*. Simpkin keeps up a running commentary to the audience, even when hidden inside a chest, and the final line of a quatrain is repeatedly his to exploit. A sample will illustrate the nature of the material. In the husband's absence, a soldier (Bluster) has interrupted the wife's seduction of the servant (Simpkin). Simpkin is now hidden inside the chest.

Bluster	Within this chest I'll hide myself,
	If it chance he should come.
Wife	Oh no, my love, that cannot be –
Simpkin	I have bespoke the room.
Wife	I have a place behind here,
	Which yet is known to no man.
Simpkin	She has a place before, too,
	But that is all too common.

Old man within.

Old man	Wife, wherefore is the door thus barred?
	What mean you, pray, by this?
Wife	Alas! It is my husband.
Simpkin	I laugh now till I piss.
Bluster	Open the chest, I'll into it;
	My life else it may cost.
Wife	Alas, I cannot open it.
Simpkin	I believe the key is lost.

While remaining notionally unseen, the clown is as free to participate in the conversation as he is to jest with the audience. The behaviour of the other characters, by contrast, is governed by the logic of the plot. In accordance with a dramatic mode that is primarily physical and mimetic, Simpkin's passions are strictly physical, with no hint of sentiment.

A textual problem arises at the end of the jig. Robert Cox, while performing the piece at the Red Bull during the Commonwealth, seems to have added two extra stanzas in which the old man returns

to beat the clown. In the earlier German texts there is no restoration of morality at the end. The husband remains in blissful ignorance, while the wife and the clown dance the finale together.[20]

These four jigs share certain obvious features, besides their common concern with adultery. They are all written as vehicles for a clown, who ends up paired with a lady. The clown always starts in a mood that is explicitly 'sad' or full of 'woe' in order to offset the mirth that follows. He starts the jig in a predicament, and the audience's pleasure consists in seeing how he extricates himself. The clown is an anti-hero in the misrule tradition, for he is the lowest of the low in all respects – wealth, status, fighting ability, even intelligence (for his ploys are never his own idea) – in everything, in short, except dancing ability.

Kemp's jigs are not wholly typical of the jig at large, so far as we can tell from surviving examples of this varied form. Some early jigs adopted the sentimental/romantic paradigm of the official drama rather than the older paradigm of misrule. In *Attowell's Jig*, a jig associated with an actor once in Strange's company, 'Dickie' and his wife are idealized representatives of a lower class, and have to fend off a wealthy, amorous gentleman. In a recently discovered manuscript jig, the hero is a poor carter, who deprives a rich cobbler of his bride. The cobbler, consistently identified by other characters as the 'clown', is the butt of the humour throughout. And in *Pickleherring's Dill Dill Dill*, extant only in German and Dutch, the clown is a prosperous miller whose wife is successfully wooed by a well-spoken suitor of unspecified status. A number of less technically accomplished German jigs exclude the clown from the adultery plot altogether, and make him a mere helper or onlooker. Two other English jigs are rather closer to Kemp's. In one elaborate piece, when a girl offers 'Thumpkin' her bed, two gentlemen try in vain to pre-empt this 'country clown'. More anarchic still is an amateur piece of *c.* 1621 in which the fool, Joculus, evades a paternity suit while two gallants are arrested for his crime.[21]

On the basis of this evidence, Kemp's jigs appear to be distinguished not only by their tightness of construction but also, in two important respects, by their content. First, they avoid the class theme. More precisely, they do not constitute an attack on the *nouveaux riches* or gentlemen of leisure. And secondly, they focus on a clown who is controller rather than butt of the humour. Where other clowns invite a simple feeling of superiority, Kemp's clown

initially appears to be a ludicrous figure, but rapidly makes everyone else appear more ludicrous.

It is the feature of all playhouse jigs, with the exception perhaps of *Attowell's Jig*, that the central part belongs to a clown figure. We must of course presume that no one person had a monopoly of post-play entertainment, for there was too much talent available. In the Chamberlain's, Pope and Bryan had backgrounds as musical entertainers and tumblers in Germany; Augustine Phillips published his 'jig of the slippers' in 1595, and was able to instruct his apprentices in the use of four different stringed instruments.[22] Nevertheless, Kemp's prominence as a jig-maker, and his function as 'clown' in the Chamberlain's Men – a function which will be examined in the next chapter – encourages us to ask further questions about the relationship between the jig and the play as inter-related forms. The jigs of Kemp in particular cannot be dismissed as coarsened and scaled-down replicas of orthodox scripted plays. The change of mode, from a predominantly verbal to a predominantly physical medium, correlates with a markedly different attitude to sexual love. In order to appreciate the function of the jig, we have to shed the assumption that the jig was an excrescence tacked on at the end of the play, and take a holistic view of the Elizabethan theatrical experience.

When we turn for comparison to a foreign theatrical form of the same period, we can perceive more clearly why the jig was an integral part of an English theatrical performance. In the public productions of the Italian *commedia dell'arte* – in the collection of forty comedies published by Flaminio Scala in 1611, for instance[23] – it is an almost unbroken convention that the marriage of socially privileged *innamorati* is accompanied in the finale by a marriage between the *servetta* and one of the *zanni*. Yet in Elizabethan comedy, the marriage of the socially privileged marks the closure of the play, and there is rarely an accompanying point of arrival for the clown. It seems to me, therefore, no coincidence that the rise of the stage jig coincides historically with the rise of romantic comedy. Shakespeare and his contemporaries wrote in the knowledge that their comedies would be rounded off by a jig, and they could therefore leave their scripts open-ended – in a sense, incomplete.

I shall return to the convention of the open ending in Chapter 8. For the moment, some Shakespearean examples will illustrate the clown's failure to pair like the gentry. In *The Merchant of Venice*, three parallel weddings conclude the play, graduated at once socially

and dramaturgically, but, at the bottom of the social ladder, there is no resolution for Launcelet, and the pregnancy of the mooress is forgotten. Launce has decided to marry the milk-maid, but the audience have not met the lady. Bottom has played a love scene with (symbolically) a bellows-mender, and he has dreamed of seduction by the Queen of Fairy. Costard and Armado have not finally resolved who will be the possessor of Jaquenetta. If the clown of the company and the clown of the jig can be identified as one and the same man, then the jig in a very important sense completes the comedy.

We do not know exactly how the transition between play and jig was effected. One text, however, gives us a particularly clear example of a dramatist planning for the clown's jig. The ever-methodical Jonson wrote the first text of *Every Man In His Humour* for the Chamberlain's Men to perform at the Curtain, and revised the text either for or after a Jacobean revival. In the final scene of the revised version, Cob and his wife appear before Justice Clement to be reconciled, but in the original version only the wife appears. The play is written for sixteen name parts, and sixteen has been shown to be the standard number for Shakespeare's company.[24] In the original version, all fifteen other characters congregate on stage in the final scene, and Clement promises that he will entertain everyone with 'the very spirit of mirth'. It is a reasonable deduction that the player of Cob is absent from the finale because he is making ready to provide this 'spirit of mirth'. Three other characters are sent off the stage prior to Clement's anouncement: Peto, in his borrowed armour, Matheo, who has been told to don sackcloth, and Bobadilla, who has been condemned to wear a 'large motley coat' as his punishment. Matheo and Bobadilla have also been told to 'sing some ballad of repentance . . . to the tune of *who list to lead and a soldier's life*'. There is no reason why we should not take Jonson at his word, or almost. These three actors are going to re-emerge, dressed in extra-ordinary costumes, to join Cob, the clown, and to sing a kind of ballad. 'Matheo', having failed to respond to Clement's challenge to 'make verses . . . *extempore*', will have a second opportunity. The transposition will be easy when these four actors make up the conventional foursome of a jig. The signs are that Jonson was trying to exert some sort of authorial control over the content of the jig or entertainment which followed his play. To what extent the actors cooperated cannot be told. By the time Jonson came to revise the play, the King's Men at the Globe had changed their policy in respect of the jig. The comic

punishments are therefore excised from the text, and Cob is brought on stage for the final scene.

Similar thinking may lie behind *Much Ado About Nothing*, a play of the same year. The actor of Don John is the only player not to appear on stage in the final act. In the final lines, it is announced that John is under arrest in Messina, and that punishments will be devised for him. Ten principals are present for the final dance, leaving two groups of three to make a subsequent 'curtain call' of whatever kind – three villains and three agents of the law. The symmetry is suggestive. Some ludicrous punishment of 'John' may have eased the transformation of Kemp/Dogberry into Kemp the jig-maker.

In *A Midsummer Night's Dream* the transformation of Kemp/Bottom into Kemp the jig-maker is anticipated in the text. Bottom promises the audience:

I will get Peter Quince to write a ballet of this dream . . . and I will sing it in the latter end of a play before the Duke.

Much uncertainty surrounds the finale of the play. It is 'Lion', not Bottom, in the authoritative Quarto text who asks the Duke if he would like to 'hear a Bergomask dance' – a dance for which the text provides no stage direction. Bottom may have been one of the two dancers at this point – but he may equally have had to wait longer before the actor could sing/dance a 'ballet'.

Because the clown appeared after the play was over, he was generally excluded from any final procession or formal dance. One example will suffice for the present. In the stage plot of *1 Tamar Cam* (*c.* 1602),[25] John Singer, in the part of 'Clown', is not brought on at the end when a grand procession of conquered races pays homage to Tamar Cam. Although six supernumeraries are drafted in to maximize numbers, Singer the Clown is kept in reserve.

The Tudor Vice traditionally had the task of mediating between play and audience, breaking down the boundary between them. The Vice's descendant, the clown, retained this function. It was his task to lead the audience out of the play and into a different type of entertainment in which vigorous participation was expected. Kemp was able to perform this task because he never submerged his own personality in the role that he played. Robert Armin was not a jig-maker. When the Chamberlain's Men acquired a new theatre, and a new clown, a change of convention becomes apparent at once. The clown in *As You Like It* is allowed to complete his wooing

within the text. The clown in *Twelfth Night* is given the final song, and the announcement that 'our play is done'. Some kind of dance may still have followed, but it did not complement the script in the same way.

When we discard the old critical notion of the unity of the text, and seek instead the unity of the theatrical experience, we find that the relationship between play and jig is many-faceted. The jig purveys anarchy to counterbalance the play's creation of moral order. In respect of plot, the jig's focus on adultery provides a denouement to follow the literal *nouement* that ends a comedy. From a sociological viewpoint, the clown's wooing recreates symmetry, reassuring the audience that the play world is relevant to the whole of society, not just to the upper segment. From another point of view, the Shakespearean hero represents intellectual and spiritual experience, while the clown represents physical experience. The play culminates in the ceremony of betrothal or marriage, and the jig represents the physical consummation that follows. From yet another point of view, we may say that the jig allows the audience to deconstruct the finale of the play. The plays are idealist in their philosophy: romantic love is presented as a perfect state that individuals can attain, despite the obstacles that they and the world erect. The jig reduces marriage to a material arrangement. Of course, we cannot ever say that the jig is moving in a direction which Shakespeare has not himself pointed to in his scripts; the jig simply pushes the logic of the clown's part an important step further.

We can now begin to grasp why Kemp was the most celebrated jig-maker of his age. Lesser jig-makers used the clown as a simple polarization of either positive or negative values, so that the clown became either the poor man or the newly rich man in a sentimental image of class conflict. Kemp's jigs neither mirrored nor reinforced the Shakespearean finale, but set up a complex relationship between two alien worlds. Kemp allows his clown to inhabit a world from which gentlemen are excluded, and where different values can therefore obtain.

I have argued that there is a close link between comedy (or tragedy) which idealizes romantic love and the clown's jig. The jig, however, followed every play, and not simply romantic plays. In order to understand the relationship between the jig and any given play, we have first to examine the deployment of the clown within the text. In two of Shakespeare's historical plays, Shakespeare relates

a major clown character – first Jack Cade, then Falstaff – to the tradition of carnival and festive misrule. Given this placing of the clown, a relationship between jig and play becomes possible. In other historical plays, including *Richard II*, written during Kemp's time with the Chamberlain's, no clown appears. I would suggest that the clown is absent because Shakespeare and his actors saw no way in which a bridge could be made between the delicate political concerns of the play and the sexual concerns of the jig. When we reach Shakespeare's major tragedies and so-called problem comedies, a different clown has been employed, with a radically different approach to his art, and the jig has been discarded.

Kemp's departure from the Chamberlain's Men marked a turning point in Shakespearean dramaturgy. I shall conclude this chapter by observing how the immediate fact of Kemp's departure, refracted through Shakespeare's imagination, was presented to the audience at the Globe.

As I observed in the Preface, when Shakespeare fails to bring on a clown amongst the 'tragedians of the city' in *Hamlet*, he deliberately reminds the Globe audience that the real tragedians who play before them have lost the services of Kemp. The relevance of this reminder emerges when Hamlet casts himself as the fool of both 'The Mousetrap' and *Hamlet*. The players within the play complain of competition from a boys' company – and it can be no coincidence that the *Paul's* boys produced Marston's *Antonio's Revenge* shortly after Shakespeare produced *Hamlet*. It may be that Marston simply expanded Shakespeare's idea, or it may be that they wrote simultaneously, each knowing what the other was about.[26] In the boys' play, the tragic hero adopts the cockscomb, bauble and habit of a fool. Hamlet's adoption of the fool's part is more subtle.

When Hamlet describes himself as Ophelia's 'only jig-maker', he is excusing his gross sexual obscenities. His posture makes his jest unmistakable when he implies that 'no-thing' lies between Ophelia's legs. Hamlet is signalling also that he has adopted the clown's role, jesting and singing to introduce the play that is about to happen. He positions himself informally, lying at Ophelia's feet, and studying Claudius's face. Placed both verbally and visually half-way between play and audience, he is 'as good as a chorus'. Mingled with puns and parody, his jests betray Tarlton's penchant for jibes and Kemp's for extempore alliteration. When the players end their play, Hamlet's clown takes the stage and plays on. The point is one that editors of

Shakespeare's clown

the play have overlooked, and the writing is sufficiently dense to warrant a commentary:

<blockquote>

Exeunt all but Hamlet and Horatio.

Hamlet   Why let the strucken deer go weep,
        The hart ungalled play,
     For some must watch while some must sleep,
        Thus runs the world away.
     Would not this, sir, and a forest of feathers, if the rest of my fortunes turn Turk with me, with two Provincial roses on my razed shoes, get me a fellowship in a cry of players, sir?

Horatio   Half a share.

Hamlet   A whole one, I.
        For thou dost know, O Damon dear,
          This realm dismantled was
        Of Jove himself, and now reigns here
          A very, very – pajock.

Horatio   You might have rhymed.

Hamlet   O good Horatio, I'll take the ghost's word for a thousand pound. Didst perceive?

Horatio   Very well, my lord.

Hamlet   Upon the talk of the poisoning?

Horatio   I did very well note him.

Hamlet   Ah ha! Come, some music; come, the recorders.
        For if the king like not the comedy,
        Why then, belike he likes it not, perdie.
     Come, some music.   (III.ii.265–88)

</blockquote>

Like the clown in the public theatres, Hamlet sings as soon as the play is over – and probably also dances to the physically expressive '*Thus* runs the world away.' The 'this' which could earn Hamlet a share in a company of players refers not only to his playwriting but also, more immediately, to his singing. Shakespeare, as we have seen, has already reminded his audience that his own clown and jig-maker recently sold his share in the Globe. Hamlet here alludes to the ceremonial costume that a dancer of jigs might wear. Feathers were always worn by morris men – or again, a fool might wear a cock's feathers as an alternative to a cockscomb.[27] Profuse roses and decorative slashing made the dancer's shoes the focus of attention. Hamlet's obsequious 'sir' – in pointed contrast to 'good Horatio' – indicates that Hamlet is mimicking the jig-maker in question.

At an obvious level, Hamlet's song refers to Gertrude and Claudius. 'This realm' is Denmark. But another stratum of meaning emerges. The phrase 'runs the world away' refers to the Globe – like

Kemp's jest in the *Nine Days' Wonder*: 'I have . . . danced myself out of the world.' The phrase initiates a sequence of thought about the clown's running off and selling his share in the Globe. The 'whole' or 'half' issue seems to relate to the fact that Kemp had relinquished shares not only in the company but also in the building – 'this realm'. 'This realm' is initially the world of 'The Mousetrap', which Claudius/Jove has just destroyed, so that Hamlet/fool must now step onto the boards. But 'this realm' becomes, by extension, the stage of the play *Hamlet*. The words 'This realm dismantled was / Of Jove himself' allude to the fact that the frame of the 'Theatre' – built by the real-life father of Burbage, alias Hamlet – was dismantled and reassembled in 1599 as the Globe. Hamlet does not proclaim himself as 'ass' as the rhyme demands but a 'patchock' – a patched or motley fool.[28] Kemp was notoriously asinine in the roles of Dogberry and Bottom, but Hamlet is setting himself up as a more voguish figure, a fool in motley. A new kind of fool was lord of the stage in the new building.

The momentum of Hamlet's clowning sweeps him on, and he demands music to accompany his performance as he launches into banal extemporal rhyming. He does not dance, however, for when the players return he imagines himself the pipe and refuses to be played upon. He ends with some manic fooling with Polonius, veteran actor and lover of jigs. Hamlet's mediation between reality and illusion is complete when he persuades the audience, as well as Polonius, to look at a cloud in the sky above the playhouse, and to imagine a likeness of first a camel and ultimately Gertrude. The clown persona can serve Hamlet no longer. When he leaves to find Gertrude in the privacy of her closet, he knows that he must now act in the paradoxical modern style. In order to be 'not unnatural', he must will that his 'tongue and soul in this be hypocrites'. He abandons the role of fool, and establishes that the patchock who now reigns here is Claudius: 'a vice of kings', a 'king of shreds and patches' (III.iv.98, 103).

As a coda to this discussion, it may be worth adding that Dick Tarlton was a Master of Fence, and that exhibition fighting was one of his professional lines.[29] The comic mode remains available to Hamlet for his final performance.

It was a significant moment in theatre history when Burbage united within Hamlet the figures of clown and tragic hero. In the sixteenth century, clown and tragic hero remained in some measure

descendants from the allegorical interlude, and each represented different fragments of the experience of a single mankind. In *Hamlet*, however, all human experience seems capable of being channelled through one unifying consciousness. Hamlet has taken over from the clown/Vice the function of mediating between play and audience. Through the sophisticated medium of the soliloquy, the audience learn to look simultaneously at and with an integral individual – an actor, that is, who represents the total experience of a human being in all its tragic and comic disorder. The formal 'clown' in *Hamlet*, the gravedigging sexton, does not realize a different area of experience, in either sociological or emotional terms; rather, he refracts and mirrors Hamlet's experience in new ways. The mad clown's assumption that Hamlet is mad makes Hamlet seem the more sane. This new clown never addresses the audience directly: his ghoulishness, and physical placing by the trap-door, make him remote. It is Hamlet who is the link between clown and audience, the one totally accessible sensibility. A complete reversal has taken place.

In *Hamlet*, symbolically, we see the jig being swallowed up and dissolved within the play. The jig became a residual form, a self-contained end-piece, once the juxtaposition of rule and misrule ceased to be the organizing principle for drama. In Shakespeare's 'dark' comedies and tragedies, the possibility of perfect order disintegrates; the celebration of anarchy ceases, necessarily, to be an admissible complement to the play.

CHAPTER 5

'The clown' in playhouse
terminology

THE LAST SERIOUS ATTEMPT to show which roles Kemp
played was that of T. W. Baldwin. The attempt foundered
because it was based upon character analysis. Kemp's 'line'
was assumed to be that of 'the pompous, countrified, blundering
clown' – and from that premise a series of highly speculative conclusions resulted.[1] My own method will be to avoid any concept of
character, and to concentrate instead upon the terminology of stage
directions, and upon structural features within the organization of
the text.

The argument of the last chapter turned on the assumption that
the 'clown' of the play-text can be identified with the comic protagonist of the jig. The argument needs to be consolidated. In this
chapter, therefore, I analyse the term 'clown' in order to show that
when it appears in Elizabethan texts it refers to the actor a company
employed specifically to be its clown. This prepares the way for an
analysis, in the next chapter, of the roles written for Kemp *qua* 'the
clown' of the Chamberlain's and later of Worcester's Men.

The term 'clown' does not appear before the Elizabethan period.
The word entered the language because it expressed a new concept:
the rustic who by virtue of his rusticity is necessarily inferior and
ridiculous. The word was evidently borrowed from Low German,
although a spurious etymology from the Latin *colonus* – 'a tiller of
the soil' – was posited by some Elizabethans.[2] The use of 'clown' to
refer to a type of comic performer is marginally later, and may be
traced back to Tarlton, in whose person the twin meanings of
'comedian' and 'rustic' were rendered indisseverable. A puritanical
treatise of 1577 exemplifies the early usage:

What is a man nowadays if he know not fashions, and how to wear his
apparel after the best fashion? To keep company and to become mummers

61

and dice players . . .? If he cannot thus do, he is called a miser, a wretch, a lob, a clown . . .³

A sequence of oppositions will best demonstrate how the term was used and defined:

No clownish or uncivil fashions are seen in him
(*French Academy*, anon. trans., 1586)

Both Clowns and Kings one self-same course must run.
(Kyd, *Cornelia*, 1594)

Clean and unclean, the gentle and the clown.
(John Davies, *Epigrams*, c. 1594)

In a fool and a wise man; in a clown and a courtier
(Jonson, *Cynthia's Revels*, 1600)

> The world's a theatre, the earth a stage . . .
> This plays an honest man, and that a knave,
> A gentle person this, and he a clown.
> (Heywood, *Apology for Actors*, 1612)

The concept of a 'clown' emerged within a neo-chivalric discourse centred on the notion of 'gentility'. The word 'gentle' has ambiguously genetic and ethical connotations, and to be a 'clown' is the obverse of being 'gentle'. An example will illustrate the point. Sir Philip Sidney is often seen as an embodiment or symbol of neo-chivalric values. In the quasi-dramatic role of the Shepherd Knight in the tilt-yards, Sidney tried to represent an ideal of the civil/courtly/gentle person – to become, in other words, a positive pole within a new moral discourse. The adjective 'clownish' was needed to define the opposite pole. The 'clown', as word and symbol, embraced the negative but excluded the positive aspects of rusticity. It is a nice paradox that Sidney the man liked Tarlton well enough to stand godfather to his son, but Sidney the literary critic mounted an influential attack on the clown's role in drama.⁴ The neo-chivalric system of values was not without its contradictions.

In the theatre, perhaps the earliest role scripted for a 'clown' is John A-droynes in George Whetstone's *Promos and Cassandra* (1578). The play is a bold attempt to wed popular theatre to a neo-classical aesthetic. The preface is a manifesto. Whetstone attacks dramatists who allow 'a clown' to use 'affected speech', and (like a Vice) to offer counsel to a king. Decorum requires that

characters must conform to type, and that 'clowns should speak disorderly'. Both stage directions and dialogue refer to John as 'a clown'.[5] The morality framework has gone from the play, and the clown is relegated to a sub-plot. In his search for a language, Whetstone constructs the clown's first scene in the form of a combat from a may-game.

Within a decade or so, 'a clown' becomes '*the* clown', and the term 'Vice' has become an anachronism. It is the Elizabethan use of 'the Clowne' that I shall examine in this chapter. In order to interpret the terminology of the period, I shall first examine the evidence offered by different categories of Elizabethan theatre practice. I shall then consider the importance of different types of text and different types of language.

BOYS' AND AMATEUR COMPANIES

In the Elizabethan theatre, 'the clown' was a skilled professional actor. We find no trace of any 'clown', therefore, in the stage directions of plays written for boys or students.[6] Boys and students had neither the technical skills nor the years in the public eye needed in order to project a clown persona – a persona distinct from and interacting with roles written into individual plays. Neither boys nor students ended their performances with a jig. Boys' and students' plays also tended to be in the vanguard of neo-classical fashion, and to be governed, therefore, by an aesthetic which saw no obvious place for the clown.

Two illustrations will suffice. Both are exceptions which point up the general rule. A representative student play is *Timon*, performed at the Inns of Court in *c*. 1602/3.[7] The list of actors' names includes 'Lollio, a Country Clown, Philargurus' son'. The etymological (i.e. sociological) meaning of the term 'clown' predominates. This is *a* clown, not *the* clown. The epithet 'Country' signifies that this clown, in accordance with decorum, has a disorderly rustic accent. Because the clown is a *nouveau riche*, the comedy can blend instruction into the entertainment. Like all the other characters, this clown has a classical-sounding name, and speaks in verse. There is nothing to detach the role from the fictive world of the play.

A representative boys' play is Jonson's *The Case is Altered*, written in *c*. 1598. Here the author's experience of working in an adult company leads him to adopt elements of the professional clown's

role. But Jonson splits the function of the clown between two characters, Onion the groom and Juniper the cobbler, in order not to create
a part beyond a boy's technical range. The boy playing Onion is
given prose dialogue, brief asides to the audience, physical horse-
play, obscenity and striking changes of costume, like many a clown
in adult plays. But Jonson makes Onion and Juniper work as a pair in
order to spare the actors monologues or sustained audience address.
At no point is the actor disengaged from the fabric of the play.
Onion, like his more verbal companion Juniper, is clownish in his
behaviour, but the technical term 'clown' is not used of him.

In the opening scene, Jonson points out to the audience the social
basis for Elizabethan conventions. Balladino, alias the playwright
Antony Munday, condemns plays with 'nothing but humours',
which please only the 'gentlemen', and states that it is his policy to
write for the one-penny entrants. Onion echoes his view, and condemns a recent play with 'nothing but kings and princes in it, the fool
came not out a jot'. The fool or clown is presented to the six-penny
clientele at the Blackfriars' as a figure who appears in the public
theatres simply to please the groundlings.[8]

In the case of well-established amateur troupes in the country,
these practical and aesthetic considerations do not apply. The actor
who played 'the fool or clown' in a libellous jig performed in Shropshire towns in around 1620 had taken that part in plays annually for
the previous twelve years.[9]

JOHN SINGER AND THE ADMIRAL'S COMPANY

Dekker picks out the three famous names of an era when he writes:
'Tarlton, Kemp nor Singer, nor all the litter of fools that now come
drawling behind them, never played the clowns more naturally.'[10]
John Taylor records that he was acquainted with 'John Singer, who
played the clown's part at the Fortune play-house'.[11] Singer was
Kemp's opposite number in the Admiral's company. The stage plot
of 1 *Tamar Cam* (*c.* 1602) gives us an example of 'the clown's part'.
Singer is cast as the drunken Assinico, a character for whom the
document twice uses the alternative name 'Clown'. The role-name
associates Singer with the fool's emblem of ass's ears. I noted in the
last chapter how Singer was held back from the finale in order to
appear subsequently with his jig.

In scripts prepared for the Admiral's company, the word 'clown',

when it appears, is a technical playhouse term. In *Englishmen for my Money* (performed 1598), the *dramatis personae* signals the double playhouse and plot functions of 'Frisco a Clowne PiSaro's man'. Upon Frisco's first two entries, the playwright provides the reminder: 'Enter Frisco, the Clowne'; and once the nature of the role has been established, he reverts simply to 'Frisco'. Another play of the same year, *The Downfall of Robert, Earl of Huntingdon*, gives us further insight into playhouse terminology. An induction sets the scene as a rehearsal of a play to be performed before Henry VIII. When the missing actor, Sir John Eltham, arrives:

At every doore all the Players runne out, some crying where? where? others welcome Sir *John*, among other the boyes and Clowne.

The 'clown', like the boys, is recognizable to the audience as a special category of player. The clown is given the part of Much the miller's son, and his first entry after the induction reads: 'Enter *Much*, clowne'. In the induction, the speech headings identify the actor, out of role, as 'Clow.'; but once the play begins, he is titled 'Much' throughout.[12] The word 'clown', therefore, refers both to a particular type of part, and to the particular actor whose job it was to take that part in the company's repertoire.

Henslowe's inventory of March 1598 is haphazard in allocating costumes to named actors or to named roles. When Henslowe enters: '5 pair of hose for the clown, and 5 jerkins for them', he is clearly referring to costumes worn by one *actor* in a series of plays. But when he adds: '1 yellow doublet for a clown', he refers to the *role* of a rustic peasant, a role probably taken by *the* clown.[13]

ROBERT ARMIN AND THE CHAMBERLAIN'S COMPANY

No one has seriously doubted that when Robert Armin joined the Chamberlain's Men, Shakespeare created a series of domestic 'fools' for him to play. (I examine Armin's roles as 'fool' in Chapter 10.) Robert Armin published his book *Fool Upon Fool* under the name 'Clonnico de Curtanio Snuffe' – Snuff, the clown of the Curtain Theatre; and the book was reissued in 1605 as written by 'Clonnico del Mondo Snuffe' – Snuff, the clown of the Globe. The book is a study of retained household fools. Within the book the term 'fool' is used throughout, except when Armin refers to a theatrical 'clown' in Lord Chandos's company – an individual who is probably Armin

himself. The same terminology characterizes *Quips upon Questions* (1600), a volume of poems based upon Armin's improvisations at the Curtain. Armin states that the book is 'clapped up by a clown of the town'. Within the poems he uses the term 'fool' when talking of himself, or picking up comments from his supposed audience, and he uses the term 'clown' only in a discussion of Tarlton's theatrical successors.[14]

In dramatic texts associated with Armin, the convention is the same. In the stage directions of the First Folio, the term 'clown' is used throughout to denote Touchstone, Feste and Lavatch. Within the dialogue, however, the term 'fool' is consistently used of these characters. Touchstone is the one complex case. Though usually termed a 'fool', he is described as 'clownish' by Rosalind (I.iii.126) and as a 'roynish clown' by the Second Lord (II.ii.8). The term in the first instance helps identify the now absent character for the audience. In the second, it places the character socially amongst the 'villains' of the court. Both instances help prepare the ground for the confusion of identities in Arden. For Touchstone 'It is meat and drink to me to see a clown' (v.i.10) because, on one plane, the actor (Armin) is identified as a man who earns his living as a stage clown, and, on another plane, Touchstone the foolish courtier relies on a rustic clown to give definition to his own gentility. The jest relies upon the existence of two now distinct senses of the word *clown*.

A conclusion begins to emerge from this discussion. The term 'fool' was the normal colloquial term for a man like Armin. The term was the obvious one because men like Tarlton, Kemp and Armin sustained their comic personae outside the playhouse walls. The term 'clown' belongs either to a specialized playhouse vocabulary or to a neo-chivalric discourse concerned with morality and class.

THE QUEEN'S MEN/RED BULL COMPANY

If we look at the history of Worcester's Men after Kemp's death, when the company passed into the service of the Queen and moved into the Red Bull, we find Thomas Greene in the clown's part. According to Greene, the spectator who will go anywhere provided 'the clown have a part' will choose the Red Bull in preference to the Globe because 'they say Greene's a good clown'.[15]

In the Caroline period, the clowns played a greater range of parts. Nevertheless, when the company at the Red Bull was reformed under

Queen Henrietta's patronage, we find William Robins taking over the comic eunuch's part in Massinger's *Renegado* and the role of 'Clem, the Clown' in Heywood's *Fair Maid of the West*, and playing the self-proclaimed 'fool' in a play of Shirley's.[16] When the Prince's Men took over the Red Bull, the actor Andrew Cane, former jig-maker at the Fortune, was described as 'the clown at the Bull' and, after the closure of the theatres, as 'the quondam fool of the Red Bull'.[17]

THE JOB OF AUTHOR: HEYWOOD AND JONSON

The problem with printed texts is that we have to distinguish between the work of the author, the scribe (if any) and the printer. Manuscript plays are helpful in leading us directly to the process of writing. The manuscript of *Sir Thomas More*[18] is particularly revealing. In the original text, written out by Munday, no 'clown' is included. In the revision, a hand identified as Heywood's has picked out the name 'Ralph Betts' from Munday's script, and has used it for a character who is labelled in all stage directions as 'clown'. Dialogue for 'Clo.' is inserted into the manuscript. When part of the play was passed over to 'Hand D' to draft, a playhouse scribe had afterwards to allocate some of the anonymous crowd speeches to 'Clown. Betts'. A further appearance was needed for the clown later in the play, and in a new scene for the Cardinal's interlude players, some lines are allocated again to 'clo.' Twice, space seems to be left for a mono-logue for the clown (Fols. 7a & 16b), and the intention was perhaps to consult with the actor. The manuscript shows how those who prepared the text for performance had the job of tailoring a part for the particular actor who played the clown. In the next chapter, I examine the particular circumstances in which this piece of revision was undertaken.

Two manuscript plays of Heywood's survive from the early 1620s. These simply confirm what is obvious from the printed texts. The playwright was expected to indicate to the company which part he intended as the clown's. In both manuscripts, Heywood casts the principal servant as clown, and systematically writes 'clown' in all stage directions.[19] Shakespeare is second only to Heywood in the consistency with which he specifies 'the clown' in stage directions. These two writers were unique in that they were sharers in the companies for which they did most of their writing, and effectively

worked as managers rather than freelance employees. They were therefore freer or better equipped than other writers to cast their plays as they wrote them, and it is probably for this reason that they use the term 'clown' so readily.

At the opposite extreme to Heywood, professional man of the theatre, we must set those playwrights who took a professional pride in the business of publication. When Jonson asks a reader 'in these Jig-given times, to countenance a legitimate poem',[20] he distances his play from the ephemeral conditions of the playhouse, and stakes a claim for the immortality of his verse. When plays are published in accordance with such an ideal, it is natural that all reference to 'the clown' should disappear from stage directions. Jonson, typically, relegates a list of principal performers to the back of each play in the Folio. The 'persons of the play', listed at the outset, are to be seen as the author's and not the performers' creation.

Two anonymous plays evince a very different attitude to publication. *Mucedorus* (printed 1598 and 1610) and *The Fair Maid of the Exchange* (printed 1607) follow the tradition of the printed interlude, and offer themselves for acting. When they place 'Mouse the Clowne' and 'Fiddle *the Clowne*' at the end of their respective cast lists, they follow the pattern of *Enough is as Good as a Feast, Like Will To Like* and *Trial of Treasure*, each of which lists 'the Vice' last.[21] The definite article distinguishes *the* clown from such types as 'A Noble man' or 'an humorous gallant'. These cast lists provide useful evidence that the clown, like the Vice, was not normally expected to double.

CONCLUSION: 'CLOWN' VERSUS 'FOOL'

In its origins, the term 'clown' was pejorative, it was affected or poetic in its use, and it related to rank. The residual meanings overlapped in the 1590s with an emergent technical value-neutral usage. It was not a colloquial term.

Like Armin in his *Quips*, Kemp in his *Nine Days' Wonder* speaks of himself as being a 'fool', not a 'clown'. Shakespeare's stage directions in *Love's Labour's Lost* refer to 'Pedant', 'Braggart', 'Curate', 'Clown' and 'Boy', but Berowne *speaks* of 'The Pedant, the Braggart, the Hedge-Priest, the Foole, and the Boy' (v.ii.543). In Shakespearean dialogue generally, the word 'fool' is used with enormous freedom. The word 'clown' is never found outside stage directions

unless used *of*, or (for ironic effect) *by* the character who is designated as *the* clown of the play. Likewise, Peter Onion in *The Case is
Altered*, Sly in *Taming of A Shrew*, and the country gentleman in the
Praeludium for *The Careless Shepherdess* all speak of their affection
for the 'fool' in plays.[22] When the Globe burned, drunken reprobates
prayed for 'the fool', and when a poet disparaged genteel Bankside
theatres, he wrote affectionately of the 'fool' of the Curtain and the
'fool' of the Bull.[23] A generation later, a group of theatre share-
holders appealed to the public on behalf of employees listed as 'our
housekeepers . . . our hired men . . . our fools . . . our door-keepers . . .
etc.'[24] The ancient word 'fool' remained dominant in everyday
usage.

Playhouse terminology was more precise than colloquial speech,
and it recognized a very clear distinction between 'fool' and 'clown'.
In Henslowe's inventory, while 'the clown' wore hose and jerkin in
many plays, at least one play required a 'fool's coat, cap and
bauble'.[25] In just the same way, Shakespearean stage directions
introduce the term 'fool' only for the wearer of the cockscomb in
Lear.[26] 'The fool' was a type of role identified by an iconographic
costume, a costume containing the insignia of 'folly'. (My appendix
to this book contains a full discussion of the 'fool's' costume.)

To conclude: we find the direction 'Enter . . . the Clown' in texts
prepared for the four major late Elizabethan companies – the Admiral's, the Chamberlain's, Worcester's, and Derby's.[27] We never find
this direction in texts prepared for boys' companies. And we do not
find the term 'clown' in colloquial usage. We may safely conclude,
therefore, that in a theatre-related context the term 'the clown' refers
always to the resident clown or fool in a professional company.
Having reached this conclusion, however, we must make two immediate caveats.

THE 'GENERIC' THEATRICAL USAGE

No generic term exists to cover the group of comic characters who
play with the clown. Occasionally, therefore, the term is used gener-
ically for the clown and his companions. In Munday's manuscript
play *John-a-Kent and John-a-Cumber*, the dominance of the principal comedian is signalled by the direction for his and his companions' first entry: 'Enter Turnop with his crew of clowns, and a
minstrel'. The word 'clowns' comes easily here because the charac-

ters are country tenants preparing an entertainment for the gentry, a proper welcome 'lest they term us clowns'.[28] In Shakespeare's closely related *Midsummer Night's Dream*, the author once writes 'Enter the Clownes' when Bottom comes on with his companions (III.i). However, when *the* clown (Bottom) is absent, we find instead a reference to 'the rabble' (IV.ii). Two additional references to 'the clowns' can be attributed to the book-keeper or editor.[29]

The plural use never obscures the fact that one person is *the* clown. In *Orlando Furioso* (performed *c.* 1591), the direction 'Enter two Clownes' is followed a few scenes later by the reappearance of one of them – we are not told which: 'Enter . . . the Clowne drest like Angelica'.[30] In *Hamlet*, likewise, 'Enter two Clownes' is followed by further directions which distinguish 'Clo[wne]' from 'other'. The 'bad' Quarto is surprisingly similar: 'enter Clowne and an other' is followed by the speech headings 'Clowne' and '2'. The reporter and Shakespeare both know which part is *the* clown's part; their problem is the lack of a generic term to embrace both the clown and his companion.

THE 'ESSENTIAL' CLOWN

Finally, before we conclude this exploration of a technical theatre term, we must observe that the term, and the convention to which it referred, were called to account at the end of the 1590s, in the wake of Jonson and Chapman's theory of humours and of plays based on contemporary London life.

London realism inevitably undermined the formal features of the clown's part. When all the characters are English, most speak in everyday prose, and witty banter is specific to a given milieu, then little remains to differentiate a 'clown' from other characters. When the essence of a given character is his 'humour' – his dominant trait fleshed out with detail – then the ambiguous relationship between actor and role, characteristic of the clown, cannot be maintained. The essence of character has to be sought within the role. While Shakespeare's plays in the late 1590s are constructed as a montage of situations, Jonson's are constructed as a montage of characterizations. The Shakespearean actor starts with the premise of a situation, the Jonsonian actor with the premise of a character.

In Jonson's *Every Man Out of His Humour* (1599), for example, most of the clown's formal functions are devolved upon Buffone, the

buffoon or jester. But we also find in Sogliardo a character whom
Jonson terms 'an essential clown', a character who is rich enough to
purchase gentility. The audience are invited to look beneath the
posturing, and see the character's essential worthlessness: symbolically, the rough skin of a ploughman lies beneath a gentleman's
garments. In a Shakespearean clown, by contrast, character is not
constructed around an essence. Bottom's experience 'hath no bottom'; his 'ballet' and 'Bergomask' dissolve into Kemp's jig. The
Shakespearean clown fulfils a given function, but the Jonsonian
clown is a given type. Jonson teaches his audience to identify the
character type when he allows the 'essential clown' to be taken for a
courtier, and conversely allows the fishmonger's son to mistake the
downright squire for a 'clown' because he does not seem to deport
himself like a 'gentleman'.[31] The traditional clown's part disintegrates when identity becomes problematic in this way.

The satirist Samuel Rowlands bears witness to a new type of
audience awareness in a diatribe against mass education and social
mobility. He enquires:

> What means Singer then
> And Pope the clown to speak so boorish, when
> They counterfeit the clowns upon the stage?
> Since country fellows grow in this same age
> To be so quaint in their new printed speech
> That cloth will now compare with velvet breech.[32]

Rowlands' satire appeared in June 1599, and its title, *The Letting of
Humour's Blood in the Head-vein*, links it to the early 'humour'
plays. Rowlands has in mind the coarse acting of players who played
arriviste types as if they were rustic boors. He perceives inauthen-
ticity in the acting because the clown-type, which served as the actor's
model, was based on a Tarltonesque convention rather than on
social reality. From the Chamberlain's company, Pope rather than
Kemp is cited. No doubt Rowlands has in mind the rendering of roles
like Stephano in *Every Man In His Humour*. Stephano exemplifies
the provincial *nouveau riche* against whom Rowlands targets his
satire, while Cob the water-bearer, in playhouse terms the 'clown' of
the play, is of no interest to Rowlands.

During the 1580s and 1590s, the presence of 'the clown' had
become a requirement in professional Elizabethan plays. There was
no clear separation between the social connotations of the term and

the theatrical, because the country clown was by definition funny, the stage clown by definition a character of low social status. At the end of the 1590s, this convention was subjected to questioning. To many people, the convention no longer seemed to be authenticated by their perception of life outside the theatre. The social-pejorative meaning and the technical-theatrical meaning were felt to be disconnected. In the decade which followed, the crisis of conventions was in a sense resolved, as two distinct meanings of the term became recognized and acceptable. When Touchstone in 1599/1600 jests upon his encounter with 'a clown', he puns upon the now two-fold meaning of the word 'clown'.

CHAPTER 6

The roles of Kemp 'the clown'

W E ARE NOW IN A POSITION to analyse the extant texts in order to establish which parts were written for 'the clown' during Kemp's time as a sharer in the Chamberlain's and Worcester's companies. An analysis of the texts will help to clarify some of the conventions governing performance.

THE CHAMBERLAIN'S MEN'S REPERTOIRE, 1593–8

The text of *The Two Gentlemen of Verona* needs to be considered apart from the other comedies of this period because, in its published state, it represents the work of a playhouse scribe. For this reason, 'Launce' is systematically referred to by his role-name only.

Clifford Leech in the New Arden edition has set out at length the arguments for believing that the existing play is the product of reworking, and that the character of Launce was not part of the original conception. He accepts that the part of Launce 'was doubtless Kempe's', and dates the revision to around the time of the formation of the Chamberlain's company.' This theory seems wholly reasonable. When Kemp and Shakespeare became fellows, equal sharers in the new company, one of Shakespeare's first acts was to take an old play and to construct a part in it for Kemp based on Kemp's routines or 'merriments'. Kemp's scenes in *The Two Gentlemen of Verona*, like his episode in *A Knack to Know a Knave*, are only loosely tied to the narrative, and give him freedom to improvise if he chooses. If the part of Speed represents the original clown part, and Launce was the replacement, we have an explanation for the Folio's rather odd classification of Speed as 'a clownish servant' and Launce as 'the like'.

From the point of view of Kemp, the role of Launce marks a transition: in later roles for the Chamberlain's, the clown becomes increasingly integrated with the narrative. From the point of view of

Shakespeare, new possibilities are established: Shakespeare is now writing for an actor whose art is rooted in minstrelsy, and who therefore knows how to dominate a stage without support from plot mechanics. This enables Shakespeare to turn aside from models provided by the Vice and the classical slave, and to create a dramatic structure based on the alternation of different modes of performance.

If we regard the role of Launce as a turning point for Shakespeare, we can look back on earlier clown types in his writing as experiments. The verse-speaking Plautine servants in *The Comedy of Errors* gave way to the prose-speaking Grumio in *The Taming of the Shrew*. Grumio's Italian name indicates that he is still of a kind with his master, and that he is conceived as a function of a master–servant relationship. Speed, in the original *Two Gentlemen*, is a part for a boy, and the boy remains a foil for the adult protagonists. The only early text which actually refers to a 'clown' in its stage directions is *Titus Andronicus*, where the clown episode takes the form of a self-contained 'merriment'. The part, as we saw in Chapter 3, was probably written for Kemp during his time with Strange's.

There is little to help us establish a chronology for the next three comedies: *A Midsummer Night's Dream*, *The Merchant of Venice* and *Love's Labour's Lost*. These plays, like *Romeo and Juliet* and *Much Ado About Nothing*, were published in early Quartos based upon Shakespeare's rough papers. The dramaturgical feature that emerges from a study of Shakespeare's speech-prefixes in these plays is the logic behind the inconsistency. Shakespeare constructs character as a set of functions, a set of relationships. The dynamics of the stage situation are more important to him than the internal consistency of a single character.

A Midsummer Night's Dream illustrates this principle most clearly. When Bottom first appears, he is 'Bottom, the Weaver' – to distinguish him from 'Snug, the Joyner', 'Quince, the Carpenter', etc. The name Bottom, like Snug and Quince/Quoins, relates to his trade.[2] From the point of view of the stage directions, the personal 'Nick' is an irrelevance. Bottom's *character* is not conceptually separable from his socio-economic status. During the rehearsal, he becomes 'Piramus' in the stage directions because this is now his function in respect of the group on stage. In his second scene with Titania, he is reclassified again: 'Enter Queene of Fairies, and Clowne, and Fairies, and the King behinde them' – and he continues

as 'Clowne' in the speech-prefixes. The social dimension operates: clown/queen is a distinction of rank. But Bottom also functions as 'clown' through initiating a visual and musical game with the fairies. He wakes up as 'Bottome' (a Folio addition), but it is as 'Clo.' that he addresses the audience and tells them he is no 'patched fool'. Again, he is 'Piramus' during the play, but 'Bot.' when he drops out of role.

In *The Merchant of Venice* and *Love's Labour's Lost*, we do not find the same juggling with reality – between court and fairyland, between play and play-within-a-play. The term 'clown' functions unproblematically as a distinction that is simultaneously theatrical and social. In *Merchant of Venice*, Launcelet is 'Clown' in all stage directions and speech-prefixes – except where conversing with his father (where the social dimension ceases to apply) and in a brief exchange with Lorenzo (where the directions echo Lorenzo's direct address to 'friend *Lancelet*'). In *Love's Labour's Lost*, only the opening stage direction and two speech-prefixes refer to 'Costard', and 'Clown' is used elsewhere. 'Clown' is not only a theatrical term here: as a synonym for 'swain', it fits neatly with a neo-classical typology that prefers 'pedant', 'braggart' and 'curate' to personal names.

Dogberry was the last clown part which Shakespeare wrote during Kemp's time with the Chamberlain's Men. The erratic stage directions in *Much Ado* are notorious. In IV.ii, Dogberry is mainly denoted as 'Kemp', but once also as 'Keeper', as 'Andrew' and as 'Constable'. Verges is 'Cowley', but once 'Const.' Clearly 'Andrew' does not mean 'Merry Andrew *i.e.* Clown' – the gloss offered by so many editors[3] – for the term 'Merry-Andrew' is not recorded in the *OED* before 1673, and there is no reason for its use. The name 'Dogberry' is used in the stage directions of only two scenes, and occurs only once in the text – as against 'Bottom' eleven times, 'Costard' seventeen times, 'Launce' eight times, 'Launcelet' twenty-seven times. We must conclude that when Shakespeare drafted this scene he had not finally settled on the character's name.

The term 'clown' is never applied to Dogberry. This is partly because he always functions as part of a group of comedians. But I have argued also that the clown convention as a whole had become destabilized in 1598. In *Much Ado*, Benedick and Beatrice conduct a comic love plot which runs parallel to the serious plot. Benedick speaks almost entirely in prose, and Beatrice terms him 'the Prince's

jester, a very dull fool' (II.i.127). Benedick is in a sense intruding upon the clown's functions.

I shall postpone until the next chapter discussion of Kemp's roles as Peter in *Romeo and Juliet* and as Cob in *Every Man Out Of His Humour*. These texts require a more sustained analysis because they have more to tell us about the relationship between writer and actor. I shall also postpone discussion of (what I shall argue to be) Kemp's role of Falstaff. Falstaff is, rightly, the focus of much criticial debate, and the character cannot be dealt with briefly. One text from the Shakespeare 'Apocrypha', however, does need to be discussed at this point in order that we may complete our survey of Kemp's roles while a member of the Chamberlain's company.

Thomas Lord Cromwell by 'W.S.' was registered in 1602 as 'lately acted', and was published in the same year 'as it hath been sundry times publicly acted by the ... Lord Chamberlain his Servants'. In the most substantial analysis of the play that I have seen, Baldwin Maxwell argues that the extant play represents the telescoping of an older, two-part play. Earlier critics on stylistic grounds offered 1592 as the date of composition. A more recent argument links it to other Tudor chronicles, and prefers a date of *c.* 1599–1602.[4] The argument from topicality, however, may simply explain why an old play warranted publication. The text is a careful one, making reference to music, to the inner stage and arras, and to a passing over the stage. It is based, in other words, on a prompt book. This seems clear evidence for believing that the Chamberlain's Men had no further interest in performing the play, and that they had no expectation that another company would now find it worth reviving. I believe that it is safe to assume that the play was written for the Chamberlain's Men (since no other company is named) and that it was written (in its first or final form) in the mid 1590s.

Cromwell's servant Hodge is formally identified as '*the* clown' by the direction for an exchange of costumes: 'Enter Bedford like the Clowne, and Hodge in his cloake and his Hat' (Sig.C4v). Hodge has all the characteristics of Kemp's clowns. He is a man of the people, a farrier's foreman from Putney, and the audience are never allowed to forget the character's local and occupational roots, even when he becomes a serving-man. When the clown takes the Earl's place in prison and is required to be 'gentleman-like', he makes no attempt at realism. Like Bottom turned courtier in fairyland, Hodge turns the scene into a game, singing and breaking into fourteeners, the old-

fashioned verse of the popular stage. I shall analyse in a later chapter the fine monologue in which the clown describes his crossing of the Channel.

WORCESTER'S COMPANY, 1601–3

I shall pass now to the four or five extant texts put together during Kemp's time as a leading member of Worcester's company. It seems safest to exclude *Nobody and Somebody* from this discussion because the text in its present state is Jacobean (see p. 40). Since these plays are not generally well known, I shall have to describe them in some detail. In the accounts which follow, I shall set out the reasons for attributing these texts to the Worcester's repertoire, I shall describe the state of the text in order to show which character is conceived as 'the clown', and I shall give a brief sketch of how the clown's role is conceived.

How a Man May Choose a Good Wife from a Bad

The play was published in 1602 'as it hath been sundry times acted by the Earl of Worcester's servants'. It is a sophisticated play with a London setting, and it proved instantly influential.[5] The play cannot pre-date the establishment of a new company in London at the end of 1601.

Prose and an emblematic name show that the clown is 'Pipkin', a domestic servant. In this bourgeois reworking of *Romeo and Juliet*, 'Pipkin' is a reworking of 'Peter'.[6] Pipkin has to announce that his young mistress is dead, and like Peter he expresses his grief through the medium of tragicomic song. The part is more substantial than Peter's, and incorporates a scene in which he joins boys at school because he has been so slow in learning. Pipkin claims to be twenty-four years old (about the age when most apprenticeships came to an end) and he mentions that he is bearded (as Kemp was when dancing to Norwich). By casting a mature actor in the part of an eternal youth, the playwright counterpoints actor against role, and breaks down the domestic realism characteristic of the text elsewhere. The convention was an old one, of course: one thinks of Tarlton's role as a cobbler's apprentice in *The Famous Victories*, and of Kemp's role as Shylock's apprentice.

The Royal King and the Loyal Subject

This play was published as an old piece by Heywood in 1637. It has long been identified provisionally as the *marshalle oserecke* of *Henslowe's Diary*, a play written by Smith and Heywood in September 1602. *The Royal King and the Loyal Subject* divides into two equal but disconnected parts. Smith and Heywood were paid equal amounts for their contributions to *oserecke*, which reached the playhouse at different times.

The first of the two plots deals with a King's paranoia about his rich Lord Marshal, a man who is wholly a 'loyal subject', but is also able to outdo the King in 'all degrees of honour, love and courtesy'. The second deals with a discharged Captain Bonevile, an embittered malcontent who resolves to try the 'humour' of those he once considered his friends.[7]

The play is clearly Elizabethan in its concerns. The Bonevile plot owes much to *Every Man Out Of His Humour* (late 1599). The action is a progress towards court, a continual exposing of humours by one who, like Macilente, is obsessed by the power of money and costume. The vogue for humour plays had passed by the end of the reign. The Lord Marshal plot is very obviously concerned with Essex, Elizabeth's Lord Marshal, executed in 1601.[8] The play is both a political attack and an exercise in wish-fulfilment. Essex had claimed to be a truly loyal subject, even in the midst of rebellion. The play enacts what might have been. When this Marshal is tried before a special court of his peers, the monarch has a last minute change of heart. The Marshal of the play, never named in the text, is a popular hero, feared by his enemies because he is 'armed by the people's love'. The play's concern with Essex gives it such thematic unity as it has. Essex, like Bonevile, spent his estate soldiering in the royal service, and was embittered by his resulting poverty.

Despite the disappearance of the Marshal's name, the identification of Heywood's text with Heywood and Smith's play of 1602 seems reasonably sound. We can pass on to examine the nature of the text. The printer seems to have worked from authorial rough papers. Heywood's epilogue does not suggest that the text had ever been revised.[9] As we have come to expect in authorial manuscripts, the clown can be referred to in stage directions either as 'the clown' or by a role-name. The logic is the same as Shakespeare's. The character is 'the clown' when he appears in a self-contained opening scene

irrelevant to the plot, but he bears his role-name of 'Cock' when he appears with his fellow soldiers. The speech-prefixes revert from 'clown' to 'Cock' immediately after the character has been addressed by name within the dialogue.

The clown is the one follower of Captain Bonevile who remains loyal. While the other characters represent false appearances, the stolid unchangeability of the clown in this play is related to the ancient roots of the clown role. Cock is not simply different in character, he belongs to a different mode of performance. 'The clown' is by definition himself, and the true/false dichotomy cannot apply. The obscenity of the clown in this play (in his opening scene, for instance, he challenges a Welshman to give an exhibition of farting) helps position him as a lower being, whose spiritual virtues cannot be measured against those of gentlemen.

Sir Thomas Wyatt

No one has questioned the assumption that this is a truncated version of 1 Lady Jane, by Dekker, Heywood, Webster, Chettle and Smith, and 2 Lady Jane, for which Dekker was paid an advance. Henslowe records the payments in October 1602. Possibly the sequel proved politically too sensitive for performance as it stood. The extant text was published in 1607, and claims Dekker and Webster as its authors, and the Queen's Men as its performers. It is a reported text, and presumably a piracy.[10]

1 Lady Jane evidently dealt with Jane Grey's reign and its swift end; the sequel intercut the story of Jane Grey's execution with Wyatt's rebellion against the Spanish marriage. The text allocates a part to 'the clown' and no personal name is given him. The clown is a fusion of two characters from the two source plays. In the first, the clown is part of the army securing Cambridge on behalf of Queen Jane. In the second, he is a member of the London trained bands, supporting Wyatt, and trying to force an entry into the city. Bret, the Captain in the first part, also reappears in command of the London apprentices.

In both plays, the clown functions as a kind of chorus, speaking for the easily manipulated, instinctual and hungry common man who takes up arms. The technique of the second play is particularly interesting. The tiring-house façade represents the city wall at Ludgate. When the Captain harangues his men, the clown throws in

comic responses directed as much at the audience as at the speaker. The audience are thereby incorporated as members of the rebel militia.

Since the text was put together after Kemp's death, we have to bear in mind that much has been cut, and that another actor's improvisations may have crept in. We have nevertheless an outline of two parts that must have been written for Kemp.

Sir Thomas More [a probable part of the repertory]

The date and provenance of the manuscript Book of Sir Thomas More have been the subject of much discussion. In a recent article Carol A. Chillington[11] has convincingly allocated the revised text to Worcester's Men. She shows that the attribution of Hand 'D' to Shakespeare has no firm foundation and flies in the face of all that we know about playhouse practice. Webster is identified as the most probable alternative. Chillington suggests that the play may be the untitled piece commissioned from Heywood and Chettle on 14 January 1603, and that Elizabeth's death may have prevented its performance. I find it wholly plausible that four of the team who collaborated on 1 Lady Jane should have got together to revise Sir Thomas More. There was obvious safety in numbers, and censorship seems to have been lax at this time. As we have seen, the company had little respect for the authority of the Privy Council. Chillington accepts the orthodox view that Hand 'B' is Heywood's, and observes that this writer seems to have supervised and co-ordinated the revision. This seems an appropriate role for Heywood, given his involvement in Worcester's company as actor and sharer as well as principal writer.

Chillington's hypothesis that the original text in Munday's handwriting belongs to the same year is to my mind untenable. She fails to explain why the censor's instructions are ignored. And she demonstrates that writers would in fact be most unlikely to work on the artistic polishing of a new text. It is far more likely that an old text remained in the possession of Heywood, or one of his collaborators, because the playhouse for which it was first intended had not been able to use it. After the Admiral's Men's 'Wolsey' plays, and after the Lady Jane plays dealing with Tudor rebellions, there was every incentive to try again. The censor had ordered the suppression of 'the insurrection wholly and the cause thereof' – but famine and im-

migration are the root 'cause' of the insurrection in *Sir Thomas More*, and these were no longer the flash-points that they had been in the 1590s: the succession and religion were now the sensitive areas.[12]

I noted in the last chapter that a part for a clown was written into the manuscript of *Sir Thomas More*. Heywood would have added the clown's part in order to accommodate his most prominent actor, Kemp. Chillington is unaware of the function of '*the* clown' in playhouse practice, and argues that the term 'clown' was used to convince the censor that the rebels were a buffoonish and innocuous bunch.[13] She ignores the plain fact that the clown is more seditious than anyone when he is made to sing:

> Shall we be held under? No
> We are freeborn
> And do scorn
> To be used so.

In the emotive hanging scene, the clown's function is not simply to lighten the mood. Rather, his humour obliges the audience to view less sentimentally and more critically the recantation of the principal rebel.

The clown's singing belongs to its context. At the end of the previous crowd scene, in which the clown is unusually silent, his brother announces: 'On May day next in the morning we'll go forth a-maying.' When the clown dominates the next crowd scene with his jesting and singing, the audience are being shown an enactment of the maying. The crowd must inevitably be dressed in accordance with the festival, and the clown presumably appears in some sort of fool's or May Lord's guise. Like Jack Cade, the clown in this play conflates rebellion and celebration. As elsewhere in the revision, when he introduced the clown's part, Heywood was concerned to enrich the play artistically rather than to satisfy the censor.

A Woman Killed with Kindness

This play was completed shortly before Elizabeth's death. The Quarto of 1607 seems to derive directly from Heywood's manuscript.[14] No character is identified as 'the clown', but formally the part belongs to the servant Jenkin.

The play reverses the norms of romantic comedy. The setting is

domestic and English, and the play begins with a wedding, followed by a sequence of improvised 'country measures, rounds and jigs': it begins, in other words, as a comedy normally ends. In the manor house where the main action takes place, there are two principal servants. Nicholas is a pompous, surly, puritanical character, and plays a crucial part in the plot. He is initially comic, but proves capable of expressing indecision in a verse soliloquy. Jenkin is a factotum rather than a valet. He remains a passive onlooker in respect of the plot, and reappears whenever household chores are involved. He signals his identity as 'clown' when he addresses the audience directly as 'my masters' and compares the real time of day in the playhouse to the supposed time in the play.[15]

The lack of an emblematic name for Jenkin is symptomatic of the fact that the clown is beginning to dissolve in the emergent mode of domestic realism. The clown nevertheless continues to have a useful function. Jenkin's voluntary or conditioned passivity helps the audience to adjust their own stance in relation to the action on stage: for the audience are now voyeurs, looking in on a private world, and are no longer bystanders in a public arena devoted to affairs of state. When Jenkin stands outside the bedchamber where the adultery is taking place, and bids his fellows: 'to bed, good honest serving-creatures, and let us sleep as snug as pigs in peasestraw', he invites the audience likewise to react as undemonstrative private individuals, more or less secure in their individual domestic lives. His wit, for this reason, is based on quiet irony – in contrast, for instance, to the brash puns and fantasies which whip up the audience of *Sir Thomas Wyatt*.

I have traced a sequence of plays in which a substantial role was always written for 'the clown'. It will be clear, I hope, from the perspective developed in this chapter, that Kemp was not wilfully turning his back on history when he decided to join Worcester's company. The company's repertoire was a radical one, both in political and artistic terms. An adequate part was provided for Kemp in each play, and the actor's talents were properly exploited, but always to the benefit of the play as a whole. Despite the assault of neo-classicists, the clown convention remained vital and flexible in these examples of late Elizabethan theatre.

CHAPTER 7

The genesis of the text: two explorations

PEOPLE ARE OFTEN MOVED to wonder to what extent Shakespeare's actors did justice to the possibilities of the text. The question is rarely framed in reverse: to what extent did the author's text do justice to the possibilities of the actors? The close working relationship between author and actor is usually ignored. I shall examine in this chapter two plays which illuminate this relationship. The existence of alternative published texts can give us insight into the methods of the writer – and, indeed, into the methods of the modern editor.

Romeo and Juliet

In reconstructing the Elizabethan play, we have to take account of three different texts. The 'bad' Quarto of 1597 (Q1) is a reported text. Scholarship has not established definitively who was responsible for getting this version into print. If one or two actors were recreating the text from memory, as is usually assumed, we should expect certain parts of the play to be better remembered than others. The fact is, however, that the text deteriorates progressively. This points to the possibility that the text was written down, during a series of visits to the theatre, by a spectator whose stamina steadily waned.[1] It is generally hard to tell whether errors in the text are attributable to failings in the reporter(s), or to accurately reported failings in the actors. It is perfectly clear, however, that Q1 records a version actually performed, and that the performance was given by a reduced cast with cuts in the text. The second Quarto (Q2), published in 1599, is mainly derived from Shakespeare's rough manuscript, but the compositor has turned to Q1 for some guidance, mainly in matters of layout. When Q2 proclaims itself to be 'newly corrected,

augmented and amended', it refers to the limitations of the earlier pirate edition, and does not imply recent authorial revision.[2] The Folio text (F) is based on Q2 (via the 1609 reprint, Q3), and changes seem to have been made by the compositor without independent authority.

All recent editors have accepted the dating of the play at 1594–6. Brian Gibbons has shown that 1593 is the earliest possible date.[3] In a recent article on the casting of *Romeo and Juliet*, Giorgio Melchiori goes out on a limb when he argues for 1593, and claims that Shakespeare drafted the first four acts without having any idea who would perform his play, but with a courtly audience broadly in mind. He finds here an explanation for the seemingly haphazard construction of Kemp's part.[4] In what follows, I shall demonstrate why I think this is a wholly mistaken view of Shakespeare's writing process.

We knew from Q2 that 'Peter' was the role taken by Kemp. Though modern editions limit him to appearing in but three scenes, including one mute appearance, Melchiori rightly notes that Kemp must have been given a more extensive part. A scene-by-scene analysis indicates what the nature of Kemp's role was.

I.ii

Q2 and F offer the stage direction 'Enter Capulet, Countie Paris, and the Clowne'. In the speech headings, the clown is denoted simply as 'Ser.' for serving-man. Q2 and F do not use the term 'Clowne' again. Once Shakespeare has established which is the role for '*the* Clowne' – i.e. Kemp – he has no need to repeat himself. This is a normal enough convention. The clown has now been cast as principal Capulet serving-man.

The comedy in this scene derives from the clown's illiteracy. He cannot read the list which Capulet gives him. He therefore traces out in the air the shapes of letters which he cannot decipher:

Here it is written that the shoe-maker should meddle with his yard and the tailor with his last, the fisher with his pencil and the painter with his nets.

The trick of reversal is similar to Bottom's. The illiterate clown emerges with a literary parody, and 'penis' is the implied synonym for the misplaced 'yard' and 'pencil'. This is not mere fooling for the groundlings' benefit. The hyper-literate spectator may congratulate

himself on noticing that the original passage in Lyly's *Euphues* concludes with the incongruity of a 'fool' discoursing of 'wit'.[5] The author cannot be faulted for any lack of care and attention in constructing the clown's part.

I.iii

Here it is Q1 which states 'Enter Clown'. This becomes 'Enter serving.' in Q2 and 'Enter a servingman' in F. Even the New Arden edition makes no mention of Q1's important variant here. The compiler of Q1 is not likely to have been in error in his observation, even if he misreports certain words. His eyes told him that he was watching the company clown: the term has no possible alternative connotation of 'rusticity' here.

The clown in this scene comes to summon the Capulet ladies to the feast. Having compressed his long message into one breath, he hurries away with a quip and a rhyme.

I.v

The clown's place at the hub of the household suggests that he is the serving-man who gives out orders to his fellows. After the direction which ends 'servingmen come forth with their napkins', the speech headings distinguish 'Ser.' from the others who are merely given numbers: '1', '2', and (in Q2) '3'. In other words, *the serving-man* in the Capulet household is differentiated from uncharacterized extras who are drawn as available from the pool of spare actors. 'Ser.' here is characterized in the same way as the figure who appeared in I.iii. For the punctuation in Q2 makes it clear that in both scenes he delivers his instructions in one burst:

Ser.   Madam the guests are come, supper serv'd up, you cald, my young lady askt for, the Nurse curst in the Pantrie, and everie thing in extremetie: I must hence to wait, I beseech you follow straight.

(I.iii)

Ser.   Away with the joyntstooles, remove the Courtcubbert, look to the plate, good thou, save me a peece of March-pane, and as thou loves me, let the porter let in Susan Grindstone, and Nell, Anthonie and Potpan.

(I.v)

The rapid delivery is offset in I.v by the steady replies of the other serving-men, who 'cannot be here, and there too'. The incongruous demand for marzipan keeps the clown persona to the fore.

II.iv–v

All texts have: 'Enter Nurse and her man', and refer in the subsequent speech headings to 'Peter'. This is a clear example of where the compositor of Q2 turned to Q1 for guidance. The reporter of Q1 used the proper name in this scene because at the start of the scene the character is addressed by name for the first time. He uses the loose term 'her man' because Juliet subsequently refers to 'thy man'. Since Rowe, the tradition has persisted that Peter is cast as 'servant to Juliet's nurse'. Yet there is no way in which the nurse, a servant herself, could technically have been Peter's employer. If Peter served in the Capulet household, he had to wear Capulet livery. The phrase 'her man' simply expresses the relationship in this scene. The nurse is here playing at being a Lady, and Peter is playing at being her personal serving-man.

Mercutio heralds the entry of the fool when he mimics obscenely the action of 'a great natural that runs lolling up and down to hide his bauble in a hole' – a moment before the entry of the stage fool. Peter's entry is visually arresting. Romeo cries: 'A sail, a sail' – and Mercutio qualifies: 'Two, two, a shirt and a smock'. I have never seen an explanation of 'a sail'. The bulky Kemp – the 'shirt' – must enter 'afore and apace', half concealing the nurse. I presume that the two comedians are taken for a boat because they enter with cloaks held up to cover their faces. Their errand is a secret one, and a Capulet servant cannot ever be seen to communicate with a Montague. The nurse calls for her fan to keep her face concealed while she talks. Since she masks her face in this way, she is naturally taken to be a prostitute.

Peter is not allowed to listen to the conversation, but keeps watch. Characteristically, the clown has no perception of the intrigues which constitute the main plot. Peter's one interjection calls attention to his prop, the dagger which he produces again in II.v. This may be read as the emblem carried by the medieval Vice. Peter's speech, as it appears in Q2, is obscene by implication, but introduces also an element of cowardly pomposity:

I saw no man vse you at his pleasure: if I had, my weapon shuld quickly haue bin out: I warrant you, I dare draw assoone as an other man, if I see occasion in a good quarrel, & the law on my side.

The version in Q1 foregrounds the obscenity and abandons the characterization:

I see nobodie vse you at his pleasure, if I had, I would soone have drawen: you know my toole is as soone out as anothers, if I see time and place.

It would be rash to take this as evidence of Kemp's changing his lines. Q1 does, however, point to the way the reporter understood the jest in performance. The clown's wooing in his jig is foreshadowed.

IV.ii

The servingman sent to fetch twenty cooks for the wedding jests that he will test the cooks' skill by having them lick their fingers. Evidence for the clown's playing this part is strong but circumstantial. He has been employed on errands twice before. He is noted as absent when 'three or four' servants enter with things for the cook shortly after in IV.iv. Just as another servant is given a guest-list, so he must be given money to hire the cooks, and he will need this money when he next appears. Finally, the convention is established that other servants may crack jokes aplenty, but only the clown has licence to jest in front of his master. (The exception that proves the rule comes in IV.iv where a servant jests *about* Peter.)

IV.iv

Though the clown character does not appear in this scene, the allusion to Peter merits further examination. When Capulet accosts a servant who is bringing on damp logs, Q2 and F have:

> Call Peter, he will show thee where they are.

The variant in Q1 is too striking to be dismissed as a compositor's error:

> Will will tell thee where thou shalt fetch them.

The 'Will' can only be Will Kemp, whom the actor or reporter has in a moment's lapse called by his real name. No critic, to my knowledge, has remarked on this reference to Kemp. The reference confirms, incidentally, that Q1 is indeed (as it claims to be) a text based on the play that Shakespeare's and Kemp's company actually performed.[6]

IV.V

This is Peter's most important scene. While Q1 has 'Enter serving-man', Q2 has the famous stage direction 'Enter Will Kemp', which the Folio compositors correct to 'Enter Peter'. This is not only proof positive that Kemp played the part of Peter; it provides also an example of the way Shakespeare's mind could not separate the actor from the role. Kemp is named here because this is thought of as *his* scene, a scene in which he no longer has to play a subordinate part.

The scene anticipates Kemp's appearance with the musicians after the play is over, when he will return to sing and dance his jig. The musicians are not regular actors. We note how completely Kemp must therefore control the dialogue:

— Play 'Heart's Ease'.
— Why 'Heart's Ease'?
— Oh musicians, because my heart itself plays, my heart is full. Oh play me some merry dump to comfort me.
— Not a dump we, tis no time to play now.
— You will not then?
— No.
— I will give you soundly.
— What will you give us?

The musicians are content to follow where the clown leads them. The impression given is of an improvisator at work. The jokes are all given to Kemp, while the stooges have not a word of wit between them.

The clown's riddle needs explanation. The riddle asks: 'Why "music with her silver sound"?' – and Peter rules out the reply: 'because musicians sound for silver'. His pay-off in fact runs: 'because musicians have no gold for sounding'. This starts to make sense if we realize that the clown, in his capacity as errand boy, has come to pay off the musicians, whose services are not now required for a wedding feast. Peter would still have the purse handed him in IV.ii because the twenty cooks are no longer needed. Dekker confirms the prop for us when a character in one of his plays quotes Peter's line and laments 'here's no music with her silver sound' as he hunts through a magic purse in search of gold.[7] Peter alone has gold for sounding because he jingles the gold in his purse as if it were an instrument. His jingling gold is the music that 'with speedy help doth lend redress' – but he is 'pestilent' enough to limit this redress to a

88

coin or two, much less than the proffered purse. I have explained the joke because no critical edition does so.

The stage direction 'Exit omnes' immediately before Kemp's entry has been taken to mean that Kemp's scene was an afterthought. This is not a necessary conclusion. The stage direction 'Exeunt manet' after line 94 surely indicates that the musicians (who have the speech-prefix immediately following) are to *remain* for a substantial period of time. The general exit is time-consuming, since rosemary has to be strewn and the arras closed (as Q1 affirms). 'Exit omnes' a mere four lines later simply indicates that the general exit is now complete. However, Dover Wilson suggests that this 'feeble' scene was not merely an addition but an interpolation, perhaps by Nashe. Melchiori suggests that Kemp may have added the scene himself. This comes dangerously close to the Coleridgean theory that the Porter scene in *Macbeth* was added by another hand to satisfy the mob.[8] Kemp may have been consulted, but he was not an afterthought.

Failing the 'interpolation' theory, critical embarrassment has generally been rationalized through the 'comic relief' theory. Granville Barker notes that the scene 'eases the strain before tragedy gets its grip on us'. A more recent apologist, T. J. B. Spencer in the New Penguin edition, agrees that the episode is probably 'an addition, providing an extra comic scene to take off the edge of lamentation for Juliet's supposed death'.[9] It is not made clear why 'grip' or 'edge' are undesirable. It is clear, however, that for generations of critics it has been unacceptable that grief should be mocked and parodied in a play which claims to be a tragedy.

v.iii

Q2 and F present editors with a conundrum. All versions agree that it is Balthasar who brings Romeo news of Juliet's death. But where Q1 has Balthasar accompany Romeo to the tomb, Q2 and F state unambiguously: 'Enter Romeo and Peter' – and the speeches are duly allocated to 'Pet.' When the Friar arrives in the churchyard, it is 'Man' whom he stumbles upon; and it is 'Romeo's man' whom the watch apprehend. 'Balthasar' first reappears in Q2 when, right at the end, he tells how he accompanied Romeo to the tomb. In a feeble effort to sort out the muddle, the compositors of the Folio send Peter off to summon the watch in place of Paris's page; Romeo's 'man', however, is still in the churchyard when the Friar arrives, so the

character who gives the final explanation is relabelled 'Boy', in the hopes, perhaps, that the reader will be too absorbed in the story to notice. Since Q1 records what happened in a performed version of the play, all editors – not unreasonably in the circumstances – return the lines to Balthasar.

The New Arden editor, Brian Gibbons, concludes that 'Shakespeare intended the parts of Peter and Balthasar to be doubled or else temporarily confused them.' Gibbons deduces that 'the actor who took *Peter* was still thought of as *Peter* even though he was now taking the different role of *Balthasar*'.[10] This view does not withstand examination. First, as Melchiori rightly perceives, the idea that Kemp doubled Peter and Balthasar does not make theatrical sense.[11] If the unmistakable Kemp reappeared as Balthasar only fourteen lines after his big scene, the audience would be confused. We have no evidence that Kemp ever doubled (in the sense of changing character and role-name). Secondly, it is absurdly patronizing to maintain that Shakespeare 'temporarily confused' his characters. Melchiori, however, can only fall back on this lame argument. He suggests that Shakespeare was so soaked in his source material, where Romeo's servant is named 'Peter', that he forgot, as he filled in stage directions and speech-prefixes, that he had already used the name.[12] Since no satisfactory explanation has been given for the state of the text in this scene, I shall offer my own.

Shakespeare's manuscript was in some disorder, and at certain points Q2 duplicates a discarded and a revised passage.[13] It is reasonable to suppose that we are dealing with two developmental layers of text here. If we read the lines attributed to 'Peter' in Q2 on the assumption that we find here evidence of a preliminary version of the play, and if we read the lines without old preconceptions, we can see that the text will provide ample opportunities in performance for the clown.

> *Enter Romeo and Peter*
> *Rom.* Give me that mattock and the wrenching iron,
> Hold take this letter, early in the morning
> See thou deliver it to my lord and Father,
> Give me the light upon thy life I charge thee . . .

Peter is obliged to carry, simultaneously, a mattock, a wrenching iron, a letter and a light – a comically difficult task. Romeo then confuses Peter with contradictory orders: 'stand all aloof . . .' – so

Peter stands – 'hence be gone . . .' – he goes – 'But if thou jealous dost return . . .' he is obliged to stop going –

> I will tear thee joint by joint
> And strew this hungry churchyard with thy limbs.
> The time and my intents are savage wild
> More fierce and more inexorable far
> Than empty tygers or the roaring sea.
> *Pet.* I will be gone sir and not trouble ye.

Following Romeo's extravagant language, Peter's rhyme yields a touch of bathos. After receiving a tip, Peter retreats, and offers another jingle to the audience:

> For all the same, I'll hide me here about,
> His looks I fear, and his intents I doubt.

He hides behind 'this yew tree here' (l.137), conveniently represented by the stage post. Peter's gaping mouth is visible to the audience, as Romeo opens the trap-door saying:

> Thou detestable maw, thou womb of death
> Gorged with the dearest morsel of the earth:
> Thus I enforce thy rotten jaws to open,
> And in despite I'll cram thee with more food.

As Romeo's hyperbole reaches new heights, Peter is down-stage of him, and ideally placed to engage in some visual by-play with the audience. The final comic touch comes when the Friar stumbles over Peter as he sleeps. The first sentence sets up the gag:

> St Francis be my speed, how oft tonight
> Have my old feet stumbled at graves? Who's there?

The speech given to 'Balthasar' at the end of the scene is in verse, like Balthasar's lines in his earlier scene, and no comic reading is possible.

The intention behind 'Peter' seems plain. Romeo's rhetoric is frankly melodramatic, and the presence of Peter – i.e. the clown – obliges the audience to reject Romeo's own account of himself, temporarily, and to accept an alternative perspective.

The facts remain, however. Balthasar is firmly established as Romeo's servant, and as a straight, verse-speaking character, in v.i. The existence of Romeo's servant was established at II.iv.3. 'Balthasar' was perceived to be Romeo's servant in the tomb scene when the play was performed. 'Peter' is cast as a Capulet servant.

'Peter' is nevertheless the name given to Romeo's servant in Shakespeare's source, Brooke's *Romeus and Juliet*. And Brooke suggests the possibility of comedy when he depicts Peter as a man of 'coward heart'.[14] A simple hypothesis accounts for these facts. Shakespeare drafted the tomb scene first. *Romeo and Juliet* was his first essay in a new genre, romantic tragedy, and it is reasonable to suppose that he wanted to get the feel of the climax in order to know what he was building towards.

With this hypothesis, everything falls into place. Shakespeare's source suggested to him that the clown must naturally be cast as Romeo's servant. This accorded with neo-classical convention, and he had already cast Dromio and Grumio as servant to the hero. But as he wrote, Shakespeare decided that this concept was wrong. In Romeo, there lay the possibility of transcending the melodramatic or burlesque norms of early Elizabethan tragedy. In Kemp, he had a clown whose presence would never allow Romeo to dominate the stage, a clown whose presence would preclude any even short-lived idealizing of Romeo's emotions. When he began the play at the beginning, therefore, Shakespeare relocated the clown as principal Capulet servant, retaining the English name of Peter. When he finally established the character of Romeo's servant in v.i, he gave this servant verse and an Italian name, to signal that this was a straight character, distanced from the immediate world of the London audience. There was no need to rewrite Peter's lines: a few cuts and appropriate casting were enough.

I have uncovered something of the genesis of Shakespeare's text in order to show that Shakespeare was never confused, only experimenting. He always worked with the needs and possibilities of his actors in mind.

We can see now how Kemp's role was constructed. Shakespeare built up the part, not around a 'characterization', or a name, or a precise household duty, but around a sequence of situations, and around on-going business with props. Shakespeare regularly constructs character in this way, and reporters of texts perceived character likewise. In the last chapter, I cited the example of Bottom. In *Romeo and Juliet*, Juliet's mother is a good example. In Q2 she is Capu(let's) Wi(fe) when Tybalt is slain and family is in question, Old La(dy) when telling Juliet to marry as she herself did, La(dy)

when preaching stoicism in face of bereavement, Mo(ther) when she talks joyfully of marriage and when she has lost her daughter. This yields the notorious outcome that she is simultaneously 'old' and under thirty. Kemp's role can be analysed in the same way. In relation to his master, old Capulet, he is 'Clown' – the company clown announcing himself, but also a social and educational inferior. When the feast is prepared, he becomes 'Serving-man', for his task is to be serving. When he appears with the nurse, he role-plays as 'her man'. His serving-man's livery is concealed, and the nurse is a fellow servant, so he becomes 'Peter'. When he joins the musicians in a scene which anticipates his next appearance, again with the musicians, as jig-maker, he becomes 'Will Kemp'.

Modern editorial practice reflects modern naturalistic dramaturgical practice: that is, the presumption that a play is peopled by 'characters' – and that the mark of a good character is to be real and convincing, which is to say, simultaneously coherent yet complex. A *real* character is taken to be one with whom actor and spectator can in some measure identify. Modern readings of the play tend to isolate the two protagonists, because only their characters seem to offer enough material for worthwhile analysis.

Illusionist assumptions carry a corollary here: namely, that the clown must be present to satisfy the mob, because the mob needs someone with whom to identify, while the tragic hero exists for the discerning. Couched in less simplistic terms, this traditional view still has appeal in many quarters. In order to avoid the illusionist fallacy, we must always keep hold of the fact that the Elizabethan theatre was a location where all social classes could gather and survey each other face to face. No spectator watched the play as an isolated individual. All spectators perceived in this environment that their own identities and moral codes existed in relation to opposites and alternatives. No one mode of organizing experience – Romeo's, a gentleman's, a labourer's, Peter's – had any overriding validity, any fixed hierarchical precedence, within the physical ambit of the playhouse.

Shakespeare's perception of the world cannot be detached from his perception of his variegated audience. It cannot be detached, either, from his perception of his own company, in which there were perhaps nine other sharers or master actors to be satisfied. He was impelled to create a play-world which contained a multiplicity of points of view – not just the Romeo viewpoint which governs

Brooke's narrative. Shakespeare rejected the obvious ploy of developing a master–servant relationship, and relocated his clown within a set of inter-servant relationships. He thereby isolated Romeo. The social fabric around Romeo is nevertheless an integral part of the play. The individual and the society are necessarily in tension.

In *Romeo and Juliet*, Friar Lawrence, the Nurse, Mercutio and the Capulets offer alternative points of view: the self-sacrificial, the reproductive, the lecherous and the institutionalized aspects of love all compete against the romantic. The clown offers a perspective which differs from all these. Romantic love is beyond his ken because he is fully occupied with work. Pleasure is wise-cracking, practical joking, stolen marzipan. He underlines the fact that musicians manufacture emotion for gain. He parodies Romeo's duel with Tybalt when he brandishes his dagger in a duel of wits with the musicians. If Romeo had heeded his wit rather than his honour, events could have turned out more happily. In all his jests, the clown's humour is predominantly physical and visual. He contrasts with Romeo, who communicates almost entirely through the medium of words. The clown's alternative viewpoint is not a dominant one, in the play that Shakespeare finally wrote, but it is a significant component in the play's structure, and will of course be reinforced in the jig.

Every Man In His Humour

Jonson's *Every Man In His Humour* illuminates in a rather different way the relationship between author and actor. As we saw in relation to the jig, Jonson wrote with the practical requirements of the Chamberlain's company very much in mind. We may take the 1601 Quarto text, the Italian version, as the text which Jonson prepared for performance in 1598.

The clown's part is manifestly that of Oliver Cob. The part owes nothing to the theory of humours, everything to the clown tradition. I have shown how Kemp's clowning is rooted in festival. 'Cob' identifies himself as a herring cob – that is, an emblem of Lent. But Cob loathes fasting days, because herring are then eaten, so Cob becomes, paradoxically, the embodiment of Carnival. In accordance with his fishy name, Cob is obliged to earn his living by carrying water: but he gains no pleasure from this Lenten antithesis of feasting and drunkenness. Cob's English name distances him from the

Italian world of the play, and he is English enough to deal in shillings and pence. A virtuoso mime routine is given him when he performs a balancing feat with his tankard to the nonsense words: 'Helter skelter, hang sorrow, care will kill a cat, up tails all, and a pox on the hangman'.[15]

The central feature of Cob's clowning is that the audience do not know whether they are laughing at or with him.[16] On the face of it, he is set up as the fall-guy to be cudgelled, scratched, knocked on the head by a door, and duped into thinking he must go to prison. Yet at the same time, he remains in control of the humour of every scene in which he appears. Cob hates tobacco, because herring are smoked, and describes how a smoker 'voided a bushel of soot yesterday, upward and downward' (II.ii.95). The audience do not know whether this is wit or lunacy. The same uncertainty is present when Cob holds up a fish and claims it for his ancestor. If he claims descent from the herring in Adam and Eve's kitchen (I.iii.13), this implies seditiously that the only logical response to his nonsense is the egalitarianism advocated by the old rhyme: 'When Adam delved and Eve span, who was then the gentleman?' Like Kemp, Cob is always capable of performing a double-take on himself. Kemp meditates in his pamphlet upon how he came to utter the high-faluting word 'congruity', and Cob asks a similar question of his audience:

I'd forswear them all by the life of Pharaoh. There's an oath. How many waterbearers shall you hear swear such an oath? (I.iii.69)

The viewpoint of the author, who cast the clown as a water-bearer, is completely effaced. The audience must look to the actor in order to determine how they themselves have been cast: are their intellects one step ahead of the clown, or one step behind?

The character of Musco ('Brainworm' in the revision) may usefully be contrasted with Cob. The inspiration for Musco owes everything to the author, nothing to the actor. Like a slave in Roman comedy, his only motivation is loyalty to the young master. His regular disguises service the plot mechanics. He announces a typical disguise to the audience:

'Sblood, I cannot choose but laugh to see myself translated thus, from a poor creature to a creator: for now must I create an intolerable sort of lies . . .
(II.i.1–3)

One must doubt whether the actor in performance succeeded in

making the audience laugh with him, and enjoy his cerebral pun. Jonson had a grand design for this character. At the end, Brainworm recapitulates his activities at length, is toasted twice by Clement, and is given Clement's robes to wear in the final procession in order to appear a triumphant Lord of Misrule. Since all these features were abandoned in the revision, we may judge that Jonson's grand conception could not be realized in performance.

We do not know what relationship the revised text, published in 1616 but written earlier, bears to a revival. We can be sure of two things, however. Jonson no longer wrote with Kemp in mind. And he no longer wrote from the standpoint of one who earned his living as an actor. As Jonson became established and known as a writer, his ideas about theatre changed. A passage in his commonplace book sets out a neo-classical view of comedy that evidently appealed to him:

Nor is the moving of laughter always the end of *Comedy*; that is rather a fooling for the people's delight, or their fooling . . . Jests that are true and natural seldom raise laughter with the beast, the multitude. They love nothing that is right and proper. The farther it runs from reason or possibility with them, the better it is.[17]

We cannot take this as an expression of Jonson's personal view, since he proved himself quite capable of fooling for the people's delight when he wrote a play for the Bear Garden in 1614. The passage nevertheless relates closely to the realist programme with which Jonson's name came to be associated. It echoes Hamlet's idea of theatre in its concern for truth, naturalness, reason and possibility, and in its scorn for the multitude. Just as Hamlet sees mere laughter as the response of 'barren spectators', so this passage disparages audible laughter.

A comparison of two passages will exemplify the new authorial attitude towards the clown's role. This exchange follows Cob's claim to be descended from a herring:

Matheo:	How knowest thou that?
Cob:	How know I? Why, his ghost comes to me every night.
Matheo:	Oh, unsavoury jest! The ghost of a herring cob!
Cob:	Aye, why not the ghost of a herring cob, as well as the ghost of Rashero Baccono? They were both broiled on the coals. You are a scholar, upsolve me that now.
Matheo:	Oh, rude ignorance! [Quarto text] (I.iii.19–24)

Matthew:	How know'st thou that?
Cob:	How know I? Why I smell his ghost ever and anon.
Matthew:	Smell a ghost? Oh unsavoury jest! And the ghost of a herring cob!
Cob:	Aye, sir; with favour of your worship's nose, Master Matthew, why not the ghost of a herring cob as well as the ghost of rasher bacon?
Matthew:	Roger Bacon, thou wouldst say?
Cob:	I say 'rasher bacon'. They were both broiled o' the coals. And a man may smell broiled meat, I hope? You are a scholar, upsolve me that, now.
Matthew:	Oh raw ignorance. [Revised text)]

In the original version, Cob's jest works subliminally. Speedy surrealistic association of ideas allows him to flummox the supercilious Matheo. The latent train of thought relates to Greene's *Friar Bacon and Friar Bungay*, where the clown nightly encounters the ghost of (i.e. made by) Roger Bacon: the ghost was made over the coals because it inhabits a brazen head. In the revised text, Jonson establishes reason and plausibility. He expands the jest so that a logical train of thought is laid bare. Cob's fantasy loses conviction when the ghost is no longer said to come to him every night. Instead, the line is turned against Cob, and refers to a fish's lingering stench. The introduction of 'sir' and 'Master Matthew' orients the player of Cob towards his interlocutor, and away from the audience. An inaccuracy is then expunged, lest anyone suspect the *author* of thinking that Roger Bacon was really burned at the stake. Cob's illogicality baffled Matheo in the original version, but in the revised text the last laugh is given to Matthew with a quibble on raw/broiled. In the passage as a whole, the audience can no longer laugh with the clown, but are required to laugh *at* Cob's grotesqueness and folly.

The same logic controls the revision of Cob's part throughout. The text has ceased to be a physical asset of the company, and has become part of the author's opus. The author must take final responsibility for what is written. Subliminal word-play on collar/choler/collier has to be ironed out and explained (III.i.135). An 'ingratitude wretch' becomes a 'monster of ingratitude' in the interests of grammar, and 'as rich as Golias' becomes 'as rich as King Cophetua' in the interests of accuracy (III.iii.52, III.i.179). A unifying style is imposed. Cob's punch lines are robbed of their throw-away brevity in a rhetorical device characteristic of the revised text as a whole.[18] A unified style is also a unified moral stance. When for instance Cob receives a

warrant for Bobadilla's arrest, his exit line in the original text is at once moronic and insubordinate:

Oh, divine Doctor; thanks, noble Doctor; most dainty Doctor; delicious
Doctor. (III.iii.117–18)

In the revision, the clown does not laugh at authority. Instead, the clerk is allowed to insult Cob with the words: 'Do not stink, sweet Oliver.' Cob does not respond, but makes his exit still cringing.

The character has become a mere 'humour', and his dimensions are within the omniscient grasp of both author and audience. The clown is not the maker but the object of the audience's laughter. The maker is seen to be the writer. Since the setting is now English, there is nothing to set the clown apart from the other characters of the play. The actor is expected to speak as a water-bearer might naturally speak, and be treated in accordance with the logic of his obsession. Jonson's small but meticulous revisions give us clues to the different way in which the Jacobean comedian was expected to approach the playing of Cob's role.

It is normal to think of the actor as the interpretative artist, the writer as the creative artist. The distinction is a false one. In *Every Man In His Humour* we can see how Jonson the craftsman interpreted his given, the clown. Jonson's training under Henslowe rendered him capable of working successfully within the clown tradition when he chose. When Jonson opted for the neo-classical mode, he opted for a different deployment of his actors' available skills and resources. In a play like *The Alchemist*, he demanded above all speed and precision as the actors submitted themselves to the dictates of a carefully wrought plot. The leisurely pace of a Kemp could have no place in an *Alchemist*. Kemp required ample stage time, not harnessed to plot, in order to make his audience think through their mutual relationship as he shifted in and out of role. In *The Alchemist*, the relationships between actor and role, actor and audience, are not in question. The assumption reigns that the actor has only to be 'true' and 'natural'.

CHAPTER 8

The conventions governing Kemp's scripted roles

BASIC CONVENTIONAL FEATURES OF THE CLOWN'S ROLE

I T IS IMMEDIATELY APPARENT that the clown's role in Elizabethan drama displays the following inter-related conventional features:

1 The clown's part belongs to a male character of low social status.
2 The clown's part is written in colloquial prose.
3 The clown is free to separate himself from the role and plot structure of the play.

A male of low status

The clown-actor always plays himself, and projects a single clown persona both inside and outside the play. It is impossible, therefore, for him to play a female character, such as the nurse in *Romeo and Juliet*.

The question of social status is more complex. In fifteenth-century English drama, prior to *Fulgens and Lucres*, we find no conventionalized markers of social status. Herod and his soldiers, Cain and Garcio, angels and souls share the same idiom and verse structure. All people are conceived as equal in the eyes of God.[1] In the sixteenth century, the Vice with increasing frequency comes to place himself as a servant to the corruptible protagonist. The Vice, as we have seen, marks out his separateness through language and costume. Meanwhile, the patterns of Roman and Italian comedy also imposed

99

themselves upon English drama. The relationship between master and slave, *gentiluomo* and *zanni*, are defining features of Roman and Italian comedy. The Elizabethan theatre tended, therefore, to present a dichotomous view of the social hierarchy.

Roman and Italian comedy commonly invert the master/servant relationship, rendering the master indebted to the servant's greater resourcefulness. The comedy thus celebrates the interdependence of all sectors of society, whilst reinforcing the idea that the divide between slave and citizen, servant and master, is the only basis upon which the world can operate. In the Elizabethan world, the division between gentleman and commoner was at once the hardest status division to define objectively, and the most critical in public social dealing. The conventions of Elizabethan popular comedy simplify this divide, and lend it a sense of naturalness and inevitability. The mental construct of 'gentle'/'clown' became a part of most Elizabethans' thought processes.

I have shown how the equivalence of 'clown' as comedian and 'clown' as low-status rustic broke down. By the end of the 1590s, the binary view of society was no longer an acceptable convention. As we shall see, Shakespeare presented in Falstaff a clown who is also a knight. Robert Armin then developed the idea that the clown is but an exemplar of the fact that all men are fools. As a jester or licensed fool, Armin placed his clown outside established hierarchical structures. Kemp, however, never ceased to define his clown as a 'plain man' in contradistinction to a 'gentle-man'. Kemp's stage names, unlike Armin's, foreground his social status: 'cock' is related to a soldier's gun, a 'bottom' is a weaver's clew, a 'pipkin' is used by a kitchen-boy, the name of a fish suits a water-bearer.

Colloquial prose

In Elizabethan drama, the provision of separate languages for protagonist and clown works to reinforce the 'gentle'/'clown' construct. While the classical slave was marked out by his mask, the Elizabethan clown was marked out by his speech.

I have traced the prose convention back through the speech patterns of the Vices in *Cambises* and *Mankind*. The clown's prose relates to his traditional function as an improvisator. Colloquial prose created the illusion of (and real potential for) sponteneity, and encouraged the audience to imagine that the character had somehow

stepped out of the yard onto the stage. The clown abandons prose only to substitute corny jingles which seem to be improvised. Cob, typically, breaks into verse only for the exit line:

> Sweet or sour, thou art a flower.
> Keep close thy door, I ask no more.[2]

In my discussions of the jig, and of *Romeo and Juliet*, I have indicated that the clown's primary 'language' is physical rather than verbal. This factor relates to his use of prose.[3] Elizabethan dramatic verse tends to function as a completed system, metrically, syntactically and semantically. The actor's movement reinforces rather than alters or extends meaning. In emotional passages dense in imagery, the actor cannot afford to divert attention from the complex interplay of words, and can only follow where the mood of the words leads him. In rhetorical verse, meaning can be reinforced by the lexicalized gestures of the orator. In prose, however, the situation is potentially different. The clown can be given a language in which links between different segments of speech are syntactically loose, and semantic gaps seal off one segment from another. There is no metre to point the breath control and emphases. The actor's movement and control over timing are necessary to fill the syntactic and semantic gaps, to indicate the impulse that prompts the words. Because the physical action triggers the speech act, the illusion is strengthened that the actor has taken over from the writer as creator of the play.

Within the prose convention, a contrast can be made between the monologues written for Kemp, which are dialogic or narrational in structure, and are organized by rhythm rather than syntax, and the elliptical, ratiocinative monologues written for Armin. Kemp's monologues are written in the idiom of the 'plain man'; Armin's are written as vehicles for virtuoso mimicry. Kemp dispenses with syntax, Armin pretends that his utterances are syntactically tight. Kemp's prose always does duty as an index of social class, but Armin's show of colloquiality gives us little coherent information about birth and breeding.

Separation from plot structure

It is easier for the clown to separate himself from the main role and plot structure of the play if he remains distanced from the intrigues

upon which the plot pivots. While Roman and Italian comedy usually present a systematic inversion of moral order, Elizabethan comedy characteristically presents an alternation of order and disorder. The sections of moral and linguistic disorder rise to their climax in the clown's jig. For the most part, therefore, Kemp's contact with the main plot remains tangential. While Speed, the proto-Clown, is given to bantering with gentry, Launce/Kemp prefers to enjoy his separate merriments. In *Romeo and Juliet* the proto-Peter knew all too well what his master was about, but the final Peter is not even allowed to eavesdrop when matters touching Juliet's *amour* are concerned. Jonson gave the clown's part to the self-obsessed Cob rather than to the ubiquitous Musco. And Heywood made a similar decision when he gave the clown's part to Jenkin, who plays no part in the plot mechanics, and not to Nick, the comic servant who is instrumental in bringing the adultery to light.

The clown's separateness is effected through plot, through language, and through his position on the stage. His use of prose relates to his characteristic use of a downstage position, close enough to all the spectators for some facial expression and breathing to register, close enough for him to seek inspiration from the audience as he seems to extemporize.

Robert Weimann has brilliantly analysed the interplay between verbal and spatial elements in Shakespeare's stagecraft. He relates the clown's command of the front of the platform stage to the Vice's use of the *platea*. He shows how Tarlton, because of his physical proximity to the audience, 'performed not so much *for* an audience as *with* a community of spectators'.[4] The clown in his scripted roles retains this intimate contact. He seems part of the community of spectators because he is physically in the centre of that community. Weimann quotes examples of direct address from Apemantus and Thersites.[5] One can see like evidence of Kemp's ability to use the downstage position in Simpkin's comments from his chest, in proto-Peter's comments from in front of the stage post, and in the clown's commentary on the siege of Ludgate in *Sir Thomas Wyatt*.

A useful linguistic marker of the clown's direct audience address is his use of the second person.[6] I have already noted that in *The Merchant of Venice* direct address is unique to the clown; an example is the imperative in: 'Mark me now, now I will raise the waters.'[7] The technique is characteristic of Kemp. Launce tells the audience: 'I'll show you the manner of it.' Simpkin: 'Gentlemen . . . you may

come to a christening.' Cob: 'you should have some now, would take him to be a gentleman'. Jenkin: 'You may see, my masters . . .'.[8] The technique is less characteristic of Armin's monologues. While Kemp constructs his audience as a community of peers, Armin acknowledges the audience only as a collection of individuals. He occasionally incorporates individual spectators into the action of the play – probably gentry sitting on stools on the stage: 'Faith, here's an equivocator . . .', 'Then have we here young Dizy and young master Deepvow, and Master Copperspur, and Master Starvelackey . . .'[9]

Another marking device which can help to separate the clown from the main role and plot structure is a naming convention. When the play has a notional foreign setting, Kemp's name is always English. I have noted Cob and Peter as examples. This convention relates in an obvious way to the clown's self-envelopment in a community of spectators. Italian names are retained for the early 'Dromio' and 'Grumio' – roles not written for Kemp. Geographical verisimilitude is likewise normally preserved for Armin's clown. 'Lavatch', for instance, requires a smattering of French before the double pun can be deciphered. Armin does not identify himself as part of the community of spectators, and does not engage in an implied dialogue with an audience of equals.

KEMP AND SINGER

In order for us to separate the individual aspects of Kemp's art from the generic, a comparative method is essential. Since the comparison between Kemp and Armin will be the subject of a later chapter, I shall here contrast Kemp with his opposite number in the rival Admiral's company.

The part of 'Clown' is formally indicated in the texts of several plays written during the period of Singer's association with the company. We may therefore assume that he plays Frisco in *Englishmen for my Money* (1598), 'Clown' in *Four Prentices of London* (by 1600), Swash in *Blind Beggar of Bednall Green* (1600), Much in *The Downfall of Robert, Earl of Huntingdon* (1598) and therefore also in *The Death of Robert, Earl of Huntingdon* (1598), and of course Assinico in the scenario of *1 Tamar Cam* (c. 1602). In another group of plays, one character emerges as an unambiguous clown figure in terms of the conventions which I have described: Pego in *Blind Beggar of Alexandria* (1596), Shadow in *Old Fortunatus* (1599),

Firke in *Shoemaker's Holiday* (1599), Babulo in *Patient Grissel* (1600).[10] An adequate stock of parts is therefore available to be analysed. With the exception of *Blind Beggar of Alexandria* – in many ways the least revealing text – all these plays were written by dramatists who were in Henslowe's regular employment, and who therefore wrote to a brief.

Kemp and Singer were different in respect of voice and manner, of body and movement, of background and experience. The principal differences between them can be summed up under three headings.

Plain/boorish

Something of Tarlton's rusticity must have rubbed off on Singer during the five years of their association in the Queen's. Rowlands informs us that Singer and Pope – by inference, unlike Kemp – spoke 'boorish when / They counterfeit the clowns upon the stage'.[11] While Kemp was proud to be a 'plain man', Singer was content to end his life a courtier.[12] These snippets of information correlate with the fact that Singer presents his character as a butt, while Kemp sets up a more complex dialectic between laughing 'at' and laughing 'with' the character he plays. Because Singer projects himself as boorish, he tends to finish the play disadvantaged. Pego is saddled with a child, Much loses his girl to Friar Tuck, Shadow is arrested, the Clown in *Four Prentices* is found fighting the heroine and is chased away. A comparison with Kemp's apparently boorish Dogberry will illustrate the contrast. Dogberry boorishly dubs himself an ass, but at the same time he secures impunity in order to call the Governor of Messina an arrant knave, to bid him correct himself, and to give him leave to depart. Kemp is never merely the butt of the humour.

A hallmark of Singer's boorishness is a trick of inarticulate roaring. Much is described as a 'roaring slave' after he has been asked to 'make a cry'. Attempts to calm Swash result in the reply: 'I do not cry, I do but roar.' And Shadow obliges nobles to 'stop his balling throat'.[13] A hallmark of Kemp's more subtle style is his assumption of melancholia. Hodge asks the audience: 'Is it not most gentleman-like to be melancholy?'[14] Simpkin starts his jig 'sad' and 'troubled at heart'. Rowland is likewise 'full of woe'. Peter yearns for 'heart's ease'. Launce contrasts his own tearful state with his dog's lack of feeling. And so on. Kemp maintains a sense of distance from a

melancholic state which, his audience must understand, is ultimately alien to the creator of mad jigs and merry jests.

Passive/active

A pronounced feature of Singer's act is his physical energy. He is given directions which exploit this energy. We find: 'Enter the Clown running', 'Enter the ladies flying, pursued by the Clown' – and Heywood gives the clown a final exit line 'I am running thither as fast as I can.' We also find: 'Enter Frisco, running', 'Shadow enters running', 'Enter Much, running' (twice). Swash goes 'running after' a thief. Firke is told to 'run, do you hear, run to Guild Hall' and exits with 'I run'; later he is told to 'frisk about, and about, and about'.[15] There is only one example of Kemp making similar haste. The exceptional stage direction which proves the general rule is 'Enter Pipkin, running'.[16] For Pipkin comes late to school; he is the school-boy who never learns, the apprentice who never completes his indentures. A flow of words always prevents him from carrying out instructions. Cob is similar. He fails to 'come running' with urgent news, and prompts the ironical comment 'I am familiar with thy haste.'[17] Launce nearly misses his boat, delays giving Speed an important message, and spends two days loitering. Kemp is adept at extracting comedy from inactivity. In his jigs he lies in a box, acts dead, or waits to be seduced. As Cock he sits passively on the bawd's knee. As Hodge he spins out the time with song and fantasy while the hero makes his escape in Hodge's clothes. As Peter he prevaricates when supposed to pay off the musicians. When Jenkins discovers the adultery, his advice to fellow servants is: 'let us sleep as snug as pigs in pease-straw'.[18] There is no difficulty in multiplying examples. While Singer may best be likened to a modern farce actor concerned to force the pace, Kemp seems closer to music hall: the audience's pleasure lies in seeing how the actor, with nothing but a bare stage, an expanse of time, and his personality, can conjure up pleasurable ways of filling a vacuum.

Kemp's physical attributes came to his assistance. His leaping indicates that he was a large man, and there is play on this in the texts. Dogberry and Verges are 'not alike' because Verges 'comes too short of' Dogberry. Pipkin describes himself as 'the greatest scholar in the school, for I am bigger than two or three of them'. Costard is

the most striking example. A 'costard' is a particularly large apple, and he plays Pompey the Great (with a pun on 'pompion'/pumpkin) because of 'his great limb or joint'. Limb and joint are indistinguishable in one of such rounded shape. He dwells on the boy's small size and cannot recognize himself in Armado's description of one who is '*low*-spirited' '*small*-knowing', a '*shallow* vessel'.[19] The speedy and ubiquitous Singer seems to have been a smaller man; there is play on the name 'Shadow' and its relation to poverty.[20] Kemp's remarkably solid physique made it easier for him to impose a still presence and to dominate the forty-foot width of the stage.

Solo entertainer/company man

While Kemp's background was that of a solo entertainer, there is no evidence that Singer was ever other than an actor in a company. Singer was a founder member of the Queen's Men in 1583 and was still with that company in 1588. By 1594 he had joined the Admiral's.[21] The implications of this difference are apparent. There is no obvious tendency to isolate Singer's clown from the plot mechanics, and roles like Pego and Frisco keep the plot moving. Singer is an actor who has no trouble playing within a master/servant relationship when required. Shadow, Swash and Babulo are ever-present alongside their employers, and do not threaten to upstage them. Kemp, by contrast, always dominates the stage. Writers do not make him cramp his style by functioning as part of a master/servant relationship, or trying so to function. When Hodge and Cock are enlisted as valets in the course of the action, it is made clear that the profession is alien to them, and their chief comic opportunities are set up when the master is absent. While Kemp characteristically dominates a group of 'clowns' or lower-class characters, Singer is characteristically an individual lower-class character, defined as a 'clown' through his relationships with social superiors.

Kemp's roles seem to be structured in order to allow him to rehearse his own sections of the play independently. Dogberry, typically, always leads his group onto the stage, and pronounces the exit line which takes them off. *A Woman Killed with Kindness* offers a striking example of playhouse practicalities. Jenkin has the single cut-off line which halts the scene of improvised dancing and takes the servant group off stage. He opens and closes the processional scene

in which servants carry supper across the stage, and he talks through
– with obvious scope for improvisation – the setting up of the card
table. Through the play the servant group never enters or exits unless
Jenkin has the cue. The convenience of this arrangement in a playhouse where only one man held a full copy of the script is obvious.
No separation can therefore be made between Kemp's playing of a
dominant character in the script and his role as one of the principal
sharers in the company. There is no sign that Singer sought artistic
and organizational independence of this kind.

Another characteristic feature of Kemp's roles relates to this independence. All his roles in the plays are structured in order to allow
for at least one short scene in which he speaks directly to the audience. Few qualifications are needed: Jenkin's monologue and Costard's two monologues remain short; Dogberry's expostulation
'would that I had been writ down an ass!' is delivered while other
characters remain on stage; and the monologue in *Sir Thomas More*
interestingly remains unscripted. The monologue is normally placed
at the end of a scene, and thus seems to provide a format within
which the clown may extemporize without risk to the rhythm of the
play or direction of the narrative. Singer's roles are not structured in
this way. Firke's single monologue is pure plot exposition. Only
Frisco has any significant amount of stage time alone with the
audience, and his speeches go little beyond scene setting. Frisco
employs second-person address in one monologue when he opens:
'Ah sirrah, now I know what manner of thing Paul's is.'[22] The mode
of address is to a proposed individual in the yard. Singer does not
share Kemp's assumption of community with the whole body of
spectators.

I have picked out a number of points which render Kemp's scripts
distinctive. In order to complete my discussion of the texture of
Kemp's clowning, it will be helpful to analyse a monologue written
for Kemp. I will use the one in *Thomas Lord Cromwell*. I have chosen
this one because the book-keeper in the playhouse appears to have
been very precise in punctuating according to the comedian's timing.
I have modernized the spelling, but retain the punctuation. The
passage is of course printed as prose, but I set it out here as verse in
order to highlight the rhythm.

Shakespeare's clown

Enter Hodge his father's man.
Hod.   Your son *Thomas*,
    quoth you,
    I have been *Thomas'd*,
    I thought it had been no such matter to a gone by water:

    for at Putney I'll go you to Parish-garden for two pence,
    sit as still as may be,
    without any wagging or jolting in my guts,
    in a little boat too:

    here we were scarce four mile in the great green water,
    but I thinking to go to my afternoon's 'unchins,
    as 'twas my manner at home,
    but I felt a kind of rising in my guts:

    at last one o' the Sailors spying of me,
    be a good cheer says he,
    set down thy victuals,
    and up with it,
    thou hast nothing but an Eel in thy belly:

    Well to't went I,
    to my victuals went the Sailors,
    and thinking I to be a man of better experience than any in the ship,
    asked me what Wood the ship was made of:

    they all swore I told them as right as if I had been acquainted with the
       Carpenter that made it,
    at last we grew near land,
    and I grew villainous hungry,
    went to my bag,
    the divel a bit there was,
    the Sailors had tickled me,
    yet I cannot blame them,
    it was a part of kindness,
    for I in kindness told them what Wood the ship was made of,
    and they in kindness eat up my victuals,
    as indeed one good turn asketh another:

    Well would I, could I, find my maister *Thomas* in this Dutch town, he
       might put some English Beer into my belly.[23]

The comedian's rhythmic patter can easily be sensed. The punctuation cuts the speech into segments (rendered above as lines) which are linked not syntactically so much as by their place in the linear progress of the narrative. As in Kemp's own writing,[24] the seg-

ments are frequently paired, both by sense and rhythm: Thomas /
Thomas'd, to't went I / to my victuals went ..., in kindness / in kindness, etc. The rhythm gives the speech momentum. There is a brief
halt at the commas for laughter, but the comedian stops for a full in-
take of breath only at the colons. The colons are set at the point where
real semantic gaps occur, where the audience has to put its imagination
to work. The clown's movement is essential here as, by some minimal
mime, he indicates that the boards of the stage are now water, that he
is a big man perched on a tiny boat, that he longs to eat but feels too
ill, that an eel seems to be climbing his oesophagus, that all he can see
as he leans over is the gunwales. The build-up to the final colon is the
longest, and indicates some acceleration of pace. The familiar question is duly posed: is this mere stupidity, or does speed of delivery
conceal a logic beyond the audience's grasp? Capitals help point the
stress: Sailors, Wood, Eel need to be visualized. A 'Carpenter' works
in wood, but he does not build boats.

There is an easy movement into second person address. As the
clown walks forward, 'quoth *you*' refers to Hodge's master in the
tiring-house, but 'I'll go *you* to Parish-garden' refers to the now
adjacent audience, presumed to share Kemp's known love of bear-
baiting. The occasional slippage into present tense – 'says', 'eat' –
indicates the double reality, the historical past of the narrative, and
the present in which the action is really taking place. At the end,
Kemp sets the scene afresh: the stage will now represent Holland. But
'this Dutch town' is of course the theatre in Moorfields where people
are enjoying the pleasures of clowns and drinking 'English Beer'.
Kemp logically seeks Thomas in the crowded yard rather than the
distant tiring-house back over the water. Kemp thus ends by drawing
the audience into the play, and at the same time indicates that he, the
plain beer-loving Englishman, does not fully belong in the artificial
world to which his back is turned.

Hodge is established in his first scene as a working farrier, and he
places himself physically close to the groundlings. We need now to
clarify how far his speech serves as an index of class. This relates to
the question of how far the clown is a representative of and spokes-
man for the groundlings. Basil Bernstein's theory of 'restricted codes'
and 'elaborated codes' is useful here. Bernstein takes 'restricted' code
to be broadly characteristic of modern working-class speech.

The speech is played out against a background of communal, self-

Shakespeare's clown

consciously held interests which removes the need to verbalize subjective intent and make it explicit . . . Verbal planning will tend to be reduced and utterances fluent. The non-verbal component (expressive features) will be a major source for indicating changes in meaning . . . The intent of the listener may be taken for granted. Finally, the content of the speech is likely to be concrete, descriptive and narrative rather than analytical and abstract. The major function of this code is to reinforce the *form* of the social relationship (a warm and inclusive relationship) by restricting the verbal signalling of individuated responses.[25]

Kemp's speech is clearly written in this 'restricted' code. Characteristic of this code is the lack of subordinate clauses, of complex verbal stems, and of the passive voice. The coined 'Thomas'd' is the exception which points to the master's speech, and to the absurdities of 'elaborated' usage. Kemp offers the normal rather than the individuated response of a man crossing the channel for the first time. He assumes that everyone eats packed luncheons and drinks beer at the first opportunity. He takes for granted a shared set of interests and identifications. Later, Thomas Cromwell will offer individuated, subjective responses to the world about him. The speech is an index of class inasmuch as it differentiates the clown's language from the verse of the master. It is not an index of class in that the clown embraces both the yard and the galleries with his gaze, and can imply an inclusive relationship which excludes no one. The language can fulfil this double function only when certain social conditions obtain in the audience, and when the actor has adequate powers of self-projection.

THE STRUCTURE OF MISRULE

In Chapter 2 I stressed the historical links between the clown's art and the amateur misrule tradition central to so many calendar festivals of the sixteenth century. C. L. Barber's study, *Shakespeare's Festive Comedy*, complemented by the work of Northrop Frye, and more recently by Neil Rhodes's *Elizabethan Grotesque*,[26] has elevated to the status of critical orthodoxy the view that Elizabethan comedy is structured by the paradigms of festival: the alternation of order and disorder, urban world and green world, Carnival and Lent. It is important to examine how the clown is integrated into this festive structure.

The clown's role within the scripted text needs to be viewed as a

progress towards the jig, the instituted climax in which the spectators participate in the enactment of misrule. As we saw in Chapter 4,
the conventions of Elizabethan romantic drama are shaped by the
balance of play with jig. In order to end, the script must always bring
to a point of closure – through betrothal, marriage or death – the
loves of the young protagonists. And conversely, it must never bring
to a conclusion the love-life of the clown. The jig does duty, in a
sense, for the physical consummation of the protagonists. But at the
same time it brings the clown's progress through the play to its
anticipated climax.

Nashe dedicated his book to 'Cavaleire Monsieur du Kempe', and
Kemp described himself in his *Nine Days' Wonder* as 'Cavaliero
Kemp, head-master of morris dancers, high headborough of
hays . . .'[27] These mock-heroic titles relate to the persona of Lord of
Misrule to which Kemp always aspires. In the jig, the clown finally
becomes Lord of the theatre, and the norms which have hitherto
governed dramatic speech, plot structure, sexual morality and audience behaviour are abruptly reversed.

When we look at the plays in this light, the following conventions
become apparent:

1 The clown's sexuality is always suggested, never demonstrated.
2 The clown's metamorphosis is either represented visually or
   prepared for.
3 The clown is excluded from the scripted finale.

Kemp's roles observe these conventions almost systematically;
Singer's observe them more casually. Singer was not famed for his
jigs in the same way as Kemp. He did not fully share Kemp's ability
to function as a point of interface between the two forms.

The clown's wooing

The clown's names often bring his potential sexuality to the fore.
'Launce' carries a staff as his emblem and uses it to illustrate the jest:
'My staff understands me.'[28] 'Launcelet' and 'Cock' are obviously
phallic, and are analogous to such names given to Singer as 'Pego',
'Babulo' (i.e. bauble) and 'Firke'.[29]

Yet the clown is consistently denied physical satisfaction. The
Roman/Italian convention whereby the servant pairs with the ser-

vant girl is conspicuous by its absence. In his Plautine *Comedy of Errors*, Shakespeare closes off the narrative of Dromio's relationship with Nell. The classically trained Chapman secures a wife for Pego. These are exceptions to the general rule that I noted in Chapter 4. Gratiano can be married off, but not Launcelet. Costard, Launce and Bottom fail to bring their wooings to any kind of conclusion. The relationship between Juliet's nurse and 'her man' is not clarified. The original Cob never comes on stage to be reconciled with his wife. Cock is dragged away from an embrace with the bawd. Jenkin pledges his hand and heart to Sisly Milk-pale, but we are not apprised of the outcome. Singer's clown fares no better than Kemp's. In *Shoemaker's Holiday*, Ralph is reunited with Jane, but Firke, the clown, only hints at a liaison with Sybil the serving-maid. Swash sings a ballad to teach his master how to seduce ladies, but there is no appearance of his own wench for whom he is too poor to buy pins. The Clown in *Four Prentices* has been banished for the getting of bastards, but his lechery is merely stated. Much the miller's son sees his beloved Jenny seduced by Friar Tuck in an unresolved sub-plot in the *Downfall*; and, in the sequel play, Much acquires tenancy of the mill, and decides he can therefore ask Jenny to marry him, but again the audience are not shown the outcome.

The clown's metamorphosis

I concluded in Chapter 4 that the clown must have worn some form of ceremonial costume in order to present his jig. It is a striking feature of many texts that the clown adopts an appropriate ceremonial costume in the course of the play. The change usually takes place in the context of a journey to court, where marriage awaits the protagonists.

We have noted that Launcelet dons an extravagant livery when he comes to Belmont (see Chapter 1). And that Ralph Betts is apparently turned into a May Lord in the context of the May Day celebrations (see Chapter 6). Bottom, while lording it over the fairies, wears a coronet of roses, the regalia of the may-game,[30] and we may assume that, when Pyramus the weaver creates for himself a striking heroic outfit. Costard is decked out as Pompey. Hodge dresses as a Lord in the Earl's coat and hat, and he makes his final entry at court as a marshal 'very fine with a tipstaff'.[31]

Dogberry must be another who dresses up for court. The stage

direction for the interrogation scene specifies that Dogberry and his fellows appear 'in gowns'; and at the end of that scene Dogberry mentions that he has *two* gowns, an indication that he is going to produce a still more impressive outfit for his appearance at court in the last act.[32] In other texts, the transformation is anticipated but never materializes. Cock starts the play in rags, and appears at court as a soldier 'in a new livery'; but in his final speech he explains that he plans to transform himself once more: 'My casque I must change to a cap and a feather, my bandilero to a scarf to hang my sword in, and indeed fashion myself wholly to the humours of the time.'[33] Launce, after a play spent journeying, never actually arrives at court, where he needs to present Julia with a new lap-dog. At the end of *1 Lady Jane* the clown resolves to use his looted gold in order to buy 'some counterfeit suit of apparel'.[34] It may be no coincidence that Peter – like Singer's Swash – makes his final exit with a purse.

An important point to notice in connexion with these metamorphoses is that the clown in no sense changes character. Kemp's Lord of Misrule always projects a double identity: the Lord of the game and the clown or social inferior beneath. This double identity is central to the creation of Falstaff, which we examine in the next chapter.

Dressing up is a feature of Singer's roles, but less markedly so. The pattern here is rather one of rags to finery to rags again in accordance with the construction of Singer's clown as butt of the play's humour.

Absence from the finale

The clown does not appear in the scripted finale of most plays because his own finale follows. We have already noted the striking exclusions of Cob and Assinico when the remainder of the cast assembles. Launce never arrives at court; Eglamour and Speed also fail to join the principals gathered on stage for the final scene. In *The Merchant of Venice*, Shakespeare establishes that the clown is at Belmont, but does not bring him on to join Antonio, the three couples, 'followers' and the musicians who assemble at the end. In *Love's Labour's Lost*, Armado introduces a final song to be sung by Nathaniel and Holofernes. The physical absence of Costard would explain why he is not mentioned. The text of *A Midsummer Night's Dream* is problematic, as we have already noted. It is likely, however, that four of the mechanicals doubled as fairies,[35] so Kemp would be almost alone in having no formal exit written into the script. The

convention is maintained in Kemp's later texts. Cock abandons the stage, declaring: 'The King, the Queen, and the rest of the Lords will use this place for their revels':[36] four couples are formally brought together, with the court looking on, and of the principals only Cock and two fellow-soldiers fail to join the revels. More strikingly still, Pipkin is the only member of the cast who does not appear in the last scene of *How a Man May Choose a Good Wife from a Bad.*

Singer is not so obviously subject to this convention, so far as we can judge from the repertory of plays which I discussed earlier in this chapter. Frisco has to pull the final strings in the plot, Shadow is needed for a pastiche morality end scene, and Chapman's *Blind Beggar of Alexandria* is consistently an innovative piece. Nevertheless, where some sense of a comic grouping exists, Singer fades into the background. Firke has nothing to say once the King comes on stage. Babulo never returns to court for the final scene. Heywood's Clown is absent from the siege of Jerusalem. The comic grouping of Much, Jenny and Tuck are, if present at all, silent when some twenty other players come on stage for the processional finale to the *Downfall.* In another interesting example from the Admiral's Men's repertory, the two principal comic servants in *Two Angry Women of Abingdon* hide at the back of the stage some twenty minutes before the end, and, although shouted for, never reappear.[37]

Edward Berry has recently argued that there is no progression within the clown's role.

> As an embodiment of chaos ... the clown is from one perspective an emblem of regression or stasis. While the dynamics of the plays are progressive and integrative ... the clown remains fixed in confusion, sometimes outside and alone ... His emblem, it seems, is not the line but the circle ... The Clown's is a natural circle, always the same, but capable of infinite renewal.[38]

Berry is right to point up the paradox that the clown is both ever changing and ever the same. However, I want to change Berry's emphasis and to suggest that there is a forward momentum within the clown's performance, a movement towards a different kind of integration.

Kemp's emblematic names contribute to the impression that the clown in the jig will complement and complete the clown of the play. The names of the clown are the opposite of carnivalesque. Carnival,

like other festivals, is associated with the eating of meat. But 'Pipkin' is a pot yet to be filled with meat, a cob herring is Lenten fare, and costard is likewise not part of festive eating. A dogberry is wholly inedible (while 'Verjuice' is just about palatable, and the commonwealth is actually sustained by plain 'Oat-cake' and 'Sea-kale'). The audience must await the moment when Kemp will slough off the desexualized, workaday, Lenten identity that the playwright has given him, and join them to become their Lord of Misrule in the festive climax that concludes the performance.

CHAPTER 9

Falstaff

I HAVE POSTPONED DISCUSSION of Falstaff until this point
for strategic reasons. I wish to argue that the Falstaff of the two
Henry IV plays is structurally the clown's part, albeit with significant modifications. If Falstaff is structurally the clown's part, it is
reasonable (I believe) to conclude that the part was written for
Kemp. As I make this claim, I have to recognize that a massive body
of criticism has accumulated around the figure of Falstaff. Readers
familiar with this critical tradition may consider that I am being
foolhardy, and reductive, in branding Falstaff as '*the* clown' of
Henry IV. I shall hope to overcome such objections by showing that
my argument follows logically from that of previous chapters, and
that the Tudor Vice/clown tradition was never more complex than
when, under pressure for dramaturgical change, it spawned 'Falstaff'. Readers familiar with the rich performance tradition that has
attached itself to Falstaff may find themselves disconcerted by the
implications for staging if Falstaff was indeed a part written for
Kemp. We have to keep reminding ourselves that Shakespeare's
plays 'work' – and have worked for three centuries – under performance conditions radically different from those of the Elizabethan
public playhouse.

Before proceeding further, I shall review the circumstantial evidence which should encourage us to believe that Falstaff was a role
for Kemp. The hypothesis that Falstaff = Kemp offers a coherent
explanation for phenomena which historians have tended to leave
unexplained.

The first piece of evidence is the disappearance of Falstaff from
Henry V. It is easy to argue retrospectively that the play could not
have accommodated Falstaff, that the account of Falstaff's death has
its due part in a unified artistic whole. The point remains that
Shakespeare reneged on his promise made in the epilogue to *2 Henry
IV*, where the dancer clearly states: 'our humble author will continue

the story with Sir John in it'. Dover Wilson noted the obvicus coincidence of chronology.[1] *Henry V* can be dated to the few months following Essex's departure for Ireland on 27 March 1599. Kemp signed the Globe lease on 21 February 1599, but had left the company by the autumn. We have no explanation of why Kemp withdrew so quickly. The argument that artistic motives alone caused Shakespeare to exclude Falstaff from *Henry V* does not threaten my case. A decision by Shakespeare to downgrade or obliterate Falstaff's part would provide a plausible motive for Kemp's sudden withdrawal from the company.

The second piece of evidence is the Quarto text of *Syr John Falstaffe, and the merrie Wives of Windsor*, registered on 18 January 1602. There seems now to be a critical consensus on two important points. First, it is agreed that the play originally was written at short notice for performance at the Garter Feast in April 1597, at the behest of Lord Hunsdon, the company's patron, elected to the order at the time.[2] Second, it is agreed that the Quarto is a reported text based on a heavily cut version of the original, and that, because their parts are on the whole accurately rendered, the original actors of the Host and Falstaff were responsible for the reporting.[3] We know of only one group of deserters who left the Chamberlain's company in the period 1598–1601, and that is the group who joined Worcester's Men: Kemp, Beeston, Duke and perhaps Pallant. We can deduce the motivation. The player of Falstaff, having left the company, would have had the incentive to restore, from memory, a playable text to serve as a vehicle for his talents. If Kemp was trying to establish himself at the Curtain in the winter of 1599–1600, if he took a group of actors to Germany in the late autumn of 1601, or whatever comparable activity engaged him in the theatrical underworld, he needed scripts, and this reconstructed script from the Chamberlains's Men's repertoire would have served. Once established as a member of Worcester's company in 1602, he would have had no further use for the script, but he would not have minded aggravating the rival Chamberlain's company through publishing. It cannot be proven that Kemp was the principal pirate, but this hypothesis offers the simplest available explanation for the Quarto's existence.[4]

A small textual curiosity in the Quarto text of *2 Henry IV* does something to corroborate the idea that the part of Falstaff was written for Kemp. Dover Wilson noted that a rogue stage direction 'Enter Will' can be explained as an entry for 'Will Kemp',[5] but he

does not explore why there is no reference to such an entry in the dialogue. The drawers are on stage, and Falstaff is supposedly supping in the next room. The text reads as follows:

Dra[wer]. Dispatch, the roome where they supt is too hot, theile come in straight.
Francis Sirra, here wil be the prince and master Poynes anon, and they will put on two of our jerkins and aprons, and sir John must not know of it, Bardolfe hath brought word.

Enter Will.

Dra. By the mas here will be old utis, it will be an excellent stratagem.

(II.iv.13–20)

Doll and Quickly enter a line later, and at line 32 Falstaff enters with a full chamber pot. The mysterious '*Enter Will.*' vanishes from the Folio text. It is plausible that 'Will' should be the actor's own name: another actor's name, that of John Sincklo, slips into the Quarto text; and Kemp's name, as we have seen, appears in the Quartos of *Romeo and Juliet* and *Much Ado*. The direction seems to cue a small item of stage business. While the drawers conspire downstage and establish suspense – the dining room is hot, they'll come in straight away, Sir John must not know the plan – Falstaff upstage enters from the dining room and exits hastily through another door to seek the chamber pot. Doll and Quickly follow their client from the dining room. The women are seeing to Falstaff's needs, and we should not expect them casually to walk out on him as the traditional staging seems to require. Unless we write off the direction '*Enter Will.*' as an unaccountable error, the logic of the staging would seem to require that Falstaff is 'Will'.

The argument that I developed in Chapter 6 yields a different, negative brand of evidence that Shakespeare wrote Falstaff as a part for Kemp. If Kemp did not play Falstaff, then we would need to establish which part was written for the clown of the Chamberlain's company. Robert Shallow has a substantial part in 2 *Henry IV*, but the part is written for a man of small physical stature (III.ii.303–7). Whether appearing as a solitary figure – Launce, Cob – or as the dominant personality amidst a group of lower-class characters – Bottom, Dogberry – Kemp would dominate the stage with his presence. We should not expect him to have played a foil like Poins. Pistol's language is too far removed from the clown's colloquial idiom. Only the role of Falstaff is congruent with other roles written

Falstaff

for the clown of the company in 1595–8. A historical point can be added to the structural argument here. The role of Falstaff can be seen as an elaborate reworking of the role of Derick in *The Famous Victories of Henry the Fifth* – the role which Kemp's predecessor Tarlton took a decade earlier.[6]

It seems to me that Shakespeare plainly relied upon Kemp's performance skills in order to create Falstaff. He could rely on Kemp to control a long monologue, and to talk at length to 3,000 people as if in a *tête-a-tête*. These skills were a product of Kemp's years as a solo entertainer, and of his particular ability to present himself as an 'honest fellow', a plain Englishman able to take everyone as his equal. Shakespeare could depend upon Kemp's ability to command the stage by creating a still, focal presence. Immobility is an attribute of Falstaff throughout Part One. At Gad's Hill he stands immobilized on his feet, persuading the audience that the level stage is in fact 'uneven ground' (1.ii.25). He is motionless when asleep, and motionless when feigning death (where later actors were often tempted to introduce redundant business).[7] When ordered to the wars by the Lord Chief Justice at the start of Part Two, his great toe necessitates an inordinately slow exit (1.ii.246). Falstaff spends Part One delaying Hal from fighting, and most of Part Two delaying his own progress to the battlefields. This corresponds to the rhythm of Kemp's clowning in a way that it could not, for instance, correspond to Singer's.

In a sense, killing time is at the symbolic heart of the role. Falstaff is like a Lord of Misrule, a personification of Shrovetide or Summer, who has power temporarily to halt the normal progress of the calendar. From one perspective, the role of Falstaff conforms to what I have called the structure of misrule, though from another perspective it undermines that structure. He has prose as a clown should, but a very distinctive prose. His social status is ambiguous: he is a common cutpurse, but at the same time a knight. In respect of plot structure, he is both separate from and bound up with the chronicle of aristocratic rebellion. Like other clowns, his wooing is unresolved. He is absent from the finale of Part Two, but this time with a crucial difference: he has been formally debarred. He anticipates metamorphosis in Part One when he resolves at the end to live as 'a nobleman should do', being yet a mere knight, but in another sense *qua* knight the clown is already metamorphosed. I shall point to the numerous references which reminded the audience of Falstaff's *alter ego* as clown.

Most readers who have followed the argument that I have developed so far will, I hope, be ready to accept as reasonable my basic thesis that the part of Falstaff was written for Kemp: in other words, that Kemp and Falstaff are one and the same. In the remainder of this chapter, therefore, I shall abandon further caveats and work from the premise that Kemp = Falstaff. I shall regard this as a hypothesis to be tested against a reading of *Henry IV*. Readers must judge for themselves whether my interpretation of the text is acceptable to them.

We must try to place ourselves in the position of the Elizabethan audience who first saw Kemp make an appearance in the role of Falstaff. In Falstaff's first scene in *1 Henry IV*, Kemp's trademarks are obvious. Like Rowland and Simpkin *inter alia*, the clown introduces himself as a melancholic (1.ii.71), the better to offset his later mirth. Kemp's characteristic slowness and passivity feed the audience's appreciation of why the time of day is irrelevant to the figure before them – a figure who has not yet been given a name. Falstaff introduces himself as a cutpurse, a traditional enough occupation for a clown. He is first named, as plain 'Jack', at l.96. The first audience of the play were therefore not apprised for some time of the fact that the clown has now been cast as a *knight*. Poins addresses Falstaff as 'Sir John Sack, and Sugar Jack' at l.110, and Hal picks up 'Sir John' in his next speech. Falstaff, however, never refers to himself as a knight, but only as 'Old Jack', 'Falstaff', 'Jack Falstaff'. Because Falstaff does not speak of himself as a knight, the audience are encouraged to think of the role as, in some sense, an imposture to which they are privy. Falstaff seems to play on his ambiguous identity when he signs himself 'Jack Falstaff with my familiars, John with my brothers and sisters, and Sir John with all Europe' (*2HIV*.II.ii.125–7). The audience may consider themselves to be familiars. There is further play on Falstaff's ambiguous status when he backs false assurances with 'as I am a gentleman' and tells the truth when 'setting my knighthood . . . aside' (*2HIV*.II.i.135–7, 1.ii.80).

The ever-present emblems of Falstaff's knighthood reinforce the sense that this is a clown in role. With a great show of formality, the page bears on at the start of Part Two the sword and buckler that are to be recognized as Falstaff's accoutrements from Part One. Sword

and buckler are manifestly not the weapons of a gentleman; quite the reverse – the short sword and buckler were part of the traditional uniform of serving-men in blue livery coats.[8] Decoration apart, they were used for sport in Elizabethan England.[9] When Falstaff calls for his page to bring him his 'rapier' (2HIV.II.iv.197), it must plainly be the item on the cushion that is fetched: a stubby sword as used with a buckler. The Falstaff illustrated in *The Wits* in 1673 bears a slender rapier, and we must beware of being misled by this later, slimmed down, gentrified version of Shakespeare's Falstaff.

When Falstaff demonstrates how the buckram rogues 'mainly thrust at me', and how he 'took all their seven points in my target thus' (1HIV.II.iv.196–8), the buckler is the focus of the comedy. A buckler was very small, and designed for parrying the side of a sword. A sportive buckler was made of two skins of leather,[10] and it is this leather which has been cut 'through and through'. It is on the tiny central boss that Falstaff claims to have received the simultaneous thrust of seven swords. The staging here confirms that Falstaff is not so much the butt of Hal's practical joke in this scene as the game-maker, the instigator of comedy.

A cudgel is the only weapon associated with Falstaff in *Merry Wives* (II.ii.269). A study of Elizabethan terminology allows us to deduce that Falstaff's 'sword' was in fact the same weapon as his 'cudgel' or 'truncheon'. Young men who fought sportive combats with sword and buckler had a choice between playing 'at sharp' or 'at blunt'. A metal sword was used for serious fighting, but for practice fights a wooden 'waster' was substituted. Stowe's *Survey of London* informs us that the masters of London allowed their apprentices on Sunday evenings to play with 'cudgels'.[11] The terms 'waster' / 'truncheon' / 'cudgel' / 'staff' are near enough synonymous in Elizabethan usage. An academic gloss of 1661 illustrates the point clearly: 'The fencer's staff or waster ... was called "rudis" [in Latin] ... because with such cudgels they practised the rudiments of fencing before they came in public to fight at sharp.'[12] Falstaff's 'sword' is therefore a traditional apprentice's play-sword, made of wood. Just as Falstaff's buckler belies his words in the 'rogues in buckram' scene, so likewise his blunt waster renders absurd his reference to 'my point', 'my hilts'. He has no difficulty in carving up his waster, and the humour in the description of Falstaff's sword as 'hacked like a handsaw' lies in the fact that this particular sword is not metallic (1HIV.II.iv.191, 202, 166).

Falstaff's name confirms the emblematic function of the sword/ cudgel. This is not a real sword but a 'false staff'. The name links him to Launce and Launcelet, who may also have used staves as a Lord of Misrule's symbol of office.[13] The short staff is a versatile prop. Falstaff can convert it to a fife and seem to play music on it (*1HIV*.III.iii.85s.d.). As an emblem it is polysemous. It signifies low rank, in contrast to the rapier which was the international mark of the gentleman. It belongs not to old age but to the sport of young apprentices. It is a play-weapon, proper to a maker of game within the play. There are phallic possibilities in the derivation 'fall staff'. The fact that Folly in the interlude *Mundus et Infans* bears a staff and buckler as his emblems helps to confirm the traditional nature of Shakespeare's stagecraft.[14]

There is reference to a different weapon in the tavern scene, where Falstaff emerges most clearly in the role of game-maker and improvisator. Hal in this scene conceives Falstaff as a Vice from an old moral interlude, dubbing him 'devil' / 'vice' / 'iniquity' / 'ruffian' / 'Satan' (*1HIV*.II.441–57). Falstaff responds to this terminology by using a 'dagger' for King Henry's sceptre. The Vice traditionally wielded a toy dagger, usually of lath,[15] and Falstaff accordingly turns himself into an emblem of the Vice. Hal assures the audience that this is a 'leaden' dagger – a toy, of no use for fighting. Falstaff's pistol turns out to be no less bogus than his sword or dagger, for at the battle of Shrewsbury the pistol case is shown to hold a bottle of sack (v.iii.54s.d.).

In the final act of Part One, Kemp/Falstaff is at the core of a sustained assault on dramatic illusion. We must again read the play as a temporal construct, and put ourselves in the position of an audience who have not seen it before. They would not, any more than Douglas, have been aware initially that the first character who dies on stage is not King Henry but Sir Walter Blunt in disguise.[16] When Falstaff 'dies', there is no clue given to the audience, whose attention must be divided, that Falstaff's death is faked:

They fight: Enter Falstaff

Falst.   Well said Hal, to it Hal. Nay you shall find no boys' play here I can tell you.

Enter Douglas, he fighteth with Falstaff, he falls down as if he were dead, the Prince killeth Percy.   (v.iv.73–5)

Hal now pronounces his twin epitaphs – over Hotspur, 'stout' of heart, and over Falstaff, stout of body. The audience could reasonably have thought that the ringing couplets with which Hal concludes signalled the end of the play.[17] Hotspur's face is covered with Hal's 'favours', and Falstaff had probably covered up his own face.[18] The direction '*Falstaff riseth up*' was (and can remain) a *coup de théâtre*. Falstaff rises up and pronounces himself no counterfeit because only dead men are truly counterfeit. The speech sets up many resonances. A third corpse is on stage – Blunt, in a costume which counterfeits the King's. More fundamentally, Falstaff/Kemp reminds the audience that the player of Hotspur is as alive as the player of Falstaff: 'how if he should counterfeit too and rise?' Falstaff's resurrection reminds the audience that the whole battle is in a sense 'boys' play'.

In Part Two, costume replaces the 'sword' as the central emblem and sign of clownishness. In his first scene in Part One, when Falstaff dissociated himself from a 'buff jerkin', the jest was that the clown now wore a fashionable coloured doublet (I.ii.45). The doublet in Part One quickly became a parody of fashion. Sartorial slashing was extended by Falstaff's own handiwork as he aimed to authenticate the claim that he had been 'eight times thrust through the doublet, four through the hose' (II.iv.164). The principal difference between a jerkin and a doublet is that a jerkin is tight to the body while a doublet is normally stuffed. The grotesque peascod doublet was going out of fashion by the late 1590s, and Fluellen seems to confirm that Falstaff wore one of these when he remembers him as 'the fat knight with the great-belly doublet'.[19] At the start of Part Two Falstaff aspires only to buying a new cloak and slops (I.ii.29). His doublet was so intimately related to his person as to be irreplaceable. He does not actually obtain the satin which he wants, and which the sumptuary code, proclaimed afresh in 1597, restricted to gentlemen and their retainers.[20]

Falstaff's reference to his 'cap' at I.ii.14 is noteworthy. Falstaff is the only English gentleman in Shakespeare's work to wear a 'cap': women, clerics, servants, common soldiers and Greeks and Romans wear them, but not gentlemen. The year of *2 Henry IV*, 1597, saw the repeal of legislation compelling all below the rank of gentleman or alderman to wear woollen 'statute caps' in lieu of moulded hats. Flat woollen caps remained part of an apprentice's uniform.[21]

Falstaff's wearing of a (close-fitting) *cap* rather than a (shaped) *hat* was an anomaly which marked out the clown as no true gentleman.

Falstaff's words at the start of Part Two invite the audience to imagine a new elegance of dress, but the action of the play yields the reverse: a progressive deterioration in Falstaff's costume.

Falstaff leaves London hoping that 'our armies join not in a hot day; for, by the Lord, I take but two shirts out with me, and I mean not to sweat extraordinarily' (I.ii.208–10). He arrives at Gaultree via Gloucestershire 'travel tainted as I am', claiming to have used over 180 post horses *en route* (IV.iii.36). He leaves the battle for Gloucestershire, and leaves there as fast as his companions can don their boots. He removes his own at v.i.51, and probably does not replace them. He arrives at the coronation 'stained with travel' because he has not had the 'patience to shift me' (V.v.21). His followers mirror his condition: they lack 'new liveries', and make a 'poor show' in their 'marvellous foul linen' (V.v.11–13; V.i.32). We need to consider how this physical deterioration was effected in performance. If Falstaff has not changed even his shirt, he probably has not changed his doublet for the coronation either. Shallow confirms that Falstaff has the remains of a doublet covering his shirt when he complains that he cannot see any way to greatness 'unless you give me your doublet and stuff me out with straw' (V.v.82). The doublet was already chopped about in Part One, and it must be in a state of increasing dilapidation after the journeys and battles of Part Two. The deterioration of Falstaff's costume is related to the idea that he is sweating. Falstaff does not plan 'to sweat extraordinarily' when he leaves London for the war (I.ii.210), but the dining room is hot and Doll has to wipe his face, comparing him to a roasting pig and exclaiming 'how thou sweat'st' (II.iv.214). During the battle, he compares the drops of his sweat to the tears of Colevile's mourners (IV.iii.12). He arrives at Hal's coronation 'sweating with desire to see him' (V.v.24). The epilogue anticipates that in the sequel Falstaff may indeed 'die of a sweat'. The purpose of this evocation of sweat seems to be to equate Falstaff with fatty meat which sweats as it cooks. Falstaff was described in Part One as a 'fat-kidneyed' 'fat guts', a 'greasy tallow catch', a 'roasted Manningtree ox', 'chops', 'brawn', a 'carbonado'.[22] The image is emblematically rich in its association both with Hell-fire and with Carnival feasting.

The tavern is a prelude to Hell. Falstaff speaks of the damnation of Dives (I.ii.34), and Pistol swears he will see Doll damned (II.iv.153).

Falstaff catalogues the damned souls: Bardolph's face is Lucifer's kitchen; the devil attends on the boy; the pox-ridden Doll is 'in hell already, and burns poor souls'; the Hostess will probably howl for breaking Lent (II.iv.329–73). The fate of the damned is sealed when the tavern is invaded by a beadle who becomes 'goodman death', an 'atomy' or skeleton (v.iv.28–9). As the Prince's 'ill angel', Falstaff follows Hal out of this environment, but he carries sherris with him, the principal property of which is to keep generating heat, illuminating the face like a beacon (I.ii.163; IV.iii.100ff.). A red face must be the principal theatrical sign of Falstaff's body heat.

The autumnal aspect of Falstaff, *qua* old man, is of course important: witness the references to St Bartholomew's Day, All-Hallows, and Martinmas (2.II.iv.227; I.I.ii.178; 2.II.ii.97). But *qua* fat man, Falstaff is not a Summer Lord so much as Carnival King, a personification of Shrove-tide. Carnival is always portrayed as a fat man. John Taylor in 1617 described how in front of lean Jack-a-Lent 'there comes waddling a fat, gross, bursten-gutted groom called *Shrove-Tuesday*, one whose manners shows that he is better fed than taught'.[23] In Brueghel's famous painting, *The Battle of Carnival and Lent*, Carnival carries a pig's head and sausages on a broche in order to do battle with an emaciated Lent. An Italian Carnival play of 1554 portrays a similar Carnival King with a necklace of sausages as his chain of office.[24] When worsted by Lent, he and his cook are thrown onto a bonfire. On the fire, Carnival claims to be melting like wax – an image which recalls the likening of Falstaff in Part Two to 'tallow', a 'candle-mine' (I.ii.157; II.iv.297). The epilogue hopes that the audience will not be 'too much cloyed with fat meat' because meat is evoked as the central symbol of Shrove-tide. The audience are reminded throughout Part Two that Shrove-tide is predicated upon the coming of Lent. The tavern is declared to be a place where meat is sinfully consumed in Lent (II.iv.340–5). In Gloucestershire, after a feast of fowl and mutton, Silence sings a song to welcome 'merry Shrove-tide', and the pace of drinking accelerates furiously (v.iii.25ff.), but the environment becomes 'barren, barren, barren (v.iii.7). As an emblem of Carnival, Falstaff inevitably must be destroyed in due time by Lent – and roasting is the proper way for Carnival to be consumed.

I have dwelt at length upon the externals of performance: Falstaff's wooden stick, his cap, his tattered great-belly doublet, his face illuminated by heat. These externals were, for the audience, ever-

present signs of the figure's status as clown. They are reminders that the actor is playing a role, and has power to create and dissolve a dramatic fiction upon the stage. The description of Falstaff in Part One as a 'woolsack', a 'stuffed cloakbag of guts', a 'creature of bumbast' (II.iv.132, 446, 323), reminds the audience that Falstaff is an actor with stuffing inside his doublet. The humour of the role is lost if it is played by an actor who really *is* obese, as Stephen Kemble's audience discovered in 1802.[25] Ben Jonson, with his concern that theatre should be a mirror of life, could not accept the more unreal aspects of Elizabethan stagecraft – as, for example, its rendering of battles: he mocked actors who

> with three rusty swords
> And help of some few foot-and-half-foot words
> Fight over York and Lancaster's long jars.[26]

Shakespeare, through giving one of his actors a wooden play-sword in pointed contrast to the metal swords of other actors, encouraged his audience to reflect upon the process of play-making, and to celebrate the power of theatre to conjure so much out of so little. The ambiguous social status of Falstaff/clown – a knight who is also a cutpurse, an aristocrat who bears the weapon and headgear of an apprentice – forces the audience to sense an ever-present dialectic between actor and role, to refrain from identifying any inner core of character where actor and role merge into one.

These techniques belong to a theatre of emblems, or signs, where the emphasis throughout is not upon character but upon the complex significance of action. Consider for example the remarkable moment at Shrewsbury when Hal, instead of stripping Hotspur's helmet of its regalia as he had promised, removes the plumage from his own helmet in order to cover Hotspur's face.[27] Hal thus lacks the normal evidence with which to confute Falstaff's claim to be the slayer of Hotspur – a false deed accomplished with a false sword. The modern audience tends to seek for 'character' – the 'true' character and emotion revealed by the action: but in this theatre there is no truth *behind* the action – there is only the complex inter-play of theatrical signs manipulated by flesh-and-blood actors. The emphasis is upon externals – a plume of feathers, sign of chivalric glory, a false sword, sign of clownishness – rather than upon qualities internal to the actor.

My argument about the clown necessarily extends into an argument about the Elizabethan theatre. But such an argument is beyond the scope of this book. I shall instead limit my focus and indicate how my interpretation of Shakespearean dramaturgy bears upon the perennial arguments which surround the 'rejection scene' at the end of Part Two.

W. H. Auden empathized with Falstaff's broken heart.[28] L. C. Knights read the scene for its moral seriousness, and drained it of its comedy.[29] Dover Wilson cast the scene as part of a didactic morality play, unaware of the carnivalesque basis of most so-called 'moral interludes'.[30] Peter Davison's theatrically aware Penguin edition of 1977 continues to conflate actor and role. Davison states that in Henry's part 'a sensitive actor can make this moment painful for *both* characters (and not solely for Falstaff) and can demand for Henry as well as Falstaff the involvement of the audience in the anguish he experiences'.[31] This is a sensible resolution in relation to modern conventions of performance. But it ignores the point that an Elizabethan audience might not be emphatically 'involved' in this way if it sees emotion not 'experienced' but *represented* by two men standing on a platform. The Elizabethan audience were not allowed to forget that Falstaff's grief was *being acted* before them.

The references to Falstaff's background at the Inns of Court supplied in the Gloucestershire scenes of Part Two can be used as support for a psychological reading of Falstaff as a rounded 'character' – in Peter Davison's words 'the very semblance of true flesh and blood'.[32] The New Arden editor comments, for instance, on the detail that Falstaff was once page to the Duke of Norfolk, that this is 'one of the many imaginative retrospective touches which so extend the living reality of the characters'.[33] We must quickly add the qualifying remark that Shakespeare constructs a biography based on a purely festive world, a world of whoring, fighting, archery and visiting the tilt-yard, a world where Shallow (alias Arthur's fool, Sir Dagonet) reports that Scoggin (Edward IV's jester) had his head broken by Falstaff. There remains, nevertheless, a sense in which, in the course of Part Two, the psychological reading acquires some validity. Falstaff is progressively established as a person with an identifiable history and social position so that he may in due course take his place as a normal English subject like all the other characters in the drama.

In the end, however, it is impossible to take Falstaff as an orthodox character. He does not take up his place in the procession of English subjects who troop off behind their monarch. Although the clown tries to participate in the procession, the official finale where he does not belong, his prescribed place is the jig.[34]

The single epilogue printed in the text in fact constitutes three separate pieces. The first is an author's prologue spoken before the Queen. The second and third are to be given by someone who is going to dance. The obvious speaker of these latter epilogues would seem to be Falstaff. A principal actor is customarily used to deliver the epilogue – Puck, Rosalind, Macilente, for instance – and there is no precedent for some anonymous boy closing the play.[35] The second epilogue opens:

If my tongue cannot entreat you to acquit me, will you command me to use my legs? And yet that were but light payment, to dance out of your debt . . .

The audience is asked to acquit 'Falstaff' of his sentence of banishment or the Fleet. The heavy man promises to be *light* on his feet when dancing to earn pardon. The third piece promises Falstaff's continuance in the sequel, and probable death from a sweat . . .

for Oldcastle died martyr, and this is not the man: my tongue is weary, when my legs are too, I will bid you, good night.

'This' is Falstaff, not Oldcastle. But 'this' is also an actor who has spoken enough script and will now begin to dance his jig.

The lack of narrative closure is a remarkable feature of Part Two. The audience are not informed as to whether Falstaff should finally be considered banished with a modest 'competence of life' to ward off poverty – as the King proclaims – or whether he will be 'very well provided for' until he can be passed off as respectable – as Prince John cynically interprets – or whether he will be carried off to the Fleet – as appears to happen on the Lord Chief Justice's orders. Shallow anticipates a hanging (v.v.63–101). If Falstaff is also Kemp the jig-maker who will bid the audience 'good night', Falstaff's own prognostication 'I shall be sent for soon at night' is not wholly without substance. Doll's part is similarly constructed. Having promised marriage to the Hostess, Falstaff makes no final choice of partners. The audience do not know whether Doll is supposed to be feigning pregnancy or not when arrested: her 'cushions' may be the character's artifice, or may be the actor's. The audience are not told

whether Doll and the Hostess finish up in prison – as Pistol states (v.v.34) – or banished – as the King implies. In a naturalistic text, this would be casual dramaturgy. In the Elizabethan theatre, with its different assumptions about dramatic illusion, this open-endedness exists for good reason: further sexual encounters await the clown after the conclusion of the scripted play.

With Kemp/Falstaff's dismissal by Hal, and his reappearance in the jig, the conventional structure of comedy is restored. Clown and protagonist are relegated to their separate spheres which, in other Shakespearean comedies, are so much more sharply demarcated. The close relationship between Falstaff and Hal is unique, and it is possible only because both figures are role-playing. While the Prince masters the argot of Eastcheap, the clown is cast as a knight. The relationship of clown and prince is contingent upon the saturnalian context, upon Hal's 'playing holidays', and games or jests are its substance: the ambush, the picking of Falstaff's pockets, extemporal play-acting. In Part Two the normative structure of alternating plots is substantially restored. Before the finale, Hal and Falstaff are engaged in some kind of dialogue for only a single scene of some seventy lines. In a restricted sense, Sidney proved to be right, the mingling of kings and clowns was in the end aesthetically unacceptable.

Falstaff and Hal meet and mingle on the plane of language. Hal and Poins abandon the verse of the court scenes and pick up prose, the mode characteristic of Eastcheap. It may be useful to look more closely at Shakespeare's linguistic strategy.

Falstaff's language underscores the point that he is, in sociological terms, the clown metamorphosed. He is familiar with all kinds of animal life, and there is no hint of an Inns of Court education. His cultural references relate to oral literature: the Bible, romances, popular theatre. The New Arden editor is in serious error when he deduces that 'Falstaff is a well-read man' on the basis of Falstaff's diagnosis of the King's illness. The words are extemporal nonsense: 'I have read the cause of his effects in Galen, it is a kind of deafness.'[36]

When Falstaff elaborates his account of the rogues in buckram, impersonates the King in the Boar's Head, or manipulates the Hostess to whom he owes money, he creates the impression that he is extemporizing, inventing verbal ploys on the spur of the moment. He shares Tarlton's skill of extracting himself from a situation of hopeless disadvantage. More specifically, the actor creates the illusion of

spontaneity through the linear structure of his sentences. Similes and unlikely comparisons are Falstaff's's stock mode. He embarks on a sentence without, it seems, himself knowing what the final object of comparison will turn out to be.

Let us take some random examples:

If I fought not with fifty of them I am a bunch of radish (*1HIV*.II.iv.183)

If reasons were as plentiful as blackberries   (*1HIV*.II.iv.234)

I do here walk before thee like a sow that hath overwhelmed all her litter but one   (*2HIV*.I.ii.10)

There's no more conceit in him than is in a mallet   (*2HIV*.II.iv.239)

The words 'radish', 'mallet' etc. are no sooner thought of than uttered. The prose utterances of the Prince, by comparison, tend towards metaphor. His quips and quiddities seem to be pre-planned:

I have sounded the very base-string of humility   (*1HIV*.II.iv.5)

The rest of thy low countries have made a shift to eat up thy holland   (*2HIV*.II.ii.21)

Would not this nave of a wheel have his ears cut off   (*2HIV*.II.iv.253)

The words 'sounded', 'shift', 'nave' are uttered in anticipation of the ensuing 'string', 'holland', 'wheel'.

Falstaff and Hal are quite unalike in their relationship to the audience. While Falstaff speaks a series of monologues straight out to the audience, Hal never speaks directly to the audience in prose but uses Poins as his confidant. Hal and his father have but one verse monologue apiece in each Part of *Henry IV* in which to give the audience a glimpse into the private determinations which guide their conduct. Hal's monologue early in Part One pointedly establishes a relationship of distance with the audience:

> I know you all, and will a while uphold
> The unyoked humour of your idleness...
>
> I'll so offend, to make offence a skill,
> Redeeming time when men least think I will. (I.ii.190–212)

The audience learn that they are henceforth to be located in the third person – 'men'. Falstaff always presumes a more intimate rela-

tionship with the audience. Phrases such as 'there's honour for you' and 'your excellent sherris' mark the continuing direct second-person address. The sense of intimacy is reinforced if Kemp delivers his monologues from the edge of the forestage.

The opening of Falstaff's monologue on sherris sack illustrates his technique. I punctuate as in the Quarto. Falstaff turns from addressing the Duke to addressing the audience without formal demarcation, and he aligns the audience with himself as he playfully disparages a Duke's title:

I would you had the wit, 'twere better than your dukedom, good faith this same young sober blooded boy doth not love me, nor a man cannot make him laugh, but that's no marvel, he drinks no wine, there's never none of these demure boys come to any proof, for thin drink doth so over-cool their blood, and making many fish meals, that they fall into a kind of male green sickness, and then when they marry, they get wenches, they are generally fools and cowards, which some of us should be too but for inflammation:

(2HIV.IV.iii.84–9)

The expression 'a man' implies both Falstaff and a representative spectator; 'these demure boys' implies a type known to both, and the audience are soon ready to acknowledge that they, like Falstaff – 'us' – are by nature fools and cowards. The first-person plural creates the sense of participation in a shared experience. Any spectator who fails to participate and laugh is implicated in the charge of green-sickness. Falstaff's speech is in 'restricted code'. The lexical range is great, but the syntax is loose, with no subordination or complex verbal stems; there is no abstraction, only concrete description. It is a feature of 'restricted code' that the speaker assumes an inclusive relationship with listeners who share his system of values. Only in the last sentence of the whole monologue – 'If I had a thousand sons . . .' – does Falstaff return to the first-person construction of his opening sentence and express an individuated sentiment.

Hal's monologue in Part One is bounded by logic: 'If . . . But . . . So . . . By how much . . . By so much . . .' Rhetorical and metrical structures place a constraint upon the character. After this speech of self-introduction, Hal remains within the closed logic of the dramatic illusion. Even in his monologue in Part Two, the sleeping King is available as his formal addressee. At the end of Part Two, Hal is the person who must expel unstructured misrule and implement order. Falstaff counterbalances Hal. In Falstaff there is a remarkable absence of rhetorical patterning. Brian Vickers helpfully contrasts the

formal symmetries of Falstaff's language when he is in some way role-playing with what Vickers classes as an 'unpatterned self-revelatory style'.[37] As the monologue on sherris continues – 'A good sherris-sack hath a twofold operation in it . . .' – a parodic element does enter in, and Falstaff can build up rhetorical symmetries. But in passages such as the one I have examined, Shakespeare achieves a quality that is not present in most other monologues written for Kemp: he achieves a prose devoid of rhetoric. The extemporal illusion is perfected – the illusion that the clown is conversing *with* rather than speaking *to* his audience. As in political morality, so in language, Falstaff breaks down the structures which Hal sets up. Language, conjoined with the staging which a given language mode requires, marks out Hal's and his father's distance from the audience. Falstaff's communality with the audience is marked out no less clearly.

We may return to Peter Davison's statement about the rejection scene. Hal and Falstaff do not exist as characters within a single, contained fictive universe. The Elizabethan audience were not detached observers peering through a proscenium at a mimesis of social reality: rather they were in a position to become an incorporated element in the *ludus*, the world of play. Burbage did not step outside the role of Hal and comment upon the action from the standpoint of a representative spectator in the way that Kemp did. In the long-established manner of the Clown or Vice, Kemp/Falstaff repeatedly ruptured aesthetic codes which other players sustained. The pain of Hal cannot be deemed 'commensurate' with the pain of Falstaff, because the pain of Falstaff is simultaneously the mirth of Kemp.

The dramaturgy of *Henry IV* draws on medieval tradition but is at the same time radically innovative. The Italian-style dramaturgy of *The Merry Wives of Windsor* has cut links with the past and is plainly less complex. The domestic middle-class setting and almost uniform prose place all characters upon a single plane. A stance of detachment is made available to the audience.

If the traditional date of *c.* 1600 were correct for *Merry Wives*, it would be easy to explain the changed character of Falstaff in terms of the role's being conceived differently for a new actor. However, as I noted earlier, it is generally now agreed that the play was written for performance at the Garter feast in April 1597 – probably interrupt-

ing the composition of *2 Henry IV*.[38] If the 1597 date is accepted, then *Merry Wives* may well have served to launch the name 'Falstaff' as a replacement for 'Oldcastle'. The question arises, how would an audience familiar with a *1 Henry IV* containing 'Oldcastle', and not yet acquainted with *2 Henry IV*, have recognized that 'Falstaff' in *Merry Wives* was the same character as 'Oldcastle'? The dramatis personae is completely new. ('Bardolph' was 'Russell' in the original *1 Henry IV*, and the name 'Quickly' appears once in Part One in a jesting context.)[39] The only link was a fat 'Sir John' with a cudgel for his insignium of knighthood. It must have appeared far more obvious, in April 1597, that the 'Falstaff' of *Merry Wives* was intended as a reworking of the original Sir John Falstaff from Part One of *Henry the Sixth*.

The original Falstaff of *1 Henry VI* was a runaway, and in the play was stripped of the Garter medal, and with it his knighthood (IV.i.14ff.). Falstaff in *Merry Wives* duly becomes the antithesis of everything that the Order of the Garter represents. His fate, of being tipped into the ditch, parodies the ceremony of degradation that awaited a disgraced Garter knight, whose insignia would be thrown into the ditch.[40] Falstaff's identity is not problematic. The courtly spectators at the Garter feast are assumed to know exactly who Falstaff is, for his world is their own. He anticipates being tried before the Privy Council for his crimes against Shallow (I.i.32, 109); he has influence with 'gentlemen my friends' (II.ii.9); and he is concerned that 'If it should come to the ear of the court how I have been transformed . . . they would whip me with their fine wits' (IV.v.89–94). It would not have been appropriate for Shakespeare to do as he did in the *Henry IV* plays and to balance honour against self-preservation, duty against pleasure, the feudal code against the common man's. Instead, Falstaff becomes the negative pole in a value system that admits of no ambiguities. The citizens of Windsor largely stand outside this value system, but Falstaff, the historical and archetypal false knight, cannot.

The character of Ford has taken the principal comic role in *Merry Wives*. He has a run of monologues in which he is both subject and object of mirth, and he has the privilege of closing the play. Ford adopts the pseudonym 'Brooke' ('Broome' in the censored Folio text). And it was William or Henry Brooke who apparently prevented Shakespeare from using the name Oldcastle. Henry was dubbed 'Sir John Falstaff' by Essex in 1598.[41] It seems to me that

Shakespeare's ploy in April 1597 was roughly as follows: I will bow
to pressure. Kemp will now play a fat knight who is definitely not
'Oldcastle', but the Brooke family name will not escape untarnished
because the central comic figure will be Ford alias Brooke.

Notionally separate in *Merry Wives*, 'Falstaff' subsumes 'Oldcastle' in *2 Henry IV*, and a single composite figure emerges. Many of
the characters in *Merry Wives* can be seen as a first draft for their
successors in Part Two. So also can the motif of heat: Falstaff is 'as
subject to heat as butter' (III.v.106), and after his hot ride in the
laundry basket he is cooled in the Thames. In the final act, the king of
Carnival is transformed and 'made a Jack-a-Lent' (v.v.128).

The circumstances of the original performance explain why Falstaff in *Merry Wives* is different from Kemp's other clowns. Something remains: he retains his 'cudgel', and a measure of second-
person address to the audience (III.v.11). But his speech tends to be in
elaborated code. The clown cannot establish communality with an
élite audience on an official occasion. Rather, the audience are
encouraged throughout to sense their superiority over the false
knight. There can be no jig and, accordingly, the narrative of the
clown's wooing is completed. His metamorphosis – into a stag – is
enacted on stage, and he is fully integrated in the play's finale.

The two-part play of *Sir John Oldcastle* provides an interesting coda
to the story of Kemp/Falstaff. The play was written for Henslowe,
and was completed by October 1599. It purports to set the record
straight by creating two 'Sir Johns': the Wycliffite hero, Sir John
Oldcastle, and the comic role of Sir John of Wrotham. The latter is a
fat priest ('Sir John' being a conventional term for a parson) who
took up the highwayman's trade after being robbed by Hal in the
days of Hal's association with Falstaff. In Part One (which alone is
extant), the comic Sir John travels with a 'Doll' who is obviously the
whore of *2 Henry IV*. Now in August 1602, when Worcester's
company entered into an agreement with Henslowe, it acquired the
text of *Oldcastle* from him. Substantially revised by Dekker, this was
the first play which the company rehearsed for the autumn season,
and was the only instance of a revival. When supper was taken with
Henslowe at the Mermaid, money was paid out for Oldcastle's and
two other characters' costumes. The next day, and two days before
props for the play were bought, the following entry appears in

Henslowe's Diary: 'Lent unto Wm Kempe the 22 of agoste to bye buckram to macke a payer of gyente hosse the some of V$^{s.}$'.[42] Kemp's giant hose moulded of stiffened cloth must surely have been intended for the neo-Falstaffian role of Sir John of Wrotham. It made sense in this instance for Worcester's Men to acquire a text already known to the public because it gave the original Falstaff the opportunity of completing the available cycle of Falstaffian roles.

CHAPTER 10

Robert Armin

A STUDY OF Robert Armin's career does much to illuminate the very different career of his predecessor, Kemp. Armin's own writings do much to document his life, and there is general scholarly agreement that the parts of 'fools' in Shakespeare were written for Armin to perform. While the idea that a performer's art could shape Shakespeare's writing has long run against the grain of the literary critical tradition, the idea that Armin was an *intellectual* influence has found a ready welcome.

The differences between Kemp and Armin were at once personal and historical. Armin belonged to a rising social group. He was an intellectual, a Londoner, and as well attuned to Renaissance notions of folly as to the English folk tradition. As an actor, Armin's skills lay in mime and mimicry, skills which could easily be adapted to a theatre based on satire and the mimesis of manners. Because he set himself up as a writer, Armin did not perceive that there was any necessary tension between the purposes of the dramatist and the purposes of the actor/clown. As a mimic and an intellectual, Armin never projected the clown persona of the common Englishman.

Let us examine Armin's career, and see how these traits emerge. Armin was the son of a tailor of King's Lynn, Norfolk.[1] His education included the study of Latin and Italian. He took a step up the social ladder when he secured an apprenticeship with the prestigious London company of Goldsmiths. Since he was free of the Goldsmiths' when he died, there is no reason to doubt that he served his full eleven-year term, which expired in 1592.

While bound as an apprentice, Armin made his name as a writer of ballads. Nashe and Harvey both bracket him with the London ballad writers Philip Stubbes – whose puritanism Armin opposed – and Thomas Deloney the silk-weaver.[2] One specimen of Armin's balladry must date back to this period, his free adaptation from Straparola

of *The Italian Tailor and his Boy*. Writers of penny ballads were a despised breed, and when Armin published the piece in 1609 he anticipated the critic who would sneer ''tis ballad stuff': he seems uncertain in 1609, however, whether he can pass off the work as a 'poem', or whether to excuse it as a 'jest'.[3] *The Italian Tailor and his Boy* is a fluent piece of popular literature, quite out of keeping with the tortuous complexity of Armin's later writing. It is designed to appeal to the London citizen ethos, and is wholly unsuited to the tastes of the dedicatee, a Scottish aristocrat at James's court. As a variant on the Dick Whittington myth, it is precisely the sort of work that we should expect from a tradesman-poet with an eye on the market. The hero is a tailor's apprentice who learns enough magic to transform himself into a variety of creatures and objects. Success comes when he transforms himself into a ruby ring, and finds his way to the finger of a princess. He metamorphoses into a naked male in her bed, and thus secures her hand in marriage.

The projection of his own personality is always central to Armin's writing and performing. Armin the tailor's son shades into the tailor's apprentice, and the goldsmith's apprentice shades into the gemstone set in a gold housing. The actor of many parts is akin to the boy of multiple metamorphoses. We may presume that he wrote the piece as a vehicle for his own skill as a singer.

After completing the term of his apprenticeship, Armin entered the service of Lord Chandos as a player.[4] The Chandos company travelled the country, and in 1595–7 turns up in the West Midlands, York and East Anglia.[5] Touring the country gave Armin the opportunity of studying village idiots and retained 'natural' fools. While much of the evidence in Armin's *Fool upon Fool* (1600) is anecdotal, he was able to give an eye-witness account of one Jack Miller, who frequented towns in the Vale of Evesham close to the Chandos seat at Sudely. Miller adored the 'clown' in the Chandos company, and it is safe to assume that this was Armin himself. We know nothing of the Chandos company's repertoire, but it is very likely that Armin played the 'clown' Robin in a pirate version of *Faustus*: a line addressed to the clown finds a close echo or parody in Armin's own stage play *Two Maids of More-clacke*.[6]

By the end of the decade, Armin was back in London. In 1600 he published *Fool upon Fool* and *Quips upon Questions* under the pseudonym 'Clonnico de Curtanio Snuffe' – Snuff the clown of the Curtain Theatre. Both works are dedicated to 'the Reader' rather

than to a patron, and Armin makes no bones of the fact that his object in publishing is profit.

These publications are usually taken as evidence that Armin joined the Chamberlain's Men before they left the Curtain in the late summer of 1599. However, Armin states explicitly that *Quips upon Questions* was 'Clapt up by a Clowne of the towne in this last restraint, having little else to do'. He can be referring only to the restraint imposed in June 1600, when the Curtain was barred to players, and the Chamberlain's Men at the Globe were restricted to playing twice a week.[7] Armin was certainly playing at the Globe by August 1600.[8] There is no reason why Armin should not have joined the Chamberlain's Men at the Globe in 1599, but at the same time have continued to find opportunities to perform solo material at the Curtain. We have already seen that the Curtain accommodated such informal material as jigs more readily than did the Globe.

Quips upon Questions, sub-titled *A Clown's Conceit on Occasion Offered*, gives us valuable insight into the Elizabethan sub-culture of clowns and their improvisatory art. We learn that Armin, like Tarlton before him, used to respond to 'themes' flung at him by the audience. An anecdote in *Tarlton's Jests*, also published in 1600, tells of an encounter between Tarlton and the young Armin, and states that Armin 'used to his plays, and fell in league with his humour: and private practice brought him to present playing'. The identity between one of Armin's 'quips' and one of Tarlton's 'jests' confirms the link between the two men.[9] While *Tarlton's Jests* is anecdotal in form, Armin's improvised material has been carefully reworked. Emblem books provided Armin with a literary model.[10]

'Quips upon questions' are described more specifically as 'moralized metamorphoses of changes upon interrogatories'. In lieu of an emblem, Armin sets down an initial 'interrogatory': a question which is read out to the clown, and which takes the form either of a riddle or of a personal reference to a particular spectator. The 'changes' are, on the face of it, exchanges between the clown and one or more members of the audience – but we may as easily conceive the clown's interlocutor(s) to be the clown himself using a different voice or voices. Since Armin's punctuation does nothing to help the reader disentangle the structure of the dialogue, reading the text becomes easy only when an anecdote replaces multivocal exchanges. The 'quip' or 'moralized metamorphosis' which concludes each piece is presented as if said or sung by the clown *in propria persona*: it is

directed either at the riddler or at the luckless subject upon whom comment has been invited. Armin prefaces his work with an address to 'Sir Timothy Truncheon alias Bastinado, ever my part-taking friend'. Armin personalizes his slapstick, and we must imagine that in performance he used it like a jester's *marotte*, endowing it with the voice of his *alter ego*. *Quips upon Questions* makes it clear that the projection of multiple identities is the staple of Armin's clowning. It is this quality which above all else sets him apart from Tarlton's eternal English peasant and Kemp's plain Englishman.

Armin's audience may ask him to comment on a man who looks angry, a drunk, a man who enters sweating, an overdressed woman, a prostitute. There may be a chance event, like a dog barking. Armin may be insulted on the grounds that he is nothing but a fool, that he is not so witty as Tarlton. Riddles may be obscene – 'what's near her?' – or philosophical – 'who is happy?' – or personal – 'what have I lost?' (an enquiry by a felon with an amputated ear). In such a situation, Tarlton set up a miniature drama, a confrontation between himself, the wily rustic, and the superficially clever spectator. Armin, however, distances himself from confrontation, slipping into the person of commentator, so that the only remaining fool is the one in the audience. Tarlton's anti-intellectualist gut responses invite an instinctual response from the audience, a mass reaction against a perceived deviant. Armin offers an idiosyncratic response to the idiosyncracies of spectators. He does not invite spectators to feel that they belong to a crowd, united as one body by a shared language and emotion. He individuates both himself and his audience.

Armin's improvisations allowed him to exploit his chief technical resource, his singing. Tarlton often sang his ripostes to 'themes', and Armin the writer of penny ballads evidently had the same ability to adapt his improvised words to popular tunes. Armin was a singer, but not a dancer. The dancing of jigs, with its required leaping and whirling, needed an athleticism which Armin did not possess. Armin's diminutive nicknames – 'Snuff' and 'Pink'[11] – indicate a physique very different from Kemp's.

Fool upon Fool, published at the same time as the *Quips*, comprises sketches of six natural fools. The book has as its running theme the distinction between a fool 'artificial' and a fool 'natural'. Armin declares that his book is 'written by one, seeming to have his mother wit, when some say he is filled with his father's foppery', and the phrasing suggests the delicate line that Armin followed in his own

fooling. He always leaves the ambiguity open, whether he is a congenital moron, like the subjects of his six sketches, or whether he is merely the artful jester. His skill lay in suggesting that his lunatic foppery might be innate.

The art—nature dichotomy relates closely to the concerns of Shakespearean comedy, and it is easy to see how the two men were able to form a working relationship. Notices of 1600, 1603, 1604, 1605, 1608, 1609 and 1610 indicate that Armin's membership of the Chamberlain's/King's company was uninterrupted. Hotson is doubtless right to read into the prologue of *Henry VIII* an apology for the absence of Armin in the role of Will Somers, Henry's fool,[12] following the actor's recent retirement.

The plagues of 1608 and 1609 probably encouraged Armin once more to communicate with his audience through the medium of print. In *Nest of Ninnies* (1608), *The Italian Tailor and his Boy* (1609) and *Two Maids of More-clacke* (1609) he chose to publish under his own name rather than his stage name, inviting recognition as an author rather than as a mere player.

The dedication of *Nest of Ninnies* to students of Oxford, Cambridge and the Inns of Court establishes the work as a bid for intellectual recognition. The book is an expansion of *Fool upon Fool*, with the same anecdotes put into the mouth of a philosopher fool, Sotto or 'Hodge', who chooses to interpret them as moral fables. In the *Quips*, the clown's aphorisms retain an aura of common sense: the clown is wise because he plays the fool for money, while others have to pay for the same privilege. In *Nest of Ninnies*, the character of the cynical philosopher-fool is a new one, one that has grown out of Armin's work with Shakespeare's company.

The next work that we need to examine is Armin's play *The History of the two Maids of More-clacke with the life and simple manner of JOHN in the Hospital*. As Hotson and Felver have pointed out, the play is constructed as a vehicle for Armin so that he can double the roles of John i' the Hospital and Tutch 'the Clowne'.[13]

In *Fool upon Fool* Armin gave an eye-witness account of Blue John of Christ's Hospital, and the play incorporates incidents from the book. The wood-cut on the title page (Fig. 5) portrays Armin in the role of John, wearing the standard blue-coat livery of Christ's Hospital. He is marked out as a fool by the objects which hang from his belt: a handkerchief to mop his dribble, and a pen and inkhorn which

THE
History of the two Maids of More-clacke,

VVith the life and simple maner of IOHN
in the Hospitall.

Played by the Children of the Kings
Maiesties Reuels.

VVritten by ROBERT ARMIN, seruant to the Kings
most excellent Maiestie.

LONDON,
Printed by *N.O.* for *Thomas Archer*, and is to be sold at his
shop in Popes-head Pallace, 1 6 0 9.

Fig. 5 Title page of Armin's *Two Maids of More-clacke* (1609).
Reproduced with permission of the Bodleian Library, from
Malone 201 (2), pp. 81, 190.

signify that this adult has yet to complete his schooling. Tutch, identified by stage directions as the clown of the play, is cast as the educated servant of a gentleman. He sheds his tattered livery-coat for disguises, first as a Welsh knight, and second as Blue John. In his final scene, Armin/Tutch the artificial fool thus becomes John/Armin the natural fool. Armin's assault on dramatic illusion pushes his own personality to the fore.

We learn from the title page that the play was acted by the Children of the King's Revels, a short-lived company which played at the Whitefriars in 1607–8. I see no reason to quarrel with the critical consensus, that the published text is a Jacobean expansion of an Elizabethan original.[14] Armin's statement in his preface:

I would have again enacted John myself, but *tempora mutantur in illis*, and I cannot do as I would

clearly does not mean, as Grosart concluded upon observing the decline of 'fool' roles in Shakespeare, that Armin was too sick to play the part. But neither does it mean, as later critics following Chambers have assumed, that Armin played in the Elizabethan version, and as a King's man could not participate in the revival.[15] The play's only virtue was that it served as Armin's vehicle. The point of Armin's preface is that the play is more 'naturally' performed than rendered in the form of a book:

I have boldly put into your hands, a Historical discourse, acted by the boys of the Revels, which perchance in part was sometime acted more naturally in the City, if not in the whole.

In the city, at the Whitefriars', the play was acted, but times have changed in 1609 – *tempora mutantur* – because plague has closed the theatres and bankrupted the King's Revels company. In playing John, Armin states:

I whilom pleased: and being requested both of Court and City to *show* him in private, I have therefore *printed* him in public   [my italics]

And referring again to the inadequacies of plays in book form, Armin reiterates his apology, wishing that he:

might put life into this picture, and naturally *act* him to your better contents; but since it may not be, my entreaty is, that you would accept *this dumb show*   [my italics]

Robert Armin

A careful reading of the preface shows us that Armin acted with the boys at the private Whitefriars' theatre, in a cut version of the text. Armin apparently clowned at the Curtain at the same time as he played in stage plays at the Globe. Here again we find him operating in a freelance capacity, now with a struggling company of adolescents enlisted as foils to his singing and impersonations. The clown not only stepped across the boundaries of the text: he also stepped across the boundaries of the dramatic company.

Armin's publications of 1608–9 can all be seen as recensions of much earlier work. Through his intellectualized version of *Fool upon Fool*, Armin presented himself as a man accustomed to consort with gentlemen of Christchurch, All Souls and the Temple. With his unperformed full-length version of *Two Maids*, Armin presented himself as a playwright. His decision to dedicate *The Italian Tailor and his Boy* to the influential royal favourite Viscount Haddington looks to be a bid for court patronage. He probably sought the kind of post that Tarlton or Singer held. Armin's claim to have received a request to play John i' the Hospital at court may or may not have substance. At all events, no patronage was forthcoming, and Armin retired into the ranks of the citizenry whence he had emerged. When he died in 1616, he had at least achieved a coat of arms. A tailor and a goldsmith were his executors.[16]

A year before Armin's death, *The Valiant Welshman* was published by 'R. A. Gent'. The attribution to Armin has been challenged, but on inadequate grounds.[17] The character of Sir Morion is an Earl's son. He is in love with the Fairy Queen, and in the climax removes his hose and doublet to reveal the fool that he truly is. Though the play's verse is lucid, Morion's prose is characteristically surrealistic. The play was performed by Prince Charles's company, who toured extensively, and whose London base is unknown. The text confirms that the play was intended for presentation in the public theatre. Since the stage directions make a distinction between 'The Clowne' of the company and Sir Morion 'the foole', we may infer that Armin wrote the play in order to make a guest appearance with a company of which he was not a member, leaving retirement in order to play the brief part of Sir Morion. The play, and the careful presentation of the text, are witness to a growing ambition to be known as a writer.

Armin's career and aspirations parallel those of the company to which he belonged. Just as the company attained prosperity, a pri-

vate playhouse and the approbation of the educated, so Armin passed from being a citizen pamphleteer and stand-up comic to being a gentleman of letters. Upward mobility was something which Armin persistently sought and partially achieved. The contrast with Kemp is striking, for Kemp always made it his priority to be popular with commoners rather than to woo the London gentry. The personal aspirations of the two clowns are inseparable from the clown persona which each presented; and these clown personas in their turn governed the kind of roles that were scripted for the two actors. While Kemp is always made to stand as a representative of the common man, Armin consistently eludes any sociological placing.

ROLES

There has never been serious scholarly dissent from the view that Armin played the fool/clown parts in Shakespeare. Armin termed himself a 'clown' in 1600, and the 1605 edition of *Fool upon Fool* confirms the evidence of the *Jests* that Armin was 'Clonnico del Mondo' – the clown of the Globe. Armin makes it clear in 1609 that he had taken over the clown's part of Dogberry from Kemp.[18] Armin's favourite role is the 'fool'. Critical readers of *Fool upon Fool* are invited to say that 'the Author may keep his six fools company' (Sig. F4). And Armin literally did this when he played the part of John i' the Hospital. John Davies confirms in 1610 that Armin does 'wisely play the fool', and duly bids him 'play thy part, be honest still with mirth'.[19] The sudden appearance of 'fools' in Shakespeare's work at the end of 1599 has always, and rightly, been linked to Armin's arrival in the company.

Armin's roles for the Chamberlain's/King's company can be divided, for the sake of discussion, into three groups. First, there is a group of clown/fool parts: parts written for the clown of the company in the character of a licensed fool from 1599 to 1605. Second, there is a small group of orthodox 'clown' parts: parts following more closely in the tradition of Kemp and Singer. And third, we can distinguish a group of unorthodox variants on the clown/fool character: that is to say, parts which undermine previously established conventions.

The first group are mostly marked out as licensed fools by their costume, but the evidence here is so complex, and the costumes so varied, that I have preferred to discuss the matter in an Appendix.

Robert Armin

The fool's 'motley' or other insignia confirm for the spectator what is implicit in the text, that these characters have a distinct socio-economic status which sets them apart from ordinary members of society. The licensed fools are as follows:

Touchstone *As You Like It* 1599	'the clown' (in the stage directions, 1623; probably derived from a prompt copy) 'the clownish fool out of your father's court' (I.iii.126) 'this natural' (I.ii.51)
Carlo Buffone *Every Man Out* *Of His Humour* 1599	'a public, scurrilous and profane jester' (in the prefatory *character of the persons*, 1600 Quarto) 'an impudent common jester' (prol. 357)
Feste *Twelfth Night* 1600/1	'the clown' (in the stage directions, 1623; probably derived from foul papers) 'an allowed fool' (I.v.93) 'the jester . . . a fool that the Lady Olivia's father took much pleasure in' (II.iv.11)
Lavatch *All's Well That* *Ends Well* c. 1602	'the clown' (in the stage directions, 1623; probably derived from foul papers) 'My lord that's gone made himself much sport out of him; by his authority he remains here, which he thinks is a patent for his sauciness' (IV.v.61–3)
Thersites *Troilus and* *Cressida* c. 1602	'Achilles hath inveigled his fool from him' (II.iii.94)
Passarello *The Malcontent* 1604	'fool to Bilioso' (*dramatis personae* in Q3, 1604) 'he keeps beside me fifteen jesters' (I.viii.45)
Fool *King Lear* 1605	'The fool' (in the stage directions, 1608 and 1623) 'Your all-licensed fool' (I.iv.198)

The relationship between Robert Armin and these seven fool roles is close: the point is underlined by the fact that when the King's Men stole the text of *The Malcontent* from a boys' company, the fool role

of Passarello had to be written in.[20] I shall focus my discussion on Carlo and Touchstone, since these are two of Armin's earliest roles for the Chamberlain's, and most of the hall-marks of Armin's clowning are apparent.

The link between Touchstone and Armin's clown role of Tutch is obvious. Tutch proves 'true metal one way, but counterfeit another',[21] and Touchstone's inanities and pretensions serve to test out the true worth of court manners. The name 'Touchstone' is strictly speaking an alias used in the Forest, as the stage direction specifies: 'Enter Rosaline for Ganimed, Celia for Aliena, and Clowne *alias* Touchstone' (II.iv.s.d.). The clown's name within the Duke's court is never specified. The audience are thus encouraged to decipher the name 'Touchstone' as an alias for the real clown, Robert Armin the goldsmith. While Kemp's clowns consistently have English names, this 'alias' is the only Shakespearean instance where Armin does not bear a foreign name. Armin does not serve as an intermediary between play and audience. In order to be a touchstone of reality, rather than a dissolver of realities, the actor needs to be distanced from the audience.

The complex relationship of clown and fool is regularly explored in Armin's fool roles, in a manner that relates closely to the actor's interests. In *Fool upon Fool* Armin's 'naturals' interact variously with a fiddler dressed as an artificial fool, a theatrical clown, a rustic dressed in a borrowed fool's coat, and an artificial court jester. If the *Touch* in 'Touchstone' is Tutch the theatrical clown, then the *stone* may be a reference to John Stone, the notorious large-headed tavern fool with whom Feste is also associated.[22] The scene between Touchstone and Corin the 'natural philosopher' develops the natural/artificial theme: Touchstone proves artificial in relation to Corin, but later in his lust for Audrey he is altogether natural. With the arrival of 'William', a theatrical dimension is added. When Armin/Touchstone declares: 'It is meat and drink to me to see a clown' (v.i.10), he reminds the audience that clowning is his – Armin's – livelihood. This other clown's name – 'William' – is repeated three times, so that the audience will not miss the contrast between the departed company clown, William Kemp, and the new fool/clown. The traditional simple-minded rustic clown is symbolically dismissed from the new Globe stage.

In *Every Man Out Of His Humour*, with a lament that he lacks Kemp's shoes, Armin/Carlo reminds the audience again that Armin

has replaced Kemp (IV.iv.128). The fool/clown relationship is again a running motif, as Carlo Buffone, the buffoon or 'jester', is paired with Sogliardo, whom Jonson terms an 'essential clown'. Carlo is a tavern fool, and the name indicates that Armin is impersonating a real tavern fool by the name of Charles (i.e. 'Carlo') Chester (i.e. 'jester').[23] Sogliardo is a social *arriviste* who believes everyone to be a 'clown' but himself. Carlo's task in the play is to show up Sogliardo as being essentially a clown, and to implicate in folly all who accept this *arriviste*'s claims to higher status.

Carlo's most interesting routine is inspired by Armin's researches. Carlo plays the part of two courtiers simultaneously: the pair salute each other politely, engage in a drinking contest, and fall to blows. The routine is borrowed from Jack Oates, in *Fool upon Fool*, who played cards with himself and caught himself up in a quarrel – and there is a partial debt also to Jack Miller in *Fool upon Fool* who does a solo performance of all the parts in a play (Sigs. A4, D4v). Self-bombardment with alternating voices is the key to delivering Armin's 'changes' in the *Quips*. A cruder and better known example of the technique is of course Feste/Topas.

As the tavern scene continues, as Carlo becomes ever more drunk, and the play rises to its climax, other features emerge which indicate how completely Jonson had Armin in mind. Jonson calls on the actor to provide some unscripted singing – '*Lomtero, Lomtero, etc.*' – anticipating the fool's scripted songs in later plays. Language breaks down, and Carlo anticipates Feste's taste for neologism: 'the whorson strummell-patcht, goggle-ey'd Grumbledories, would ha' *Gigantomachiz'd . . .*'.[24] And the fool turns philosopher, citing a nonsensical 'axiom in natural philosophy' to demonstrate that pork-eating is the only rational alternative to cannibalism. Finally, Carlo rails at Puntarvolo, provoking his victim until he can stand it no more. When Jonson conceives Carlo/Armin as having for 'religion his railing, and his discourse ribaldry', Jonson prepares the way for the ribald Passarello and the railing Thersites.

Physical grotesqueness is essential for this type of fool. Carlo has a greasy face like a glue-pot. Thersites is a 'botch of nature'.[25] Armin revelled in the physical qualities of his fools. John i' the Hospital, for instance, was

> Something tall, dribbling ever, body small, merry never:
> Splay footed, visage black; little beard, it was his lack.[26]

Armin knew how to present his naturals as creatures more animal than human. He clearly had a physical affinity with dogs in particular. Jonson terms Carlo a 'feast-hound or banquet-beagle', and Carlo is twice dubbed a 'ban-dog':[27] at the end of the tavern scene he is beaten, stripped of his clothing, and made to crouch down like a 'cur'. This scene is imitated in *Troilus and Cressida* II.i, where Thersites is beaten by Ajax: Thersites is dubbed a 'dog' twice and 'cur' three times, and he responds to his beating by threatening Ajax's heels. Lear's fool reproduces the image, responding to Lear's whip with the jest 'Truth's a dog must to kennel'.[28] There is a marked contrast here with the kind of clown Kemp played. Kemp's clown remains obstinately anthropomorphic. On the stage, Launce does not degrade himself, but elevates his dog to the status of a human.

Armin's shape and size gave point to the recurrent image of the cringing dog. His principal physical traits were ugliness and dwarfishness. The nicknames 'Snuff' and 'Pink' are diminutive, as we have noted already,[29] and other references allude to his smallness. Macilente envisages Carlo creeping like a serpent or scorpion. John Davies makes a rhyming comparison between Armin and an itchy 'vermin' – in similar vein to Thersites, who envisages being a 'louse'.[30] The name 'Passarello' means 'little sparrow' – Armin's own name is 'Robin', but a sparrow traditionally is thought to be more lecherous. Armin seems to have impersonated another small, ugly animal in the role of 'Frog' in *Fair Maid of Bristow* – a play performed by the King's Men in c. 1604. A number of verbal jokes play upon Armin's size. As a parson in a gown, Feste is 'not tall enough to become the function well, nor lean enough to be thought a good student'. And Lavatch declares 'I am for the house with the narrow gate, which I take to be too little for pomp to enter.'[31] Finally, we may note that Armin's appearance as an adult with a boys' company is without parallel.

Armin was obsessed with natural fools because he himself, physically though not mentally, *was* a natural fool. This conclusion will appear alien to any reader who conceives of Shakespearean drama in relation to a modern repertory company. For Armin's contemporaries, the clown's deformity was too obvious to require direct comment. The history of the dwarf-fool can be traced from the Court of the Pharaohs, through the *Morio* of the Roman Empire,[32] to Little Tich in the Music Hall. A comparison with such forms as the mediev-

THE little childe, is pleaſde with cockhorſe gaie,
Althoughe he aſke a courſer of the beſte:
The ideot likes, with bables for to plaie,
And is diſgrac'de, when he is brauelie dreſte:
   A motley coate, a cockeſcombe, or a bell,
   Hee better likes, then Iewelles that excell.

PROMOOTE the foole, his folly doth appeare,
And is a ſhame to them, that make him clime:
Whoſe faultes, before coulde not bee ſeene ſo cleare,
For lowe eſtate did ſhadowe euery crime:
   But ſet him vp, his folly ſoone is harde,
   Then keepe him doune, let wiſe men bee prefer'de.

Fig. 6 Two fools from Whitney's *Choice of Emblems* (1586).
Reproduced with permission of the Bodleian Library, from
Malone 748 (2).

al interlude, *commedia dell'arte* and Renaissance court entertainment makes it obvious that Armin was cast as the clown/fool because of his looks. In Skelton's *Magnificence*, Fancy, the Vice who puts on the coat of Folly, is a dwarf.[33] Duchartre reproduces plates of a French dwarf Pulcinella and a Dutch dwarf Arlecchino.[34] Queen Elizabeth followed in the tradition of the sixteenth-century courts of Paris, Mantua and Ferrara when she kept a dwarf in her court from 1578 to the end of her reign: her dwarf, a woman named Thomasina, was dressed sumptuously in velvet and satin.[35] Geoffrey Whitney in his *Choice of Emblems* (1586) (Fig. 6) illustrates the two dominant conventional images of the performing fool in Elizabethan England: the first is the idiot in motley, wearing the costume emblematic of folly; the second is sub-human rather than child-like, a stunted grotesque with webbed feet.[36] Anyone could be an 'artificial' fool by dressing up in the motley uniform of the 'natural'; but artificially to simulate the dwarf-fool, Whitney's second fool, was impossible. Armin can be revealed as a fool when he dresses in motley, like Touchstone or Lear's fool; but he is also revealed as a fool when he is stripped naked, like Carlo Buffone or Sir Morion. Armin's obsession with natural fools, and the doubt which he always projects as to whether he is not in some sense a 'natural' himself, simultaneously derives from and exploits Armin's own stunted physique.

Armin's physique determines the particular character of his clowning. The pompous or parodic utterances of a man with total vocal control are counterpointed by a deformed body. This is the quality that allows Carlo's parodies to: 'more swift than Circe . . . transform any person into deformity' – to render a human's action into a pig's action. As Jonson explains elsewhere, dwarves are popular 'for pleasing imitation of greater men's action, in a ridiculous fashion'.[37] Shakespeare took advantage of this potential for ridiculous imitation when he wrote for Armin such routines as Lavatch's repetition of 'Oh Lord, Sir!' and Touchstone's account of a courtly quarrel.[38] The lines are written on the assumption that body and voice are set in opposition and speak, as it were, different languages.

A series of orthodox clown parts may be taken as a second group of roles written for Armin. I use the term 'orthodox' in the sense that the character is marked out in the text as the 'clown' of the piece, and is not a 'fool' in any socio-economic sense. My classification remains to a large extent arbitrary. Pompey, for instance, invites being classified as a 'fool' when he is paired against the dehumanized Barnar-

dine. Brothels and prisons are likely enough places for the demented to find some kind of occupation.

The text usually makes an association plain between the stage clown and Armin's identity as a fool. Frog in *Fair Maid of Bristow* establishes the Armin trademark when he quotes 'that worthy philosopher Hector' to the effect that 'the words of the wise do offend the foolish', and when he finishes his appearance by singing a ballad.[39] By the same criteria, Macbeth's Porter – again, not labelled as 'clown' – can be placed in the same category as Armin's tavern fools and railers – though the morality tradition lends the character an added dimension. In *Miseries of Enforced Marriage* – a play of 1606 in the King's Men's repertoire – the 'clown' is dressed and cast as a servingman, but he is identified as a 'philosophical fool': the clown compares himself, 'a fool by art', to other men who are 'fools by nature'. He is addressed as 'Robin' because that is Armin's own name, and he arrives in Yorkshire after a long journey from London singing in terms that allude to Kemp's famous journey to Norwich.[40] There is more personal allusion in *Hamlet*: when the grave-digging 'clown' gives Hamlet the skull of the King's jester, the actor Armin is able to pay a vicarious tribute to his mentor Tarlton.

Less innovative are the roles of 'clown' in *Othello* and *Antony and Cleopatra*. The former, like Peter, banters with musicians. The latter, like the rustic clown in *Titus*, has a short scene before the tragic climax.

The pursuit of Armin's roles becomes rewarding when we pass from these orthodox clown roles to a group of what may be termed latent clown parts: parts where the clown's new guise was obvious to the original audience, but where the clown's identity is not obvious to the uninitiated reader. We have seen that in all Shakespeare's plays subsequent to *Richard II* and prior to *Henry V* a substantial part was written for Kemp, his entitlement as clown of the company and a sharer. I propose to work from the same premise, and to pursue the logic that Armin, as clown and sharer, had to have a part in every play subsequent to Kemp's departure. Theatrical conventions are rarely static, and we must take note of chronology in order to see how each part written for Armin was a variant upon what had gone before – how each part in some new sense involved a bending of the rules.

The obvious role for Armin in *Henry V* is Nym. This is a reworking of a character from *Merry Wives* who made no appearance in

2 *Henry IV*.[41] In *Henry V*, Pistol, red-faced Bardolph and Nym are conceived as a trio of physically grotesque 'antics' (III.ii.31). Nym's 'rapier' is evidently as ridiculous a prop as Falstaff's, and again serves as a clown's insignium (II.i.7–9, 56). Like so many of Armin's clowns, Nym is given canine attributes: he is an 'Iceland dog', a 'cur', an 'egregious dog', a 'hound' and a 'tyke' – or perhaps diminutive 'tick'.[42] The actor's lack of stature is the focus of the jest 'Thy spirits are most tall', and probably the explanation of why he cannot kiss the hostess's mouth (II.i.68; II.iii.61). Nym's dialogue is idiosyncratic: his staccato ratiocinations have reminded a recent editor of Pinter.[43]

The quest for '*the* clown' in Shakespeare's tragedies does not always point to cameo appearances. I believe that the substantial roles of Caska, Menenius and Cloten are conceived as clown parts. The allusions and staging rely, I think, upon the audience's familiarity with the clown convention.

Shakespeare's Caska owes little to Plutarch, and is written into the play as a role for the comedian. Caska delights in his description of 'mere foolery' as he describes Caesar's rejection of the crown, and his description of impossible portents sits well in the mouth of a man associated with playing demented idiots.[44] When Cassius remarks that Caska is 'dull' and lacks 'those sparks of life / That should be in a Roman' (I.iii.57), the audience are reminded that Armin *qua* fool is different from other actors. The artificial fool – Armin – always lies behind Caska's façade of idiocy:

> What a blunt fellow this is grown to be!
> He was quick metal when he went to school.   (I.ii.292–3)

The allusion is to Armin's background as a goldsmith. Once we perceive that the part is Armin's, aspects of the performance become clearer. Caska's description of the tempest is a burlesque, a piece of play-acting: 'It is *the part* of men to fear and tremble', he declares. 'You look pale, and gaze / And *put on* fear, and *cast yourself* in wonder', he is told (I.iii.54, 59–60; my italics). Armin's little legs betoken insincerity when he joins the conspiracy:

> Hold, my hand...
> ...I will set this foot of mine as far
> As who goes furthest.   (I.iii.117–20)

A further visual sign of clownishness is the 'sword' which he waves about in the tempest. Like a bauble, he uses it to obscene effect the moment before the conspirators shake hands, demonstrating how the sun rises higher and higher in different directions (a most important consideration in the Globe's design).[45]

Menenius is equally at odds with the conventional Roman mould, and the character owes equally little to Plutarch. Menenius is the fool who loves to prove his audience fools likewise. Though the plebeians will be 'accused of folly' if they do not change heart, it is the tribunes for whom he reserves his traditional fool's logic. He invites them to look inside themselves: 'Why then you should discover a brace of unmeriting, proud, violent, testy magistrates (alias fools) as any in Rome.' A tribune responds: 'Menenius, you are known well enough too.' Menenius duly concedes: 'I am known to be a humorous patrician . . .', but meditates upon the question of how his face can be 'known well enough' as a fool's – for if he is contemplating two fools, this image will be mirrored in his facial reaction.[46] The evidence points to Menenius being the company fool, but the identification must remain speculative. It may be that Menenius's 'cap' identifies him emblematically as the clown, since caps elsewhere in the play – as in Elizabethan England – are items of plebeian attire.[47]

From senator to patrician to prince: Armin's climb up the social ladder is completed in pre-Roman Britain. The Folio's alternative spelling 'Clotten' suggests the pronunciation and implications of the name. Cloten cannot do arithmetic, and is conceived as mentally retarded. During Cloten's first two scenes, the audience are reminded of his extra-textual identity as the Second Lord provides them with a running commentary, jesting on Armin/Cloten's stature with the words:

till you had measured how long a fool you were upon the ground

alluding to the cockscomb and ass's ears that Armin ought properly to be wearing, and harping on Cloten's latent status:

You are a fool . . . therefore your issues being foolish do not derogate.[48]

Cloten debates with Imogen whether a 'fool' is 'mad', and refers the audience to his double identity when he speaks of his paradoxically noble and 'natural' person (II.iii.98; III.v.137).

Armin's physique is again the key to the performance. In his first appearances, Cloten is playing games, and refuses to change his

stinking shirt, but taunted by Imogen he dons the costume of Post-humus. Posthumus is particularly good-looking ('*First Gent.*: I do not think so fair an outward . . . Endows a man but he'), and Cloten is instantly recognizable as a fool since 'time hath nothing blurred those lines of favour' (I.i.22; IV.ii.104). There is much play upon the fact that Cloten's elegant costume does not and cannot fit, despite Cloten's assertions to the contrary:

How fit his garments serve me . . . the lines of my body are as well drawn as his; no less young, more strong, not beneath him in fortunes, beyond him in the advantage of time, above him in birth . . .   IV.i.1–12

What the audience sees with its eyes is a grotesque clown, older, thicker-limbed, *beneath* Posthumus in height and *beyond* him in girth. Guiderius, like the audience, is able to see that Cloten is 'made' by the tailor and is but a 'fool' (IV.ii.81–5). Stage dummies are recalcitrant props when used in an attempt to evoke pathos. But a dummy of Armin/Cloten might legitimately be misshapen and hang awkwardly when carried, a grotesque image counterpointing Im-ogen's expressions of grief. Her claim to recognize 'the shape of's leg' and her lover's 'brawns of Hercules' is rendered tragicomic.

In these three Roman plays, Armin's fool identity is clear and obvious once we learn to seek it, but, because of the transmission of Shakespeare's work through text rather than performance, the actor's function has been ignored. Shakespeare's casting has crucial implications for interpretative study. For instance, if the Menenius who presents the fable of the belly and limbs is himself a clown with a markedly ugly body, then the organic theory of the state which he propounds is undermined. The audience will not interpret the speech as part of Shakespeare's philosophy of life, but will begin to glimpse an uglier ethic of self-interest that underpins patrician absolutism. The post-Elizabethan, neo-classicist tradition of criticism and per-formance perhaps has been reluctant to accept that Shakespeare could weave a comic character into tragedies in this manner. How can Caska make phallic gestures at the moment when the audience is supposed to sense the tragic error of the conspirators? How can Imogen's grief be made to seem convincing if her supposed lover's body is of a different and ridiculous shape? Is such behaviour plausible? To formulate such questions would be to pre-

suppose an Aristotelian/naturalist theatre based purely on verisimilitude, and to ignore Shakespeare's ability to mingle contradictory modes.

King Lear provided Armin with his last straight 'fool' role. It was a classic climax for Armin inasmuch as the historical English setting allowed him, for the first time in the extant repertoire, to don the traditional motley and cockscomb of medieval tradition.[49] Armin's researches and observations of real-life idiots had hitherto led him away from the old emblematic stage tradition. With Lear's fool, Armin's cycle of fool roles came full circle. Afterwards followed a cluster of variations or inversions. Armin abandoned a fool's uniform in order to play opposite a designated 'fool' who served as his mirthless stooge.

In *Volpone*, Armin's part is not the hermaphrodite 'fool' with his bauble but – as is now obvious – Nano the dwarf. Armin the philosopher catechizes the 'fool' about the migration of his soul. Armin's singing is exploited when Nano plays zany to the mountebank.

In *Timon* the true fool, Armin, is the Cynic philosopher Apemantus. Armin's dog-like attributes lend themselves well to a 'cynic' (Greek *kynikos* = dog-like). Four characters dub the cynic a 'dog' before his major scene with Timon.[50] In this, Timon repeatedly dubs the cynic a beast or dog, while the cynic tries to prove Timon a fool. Timon represents the cynic as a natural fool: 'bred a dog', 'rogue hereditary', 'issue of a mangy dog' – while the cynic terms Timon 'the cap of all the fools alive', an artificial fool.[51] The force of the debate is clear only when we recognize that Apemantus physically resembles a dog because he is the stunted Robert Armin, while the misanthropist – Burbage presumably – degrades himself artificially. This major debate is anticipated in a short interlude in which Apemantus appears with a publicly recognized 'fool' whom he is taking as a symbolic gift to Timon. This one is a retained fool, learning to play his part in the way society demands, and responding to themes given him by a stage audience. Apemantus, meanwhile, takes the role of sour commentator upon the fools of the world, like Sotto in Armin's own *Nest of Ninnies*.

In *The Tempest*, Armin's part is that of Caliban, the 'salvage and deformed slave', and his foil is Trinculo the 'jester'. Armin's deformed or animalistic shape is exploited to the full with the creation of this 'misshapen' or 'disproportioned' whelp-mooncalf-fish. While

the physically deformed fool is astute enough to know when a song is out of tune, the jester in his 'pied' or 'patched' uniform utters jokes so feeble that they are funny only through their failure. The pair are set up as rivals. While the jester laments that 'a monster should be such a natural!', the monster learns the true nature of the man he comes repeatedly to dub 'fool'.[52]

An understanding of Shakespeare's casting is particularly important here because performers are so often confused by the assumption that Trinculo ought to be the laughter-maker. Caliban tends then to be taken either as melodramatic villain or as the receptacle of subconscious authorial sympathies, while the direction 'deformed' is glossed over. The trio of bullying drunk, simpleton and freak can be seen historically as a reworking of the comic trio in *Twelfth Night*, modified by the conventions of the Jacobean antimasque. Trinculo's motley has its iconographic parallel, too, for when Sir Andrew is given 'a bloody cockscomb' by Cesario, the character's lank, hanging hair completes the effect of a fool's hood (*Twelfth Night* v.i.170–206).

I have left *The Winter's Tale* until last because of a textual problem, and because it reverts to a theme of ten years earlier. Following the apparent loss of the prompt-book, the play was printed from a transcript by Ralph Crane, a scribe who prepared scripts with the reader rather than the actor in mind. The designation of one character as 'Clowne' in speech-prefixes and stage directions owes nothing to playhouse practice.[53] Armin's part is that of Autolycus, and, as in *As You Like It* and *Every Man Out Of His Humour*, the foil for the stage clown is an old-fashioned rustic 'clown'.

There is no reason in terms of plot why Autolycus should once have been a servant of Florizel and worn three-pile velvet, since Florizel never recognizes Autolycus, nor listens to him – as Autolycus reports – when he broaches the matter of the clown's farthell (iv.iii.621ff.; v.ii.114ff.). The point of informing the audience that Autolycus is an ex-courtier is to remind them that the *actor* is a celebrated player of court fools. Since fools are regularly whipped, Autolycus was 'certainly whipped out of court'.[54] In effect, the fool adopts the peddler's role as an incognito, which deceives Bohemia but not the audience. The stage figure has a double identity. Like Touchstone, Autolycus/Armin is delighted by the man he terms 'my clown' (iv.iv.606). A new variant in this play, written in the socially mobile Jacobean world, is that, in their last scene, the stage clown

has to humble himself and accept patronage from the old-fashioned rustic clown. The casting conceals an in-joke, for Armin the previous year had published a specimen of his own balladry in an apparent bid for court patronage. Armin's own multiple identities – as writer of ballads, tradesman, fool, King's servant, would-be courtier – are refracted through the assumed role or alias of Autolycus.

The key to the humour is again visual. When Autolycus first appeared in rags, Forman – observing Armin's diminutive size – noted the likeness to a pixie.[55] Like Cloten, Autolycus dons the clothes of the glamorous hero, and the effect is to render both clown and clothes absurd. Even the Old Shepherd can see that the 'garments are rich, but he wears them not handsomely'. An important joke is set up when the rustic clown declares that if Autolycus 'had but looked big' and spat on his opponent, he would not have been robbed. Before the clowns make their final exit of the play, the rustic clown offers to perjure himself and swear that Armin/Autolycus is 'a tall fellow of thy hands', echoing the phrase 'tall fellow' four more times.[56] The irony is that the rustic parvenu appears to the spectator's eye every inch a courtier, while the diminutive erstwhile courtier can never do so.

We have now completed our survey of all the plays for which Shakespeare bore sole authorial responsibility, from late 1599 onwards. Always, a role was created for Robert Armin, and the humour gained much of its point from the spectators' previous acquaintance with the actor.

In Jacobean 'city comedies', the Jonsonian or social-realist aesthetic makes Armin much harder to trace. He may be taken as Mounsieur Civet in *The London Prodigal* in *c.* 1604 on the grounds that he is repeatedly described as a 'little man', and that his rival in love claims punningly to be not an 'armine' but a beggar.[57] Armin is named in the actor list of *The Alchemist*, where fairly certainly he is Drugger. Asked if he has 'credit with the players', Drugger responds 'did you never see me play the fool?' (IV.vii.89). But in plays like these, prose ceases to serve as a marker of the clown's part, and extra-textual allusions to the actor's identity seem to have little place. In plays which aspire to provide, according to the neo-classical prescription, a 'mirror' of London life, the clown recedes into the two-dimensional plane of the mirror. The spectators are taken to be gazing *at* the mirror from a position of detachment. It is no longer the clown's task to remind them that plays are based on a system of

conventions, conventions continually recreated by virtue of the active presence of the audience.

THE CLOWN CONVENTION

We shall now return to the conventions which I set out in Chapter 8 as governing the Elizabethan clown's role. We must see what became of these conventions in the hands of Robert Armin.

Low status

A 'natural fool' might be of high status by birth. Such people, if possessed of property, became wards of court, and others could 'beg' them from the Crown in order to look after their persons and manage their estates. It is implied that Passarello has been 'begged' in this way.[58] While a 'clown' – leaving aside the special theatrical usage – can be defined negatively as one who is not a gentleman, a 'fool' is simply one who is not wise. The freedom given to an allowed fool consists precisely in the fact that he is allowed to stand outside social hierarchies. For this reason, the social origins of Armin's stage fools are always left mysterious.

Armin's physique rendered him absurd when imitating fashions or learning, which, in a normal man, might command uncritical approval. From mimicking the manners of gentry, as Armin did in the roles of Touchstone and Lavatch, it was a logical step for Armin to be cast directly as a high-status character – like Menenius or Sir Morion. Though the identity of the actor remained clear to the audience, the term 'clown' became problematic at this point.

While Shakespeare fostered the dichotomy of clown and role, would-be progressive writers like Jonson ceased to do so. When a new generation began to construe society as an assemblage of autonomous individuals, there was no cause to construct the clown as the representative of a class. Within a homogenized dramatis personae, the clown's identity dissolved away.

Armin was a pioneering realist in his study of how fools actually behaved. His stage fools were based on observation rather than on the recreation of an emblematic stage type. At the same time, and paradoxically, Armin's interest in fools allowed Shakespeare to tap one of the richest veins in the medieval dramatic tradition: the idea that the Vice reveals vice to be folly. At the same time again, Armin

was attuned to the intellectual tradition of the Renaissance which declared, with Erasmus and the Fool Societies of France, that the fool had his own species of wisdom, and could be used as a double-edged tool in order to satirize human manners.

Kemp rooted his clown persona in the common-sense values of the 'plain man' in contradistinction to all heroic values associated with gentility. The drift of Armin's fooling, however, is towards the universality of folly. *Stultorum plena sunt omnia* is the motto to *Nest of Ninnies*. Armin may draw out the foolishness of courtly behaviour, but he never sets up alternative values of his own. His bestial fools cause the audience to reflect on what it is to be human beings. Foolishness is seen as universal, not as the prerogative of any single class.

Colloquial prose

The language of song is always at Armin's disposal. In Cloten's serenade, typically, a delicate though obscene lyric offsets the ugliness of the singer's body. The extant setting for Armin's song implies that he was a counter-tenor, a detail seemingly confirmed in the preface to *Nest of Ninnies*.[59] The high singing voice adds to the anomaly, and to the sense of Armin's multiple *personae*, at once elegant and ugly, at once boy and man.

If Kemp ever sings, his songs appear spontaneous: Armin's songs, by contrast, are elaborate set-pieces. Armin's speaking, likewise, does not suggest in any pointed way that the actor is extemporizing. His part is too closely interwoven with the main action of the play. Indeed, there no longer seems to be a dichotomy of poetic and extemporal styles in the plays at large after about 1600, for the verse no longer proclaims itself in the same way as a poetic discourse. Armin is not rigidly confined to prose. When playing high-status characters – Caska, Menenius, Cloten – prose remains the norm, but passages of parodic verse begin to shade into the regular verse of other characters. The convention is finally inverted when Caliban is given predominantly verse: the natural fool, who has been given his language by Miranda, is thus differentiated from the spiritually grotesque artificial fools who speak only prose.

Armin's prose is constructed primarily to suit the actor's idiosyncratic speech patterns. Cloten is identified by 'the snatches in his voice, / And burst of speaking',[60] and this provides the clue to

Shakespeare's clown

Armin's characteristic rhythm. As Tutch, as Sotto, as Cloten, Armin's prose is halting rather than flowing, full of parentheses and subordinations, and held together by an always elusive intellectual logic. The prose is playable only because it allows the actor to employ a different register for each 'burst of speaking', and to suggest a multiplicity of voices engaged in an internal dialogue.

Two randomly chosen passages will serve to illustrate the point. Both are obscene.

Tutch: Change your mark, shoot at a white, will say, come stick me in the clout sir, her white is black, 'tis crept into her eye, and wenches with black eyes the whites turned up are but as custards, though they seem stone cold, yet greedily attempted, burning hot, and such a wench is she sir.

Cloten: How fit his Garments serve me? Why should his Mistress who was made by him that made the Tailor, not be fit too? The rather (saving reverence of the Word) for 'tis said a Woman's fitness comes by fits: therein I must play the Workman, I dare speak it to myself, for it is not Vainglory for a man, and his Glass, to confer in his own Chamber; I mean, the Lines of my body are as well drawn as his.[61]

Both passages aspire to prove a point: 'she loves you', 'the clothes suit me'. Both have surrealistic elements – eyes compared to custards (by association with egg-whites), consultation with a mirror. Both passages involve a splitting of the speaker's identity: Tutch becomes an imaginary arrow, Cloten moralizes 'to myself'. The argument in the Shakespearean passage is less elliptical, but is still hard for the listener to disentangle. (Who made the tailor, God or Posthumus?) Though the argument is obscure, in both passages the obscene drift can be made clear in performance.

Language helps the audience to read the character as Armin-as-Cloten. Consistency of characterization is not Shakespeare's objective. Cloten carefully signals a pun – 'fitness comes by fits' – in which *fits* may refer to bodily shapes or bodily cycles. This is not the speech of a mentally subnormal youth. Some editors have deprived Cloten of his delicate serenade (opting for the theatrically weak idea that a professional singer is brought on) because they have found the character's inconsistency otherwise impossible to stomach. Armin's juggling of natural and artificial folly is of course wholly consistent within the framework of Armin's clowning.

I have argued that Kemp used a syntactically 'restricted' code. This

code linked Falstaff to Kemp's other clowns. Armin obviously uses a syntactically 'elaborated' code – though his lexical range may be narrower. While Kemp's talk is narrational or descriptive, Armin's is analytic. Falstaff's monologue on 'sherris sack' contains a single piece of formal reasoning: 'Valour comes of sherris. So . . .' – but Armin makes logical leaps at every point. Armin's speech does not link him to a proposed audience belonging to the same social group as himself, and sharing his mode of organizing meaning. Armin does not talk *with* but is heard *by* his audience. During Cloten's speech, the implied location contracts, temporarily, to become the privacy of Cloten's chamber. Armin's language denotes an individuated mode of perception. His language sets the fool apart from plain ordinary men.

The word 'you' as a marker of direct audience address is never found in Armin's speeches. Armin talks to his own alter ego rather than to the audience. *Cymbeline* again offers a good example of how the fool is put on display rather than used to establish communality with the audience. For the Second Lord is used in the function of intermediary between the audience and the freakish Cloten. At most, as in his *Quips* so in the role of Macbeth's Porter, Armin will point to individuals in the audience, and play upon their individual faults. The actor is confined to being a parodist, hiding his own identity behind impersonations rather than offering it up to the audience.

Plot structure

As a life-long solo performer, Kemp tended to dominate the stage whenever he appeared. For this reason, as much as for reasons of dramaturgical tradition, Kemp's roles were constructed in accordance with a principle of alternation so that the clown became the dominant figure in a sub-plot. Armin's attributes were better exploited in a different way. For a simple physiological reason, he could not so easily command the stage in a long monologue. He was of much more use as a foil, or as a distinctive individual who lent visual interest to a group.

Armin is thus often used to complete a balanced threesome of fools: with Lear and Poor Tom, with Elbow and Froth (whose names suggest their physical attributes), with the hermaphrodite and the eunuch, with the butler and the jester, and so on. The physical matching is usually lost to us. He was paired with the distinctively

lanky Bilioso in *The Malcontent*. The names suggest that 'Aguecheek' was gaunt, 'Belch' well filled out. Armin is often the foil to a 'clown' who is better endowed physically, worse endowed intellectually – Corin, Sogliardo, the Bohemian clown. Or he may be the foil to an 'artificial' or man-made madman – Hamlet, Lear, Timon. Because he did not dominate a group, but completed it, he could be woven into the action in an almost endless variety of ways. At one extreme, he could be used to provide an interlude: the clown's function in *Othello* must be to provide an unscripted *entr'acte* song when he enters with the musicians. At the other extreme, he could be used as a lynch-pin of the plot. His limitation as a performer, however, was that he did not have the presence or range needed to sustain alone the role of principal comic in a comedy. Malvolio, Parolles and Lucio supplant Armin's clown in this respect.

I related Kemp's and Singer's clown roles to the paradigm of the English festival. Their clowns are Lords of Misrule who perform in perpetual anticipation of their reappearance as lords of the stage in the jig. Armin was not of a build to perform jigs, and his roles are not constructed with reappearance in mind. His roles are subject to 'closure': Touchstone is joined to Audrey, Cloten and Lear's fool are dead, Lavatch makes his journey to court and returns home again, Feste, whose sport with Malvolio is done, announces that the play 'is done'.

The metamorphosis of clown to gentleman is still a recurrent feature. Touchstone enters the forest in a new fool's coat which allows the rustics, though not Jaques, to take him for a courtier. Feste becomes a priest, Autolycus and Cloten don the hero's finery. Passarello acquires a sumptuous velvet suit (see Appendix). The motif is finally inverted in *The Tempest*, where Caliban refuses all urging to dress up in the finery which hangs before him.

These disguises do not serve to turn Armin into a Lord of Misrule, however, for Armin's clown stands in a quite different relationship to the festive paradigm. In the English festival, the fool and the Lord of Misrule are always distinct characters. The fool was attached to the morris men, and danced with them, but out of formation. The dances were performed in honour of the reigning Summer Lord. The 'Lord' was an ordinary person, of low status in the community and given temporary honours. The fool's part required a recognized specialist. The Lord's costume was improvised, marking the normality of the man beneath the costume. The fool's outfit was kept from

Robert Armin

year to year, and signalled the uniqueness and abnormality of the wearer (see Chapter 2).

Shakespeare never ceased to draw on the festive paradigm when organizing his clowns' roles. 'Cavaliero' Kemp, the 'Lord of Misrule', was allowed to develop an alternative order, unromantic, libidinal and egalitarian – an alternative to the dominant order of the gentry. Armin, however, played the fool's part. Just as the fool stayed outside the ordered formation of the morris, and did his utmost to point up or provoke imperfection in the regular dancers, so Armin's stage fools remain perpetual outsiders. Just as the morris fool beat the dancers and watchers with his bladder, so Armin railed at the fools of the world. Kemp's art lay in convincing the spectators that he was their elected representative, chosen in order to play out their most mischievous fantasies, because he was one of their number. Armin's art lay in being different, so that through parodying normal men he could point up the follies of normal men.

CHAPTER 11

William Kemp and Harry Hunks: play as game, actor as sign – a theoretical conclusion

T O WRITE AN ACADEMIC MONOGRAPH on the Elizabethan clown is, on the face of it, to offer a contribution to
our stock of objective historical knowledge. It is also, impli-
citly, to argue for a shift in academic priorities. It is to argue for the
importance of studying the actor as much as the writer, for studying
performance simultaneously with text, for studying popular culture
as much as (to give but some of the antonyms) high/official/elite/
aesthetic/canonical culture. More specifically, it is to argue for a
different approach towards reading an Elizabethan dramatic text. I
shall set out in this chapter some of the theoretical conclusions to
which my research into Kemp has led me.

The *locus classicus* for the ahistorical literary perspective on the
clown is surely Coleridge's commentary on the Porter scene in *Macbeth*:

This low porter soliloquy I believe written for the mob by some other hand,
perhaps with Shakespeare's consent – and that, finding it take, he with the
remaining ink of a pen otherwise employed just interpolated it with the
sentence 'I'll devil-porter it no further' and what follows to 'bonfire'. Of the
rest not one syllable has the ever-present being of Shakespeare.

The elitist essentialism is unabashed.[1] Because the play is *essentially*
a tragedy, comedy is inadmissible. Through the characters, Coleridge can probe the mind of the author, the ultimate object of
enquiry. For Coleridge, the physical circumstances of performance
are an unfortunate constraint upon the writer, and he echoes Hamlet's viewpoint when he laments the influence of the 'mob'.

The Romantic theory of artistic creativity takes as its fixed point of

reference the unitary imagination of the single artist. So long as the accepted task of the critic was to seek out the moral purpose of the text, the unity of the play's construction, truth and consistency of character, the inspirational kernel which generated the play's themes, then the clown remained an embarrassment. The theory of 'comic relief', with its mysterious cathartic overtones, was evolved to conceal a conceptual vacuum. The clown escaped from marginalization only when such critics as C. L. Barber, Northrop Frye and Robert Weimann began to show how Shakespearean comedy was patterned by the popular festive tradition, and not by classical notions of form.

Since the Elizabethan period the dominant aesthetic codes, neoclassicism, Romanticism and naturalism/realism have all stressed the individuality of the creative artist. In post-Elizabethan theatre we seem, therefore, to find two possibilities. Either the author (or latterly the director as surrogate author) has been the supreme creator, in which case the actors have been subservient to the authorial vision (the directorial 'concept'). Or, alternatively, the actor has dominated (Garrick, Irving, stars of Hollywood) and the text has become subservient and malleable. Brecht was the decisive innovator in the twentieth century who projected a creative fusion of the actor's and the writer's art. The Brechtian dramaturg worked as part of an ensemble. The actor did not vanish into a role, but took responsibility for its presentation, always registering a point of view about the moral actions represented. Brecht provided an intellectual framework which makes it easier for us now to accept that a piece of Elizabethan theatre was a collaborative creation. In the post-Brechtian era, it is possible to look back and discern a historical milestone when – in Rosencrantz's phrase – 'the poet and the players went to cuffs', when in one significant instance a rift set apart Kemp the player and Shakespeare the poet.

Like the Coleridgean literary critic, actors and directors have tended to see their task as being to interpret and respond to the latent meanings of a classic text. My own working assumption in this book is that the text encodes an action. Hence my subject is neither the text ('Shakespeare's *Hamlet*') nor the actor ('Kemp') but the historical theatrical event. The only meanings of the play are those which a given reader/performer/spectator constructs in given physical circumstances.

I have tried to bridge historical and literary modes of thought: that

is, to marry an interpretative historiography to a historical criticism. For most of this century, a positivist historiographic tradition and a subjectivist critical tradition have stood at once divided apart and symbiotically linked. In practice the material reality of the timber-framed playhouse has served to validate the essentiality of the human imagination. Both the Globe and the text of *Hamlet* are man-made objects, yet one has for the most part been subject to analysis in terms of historical *fact*, the other to analysis as the expression of *ideas*.

The symbiosis of positivist historiography and essentialist criticism may be illustrated, at the risk of parody, by Ronald Harwood's BBC television series *All the World's a Stage*, screened in 1984. Harwood is a popularizer, recycling the work of more sophisticated theatre historians. One can see, refracted through his work, how a positivist historiography can so easily serve to reinforce an essentialist critical enterprise.

The series began with a programme devoted to Harwood's own West End and Broadway success *The Dresser*. In the following episodes, Harwood, the series presenter, constructed a teleological historical tradition in which parallels with present modes of performance were discovered at every point. Balinese, Roman and neo-classical theatre were all ransacked in order to validate the contemporary practices of Broadway and the West End. The parameters or frame for Harwood's enquiry were created by the notion of the 'stage' – and the metonymy is significantly ahistorical. A personal credo determines the frame:

What matters in the present is that games and sports represent alternatives to the pressures and concerns of our daily lives, while the theatre – though it may also work in this way – has the essential but opposite function of helping us remember who we are and where we are. In that sense, its ties to religion are unbroken.[2]

Harwood's presentation of historical fact is thus used to construct an idealist notion of 'theatre'. This idealized theatre, it is claimed, makes us recognize who we (really) are, but it does not make us who we are because it is not part of 'our daily lives' Theatre is presented as a quasi-religious phenomenon, easily separable from other activities involving spectator and performer.

There are obvious alternatives to Harwood's model of culture as the locus of detached and mystical contemplation. One does not have to be an aesthetic reductivist in order to view Elizabethan

theatre as a material social process. But one needs for this purpose a methodology which can deal with all types of performance, one which can analyse the clown and the tragic hero on, as it were, equal terms.

If we are to refute Harwood's idealist model of culture, we must jettison at once his dichotomy between two forms of play – theatre and sport. The point needs to be illustrated by example, and I shall choose an example that will make the point forcefully. The reader is asked to forgive me if I deviate from my theme of the clown, and examine some non-human Elizabethan performers. I shall make an excursus into Elizabethan animal-baiting, and bear-baiting in particular, because Elizabethan stage plays and baitings are, from a sociological/historical perspective, so obviously congruent activities. The purpose of my excursus will be to illustrate a fundamental argument about the parameters which we today impose upon 'drama', and about alternative ways of analysing dramatic performance.

To place Elizabethan theatre and Elizabethan bear-baiting within a common frame may well seem a perverse or cynical activity, an insult to 'common-sense'. The yoking will be unacceptable to those who have learned to polarize reality in terms of such oppositions as:

culture	:	commerce
civilized values	:	barbarity
art	:	philistinism
plays	:	games
Shakespeare	:	bears foaming at the mouth
high	:	low

These polarities, which appear to many to be the product of mere 'common-sense', are reinforced by the structures of traditional academic institutions. And it is precisely this kind of 'common-sense' polarization that has resulted in the critical dismissal of the clown as mere 'comic relief', as 'low' entertainment peripheral to the 'real' concerns of the play. I shall therefore argue that bear-baiting and theatre-making are, historically, homologous activities. I shall do so in order to challenge an established critical discourse which isolates a game from a play, sport from theatre, clown acts from deep or significant art. (And perhaps, in case there is any need, I should make my moral position clear at the outset: one can understand the fascination of bear-baiting without approving the suffering of animals, just as one can admire *Macbeth* without approving the theory of Divine Right.)

The congruence exists on almost every level. Legally, bearwards and players had a common status. Architecturally, the baiting ring is the obvious ancestor of the circular, tiered playhouse. The theatre pricing system was based upon a principle established in the baiting ring.[3] The Hope was eventually built to double as both 'play house and game place', and a visitor might complain when he found

> Instead of a stake was suffered a stage
> And in Hunks his house a crew of players.[4]

The theatrical entrepreneurs Henslowe and Alleyn leased the Bear Garden, and in 1604 obtained a royal patent as Masters of the Game of Bears, Dogs and Apes.[5] Theatre and Bear Garden competed for audiences, and in 1591 plays were banned on Thursdays to create an audience for 'bear-baiting and like pleasures which are maintained for Her Majesty's pleasure'.[6] Bear-baiting attracted an audience from all social classes. At one end of the scale were tradesmen, servants and lower-class women, but bear-baiting was also a royal sport. A fashionable gentleman, according to John Davies, had to make up his mind whether to go 'To Paris Garden, cock-pit, or the play'.[7] Tourists like Platter, Hentzer and De Witt were attracted to both Bear Garden and theatre. The bears, like the players, were summoned to Whitehall if the monarch wished to be entertained, but many aristocratic visitors – like the Duke of Württemburg, the Duke of Stettin, the son of the Landgrave of Hesse, and the Duc de Biron (escorted by Raleigh) – visited the public Bear Garden.[8]

The baiting of a bear did not, any more than the suffering of a Shakespearean tragic hero, offer the audience an emotional orgy. It allowed the audience to construct meanings, to clarify values. We need only to examine the language in which people justified baitings for the point to be clear. Sir Thomas Wyatt thus explained to a Spaniard the rationale for courtiers engaging in cock-fighting:

Leaving aside the diversion which the contest affords, I say that there is not a single prince or a captain one might find among the spectators who, contemplating how fervently these little animals seek for victory at the expense of their own lives and with no profit in view, even if he were of a cowardly nature, would not recover a positive strength of spirit to vanquish his foe or to die bravely whenever it is necessary to fight for one's children's sake, for religion, for one's sacred places, or for the honour and salvation of one's country.[9]

It is clear from this reported conversation that there is no paradox in

a high-minded Protestant, a writer of 'high' love sonnets, also being a devotee of 'low' cock-fighting. Bear-baiting was justified in much the same terms. John Taylor put the case a century later:

> For whoso'er comes thither, most and least,
> May see and learn some courage from a beast.[10]

The vocabulary used for describing a fight confirms that people used animal combat in order to give meaning to human activities. The pity and fear of tragedy are immediately in evidence. A Norwich cock, fighting at Shrovetide in c. 1606, fought 'valiantly' against a 'cruel' adversary although his body was *pitifully* injured.[11] Taylor lamented that the closure of play and game houses in 1637/8 deprived the public of a bull who would 'knit the brow with terror'. This is a bull who fights with 'valour' and 'scorns abuses', he is by nature 'headstrong', but can act 'politicly'.[12] The moral/psychological categories are potentially complex. Stowe's *Chronicles* describe the 'noble part and courage' of a lion baited before the King in 1604. James himself identified the lion as king of beasts, and Prince Henry had the winning dog given a place at court in reward for his heroism.[13] James's taste for lions, in preference to the bears favoured by Elizabeth, demonstrated a new courtly exclusivity.

The name 'Jackanapes' served to personalize the monkey. The ape was used to supply farce, which, as in the theatre, followed after the exhibition of noble suffering.[14] The ape was intended to look like a scaled-down, grotesque human being, an illusion furthered by setting him on a scaled-down horse, a pony of some five hands.[15] The ape's screams at the end of the performance made human suffering finally appear risible rather than tragic.

The bear became the focus of commercial baitings. Because of his erect fighting posture – he can 'cuff a dog off with his foot-like hand', notes Taylor – he easily attracts anthropomorphic language. For Taylor, the bears in their 'Rotundius College' learn art and knowledge in the form of dancing, acrobatics, practising wards and postures. The bear is like a watchman in his rug gown, or an officer in collar and chain, and becomes finally a metaphor for the troubled commonwealth.[16] Robert Laneham at Kenilworth saw the bears as members of a jury. The largest was the foreman, and displayed due 'wisdom and gravity'. In combat, the 'force and experience' of the bear were admired.[17] The Bear Garden in 1590 housed such grand Old Testament sufferers as Jeremy, Sampson and Daniel.[18] In 1638

such roguish bears as Robin Hood, Don John and Moll Cutpurse owe something to stage characters.[19] The most celebrated bears, like Sackerson, George Stone and Harry Hunks, can be spoken of as familiars by Captain Otter or Davies's law student Publius.[20] *Aficionados* shared and developed a publicly available understanding of each bear's individual character. Bulls, by contrast, were not given such obviously human names.[21]

In certain circumstances, men could substitute for animals, and vice versa. In the Bear Garden, human actors were involved in the comic but skilled routine of whipping the blind bear. This 'company of creatures that had the shapes of men' – so Dekker describes them – are termed by Nashe 'the Colliers of Romford'. Dekker likens the men to beadles, Nashe to aldermen who 'hold their corporation'.[22] The ritualism is apparent, but we have not enough information to decipher the meaning.

Bears, equally, could take over the function of actors. In 1610 the Duke of Savoy presented King James with two white bears, and these were used at New Year to draw Prince Henry's chariot in the masque of *Oberon*.[23] A white bear was introduced into the King's Men's revival of *Mucedorus* which took place at court probably a month later.[24] And in all likelihood it was the same white bear which found its way into *The Winter's Tale* at just this time. The King's Men must have participated in *Oberon*, for they also borrowed from it the dance of satyrs which they announce as having been 'danced before the King'.[25] There would have been little interest if an ordinary bear had been brought onto the stage, but the polar bear was a novelty. If this hypothesis is correct, then we can see how Shakespeare used the bear-as-actor to convey subtleties of meaning. The whiteness in its theatrical context signifies the cruel winter of *The Winter's Tale*: the bear's exit heralds scenes of spring and pastoral regeneration. The white bear connotes purity, also exoticism, also – as a royal possession – the royalty of the foundling. The Bear, like Perdita, is a complex sign.

Shakespeare is also capable of constructing the actor, emblematically, as a bear. The Earl of Warwick in *2 Henry VI* puts the bear and staff, his family crest, prominently on his helmet (v.i.205). Both language and performance reinforce this construction. York terms Warwick his 'bear', and he himself becomes the bearward. Clifford is likened to a dog who is too terrified to attack the bear.[26] There are several clues to the way performance pointed up the emblematic

association of Warwick and bear. Suffolk's attack on Warwick's 'demeanour', and his statement that Warwick is the product of a graft from a crab-tree, imply a striking ugliness (*2 HVI*.III.ii.209–13). References to Warwick's long coal-black hair, piercing eyes and deeply wrinkled brow confirm the importance of the physical presentation. He stamps to express his will, waves his arm to demonstrate power.[27] The actor's 'roaring' is associated with his bear-like quality, and he seems to roar himself hoarse calling for Clifford-as-dog (3.v.vii.12; 2.v.ii.1–7). If one conceives a piece of theatre as a physical rather than a verbal construct, then one can see a very precise congruence between the drama of the playhouse and the drama of the baiting-ring. In Part Three Warwick withdraws from the battle exhausted, but is goaded into giving fight once more. Warwick's physical (and political) power is tested to the limits, the limit marked by a death scene in which the actor is brought on with a mangled body, his body and face besmeared with blood and dirt. Within the theatrical mode, speech largely replaces the language of roaring, and the performer's injuries are merely simulated. But the audience's reading of the two symbolic enactments – Warwick's defeat on the stage, the bear's defeat in the ring – can remain homologous in many important respects.

No more than the bear-baiting was the play a simple reproduction of social reality: both formed part of social reality. Spectators invested both bear and human actor with significance, they constructed meanings around his *agon* or contest. Neither play nor baiting had a 'real' meaning. In 1610 one spectator, Henry Jackson, could see in the death of Desdemona an example of decorum: 'she' played her part admirably, and moved him to pity. But a Puritan like William Crashaw would rather have seen the same performance, in which a male actor counterfeited a woman by his apparel, as a manifestation of Babylon.[28] Likewise the 'valour' of the bear seen by the approving spectator could be seen by the Puritan as the response of a 'poor beast' to man's foolish pleasure.[29] The organizers of the spectacle in either case encouraged the audience to construct one set of meanings and not the other. Subsequent critics may accept or reject the offered meanings. Most modern critics accept the Puritan reading of bear-baiting and reject the Puritan reading of theatre.

This argument has an obvious bearing upon an analysis of the clown. A performance encouraged the audience to construct meanings around the clown. Henslowe and Shakespeare deployed clowns,

just as they deployed bears, to create a flesh-and-blood spectacle capable of yielding complex meanings. The first job of the historical critic must be to reach for the signifiers – costume, voice, eye contact with audience, etc. Only by this means can we grasp at that which was once signified, and distinguish past from present significations.

A semiological approach to performance is bound to stress that a play is a kind of ritual. Like a bear-baiting, an Elizabethan play was a repeated symbolic action which regular spectators/participants learned to read in order to construct complex meanings. Each text and each performance were in one sense unique, but in another sense the governing formula changed only slowly. I have concentrated in this book upon one aspect of the governing formula. I have argued that Kemp's roles were consistently shaped by the 'structure of misrule', and that decaying calendar festivals offered a paradigm for Kemp's activities on stage. In order to develop a critical approach to the play as a symbolic action, and to the clown's ritualized function within the play, it is necessary to draw upon the methods of anthropologists and other cultural theorists. In the next section of this chapter I shall therefore examine the work of a number of writers who, within their different disciplines, have examined carnivalesque enactments of misrule. I shall examine what ways forward they suggest for an enquiry of the kind that I have made in this book.

The historian Peter Burke, in *Popular Culture in Early Modern Europe* (1978), exemplifies many of the pitfalls of the liberal–humanist stance. Burke distinguishes a 'high' or 'great' culture, transmitted orally. He perceives, rightly, that through the sixteenth century the European nobility were involved in a shared popular culture. But he makes the modernistic assumption that: 'For the elite, but for them only, the two traditions had different psychological functions; the great tradition was serious, the little tradition was play' (p. 28). Burke fails to acknowledge that the nobleman who pens a sonnet, participates in a masque, or composes a Latin epigram is engaged in a form of play. He bases his analysis of 'popular' culture upon a preconception as to which *forms* are popular. He refuses to concede that Shakespeare was a popular dramatist (p. 96), but he allows an activity like bear-baiting to pass off as a popular mode. His methodology cannot deal with the fact that bear-baiting was in its roots an aristocratic pastime with the practical purpose of training

dogs to fight in war, and with the subsidiary purpose of allowing gentlemen who owned mastiffs to display their wealth publicly through gambling.[30] The people came to Paris Garden to participate in aristocratic culture, and not vice versa. Cock-fighting likewise was transformed from a boys' game to a national sport because Henry VIII developed a taste for it.[31] Burke's 'popular culture' shades out of being a sociological category into being an ethical one.

Burke's analysis of the European carnival is a psychological one. He perceives the symbolic and polysemous nature of carnival, but his pan-European methodology obliges him to seek universalist explanations. He asserts that violence and sex are 'more or less sublimated into ritual', and that carnival functions as a 'safety-valve' which allows 'a controlled escape of steam'.[32] A carnival which precipitates social upheaval can then be seen as dysfunctional. In his theoretical approach, Burke has made little advance upon Enid Welsford's classic study of fooling published in 1935. He echoes Welsford's pivotal text, a French apologia of 1444 which justified the Feast of Fools on the grounds that wine barrels must be opened from time to time to prevent them from bursting.[33] Safety-valve theory, and its literary-critical correlative, comic-relief theory, rest upon a model of society, and the individual as society in microcosm, being a fermenting, amorphous mass held in place by external force. The medieval idea that the spirit must govern the flesh anticipates the Freudian idea that the ego governs the id. The implication is that repression is a necessary condition of personal and political survival. The emphasis upon interiority correlates with a modern theatrical norm according to which the actor's skill is supposed to lie in revealing the 'character' that lies *within* or *beneath* the external representation offered to the audience. The social-aesthetic categories high/low and popular/serious are an integral part of this twentieth-century conceptual system. Welsford deals with Kemp in a sentence, but devotes seventeen pages to Lear's fool: within the higher form of tragedy, within the imagination rather than the flesh, the apotheosis of the fool is realized. Burke works within the same conceptual system when he performs a converse operation, welcoming Tarlton to his pages, but banishing Lear's fool.

The anthropology of Victor Turner offers a useful alternative:

It is as though there are here two major 'models' for human interrelatedness, juxtaposed and alternating. The first is of society as a structured, differenti-

ated, and often hierarchical system of politico-legal-economic positions with many types of evaluation, separating men in terms of 'more' or 'less'. The second, which emerges recognizably in the liminal period, is of society as an unstructured or rudimentarily structured and relatively undifferentiated *comitatus*, community, or even communion of equal individuals who submit together to the general authority of the ritual elders.[34]

Individuals and societies need to involve themselves both in 'structure' and in 'anti-structure' or '*communitas*'. Unlike Burke and Welsford, Turner sees society as a process rather than a constant. He argues that no society can function adequately unless it sets up a dialectic or oscillation between these two modalities. An extreme of the one generates an extreme of the other.

Turner's dialectic offers possible ways of looking at Elizabethan theatre. *Communitas* is normally to be located on the margins or interstices of structure, it is associated with 'liminal' activities such as rites of passage. The Elizabethan theatre is not significantly liminal in respect of the calendar – except in the case of court and private performances, and except in its symbolic representation of such moments as Twelfth Night or Midsummer Night. It is physically liminal, however, set in the interstices of London and Surrey or Middlesex. Within the theatre, the clown is a liminal figure in relation to the physical margins of the stage. He locates himself in the interstices of the plot. And he dominates the liminal period of the jig, when the play gives way to ordinary living. The theatre building is an almost unique gathering point where the social classes come together, and inside that building the clown separates himself from the structured language of verse, and from the structure of the narrative fiction, and appears to set up with the audience a communion of undifferentiated, equal individuals. In Turnerian terminology, the clown strives for *communitas*, for the breaking down of structure. Turner's analysis allows us to see the play as a social process, and the clown's liminality as a necessary part of that process.

In Turner's language, the clown is a multivocal symbol. Clowns are prime examples of figures who, 'representing the poor and the deformed, appear to symbolize the moral values of communitas as against the coercive power of supreme political rulers'.[35] Turner argues that symbolic inversions such as those associated with a Lord of Misrule offer an apprehension of *communitas* to the structurally superior, whose lives are dominated by the need to maintain structure, and at the same time offer symbolic structural placing to the

structurally inferior, whose lives are dominated by communal values and ways of living.[36] It follows from Turner's argument that when theatre audiences became segregated, when the structurally superior patronized the private playhouses whilst the structurally inferior dominated the open-air houses, the social structure was no longer on public display in order to generate the opposite modality of 'anti-structure'. When the social group gathered in the theatre is homogeneous, no dialectic can be set up between structure and *communitas*. In the course of the Jacobean period, the clown gradually ceased to be the instigator of *communitas*. As a symbol, he became univocal.

There is much that is valuable in Turnerian anthropology. But flaws appear when Turner seems to suggest that those whom society renders structurally inferior obtain vicarious emotional satisfaction from inversionary rituals. Safety-valve theory begins to reappear, riding on the back of a functionalist assumption that the status quo is a contained, self-regulating system. A 'symbol' ceases to be the same thing as a sign. The notion of *communitas* becomes invested with transcendental value, and betrays its origins in Buber's theology and in the multiple liberation philosophies of Sixties America.

Where Turner's anthropology ultimately idealizes the spiritual liberation of the individual, Mikhail Bakhtin's analysis of Renaissance carnival displays its Soviet origins when it ascribes almost metaphysical status to the voice of 'the people'. With this caveat, Bakhtin's argument that people use the symbolic language of folk humour in order to voice 'unofficial' views is a valuable counter to the functionalist argument. Against a 'serious' official culture (not unlike Burke's), Bakhtin sets an unofficial culture based on laughter. Unlike Burke, Bakhtin sees the non-serious culture as holding a 'meaningful philosophical content'. Bakhtin is emphatic that no festival can exist unless it has a spiritual or ideological dimension.[37]

Bakhtin's materialism leads him to interest himself in carnival's obsession with the human body. While classicism, or the language of officialdom, represents the human body as a unified, closed system, the unofficial language of medieval carnival concerns itself with the grotesqueness of body fluids and excrement, with bodily orifices and protuberances. This second language stresses that the human individual is not a self-contained system, but is ecologically bound up with the earth. One person is not divided from others as a unique 'character', but is joined to others through being part of a self-

reproducing cosmic system. Bakhtin's comments on Sancho Panza can be applied equally well to the Elizabethan clown. Sancho's paunch or *panza* conveys the carnivalesque spirit. His greed has not yet historically acquired a 'private, egotistic and alienating character'. Yet in Cervantes 'private' bodies are beginning to be divided, atomized, individualized. In the Renaissance moment, the private and the universal are 'blended in a contradictory unity'.[38]

Bakhtin clarifies the point that the clown's task in performance is precisely *not* to create a character. His task is to project himself bodily, exploiting the grotesqueness of his 'scurvy' face and his stunted or lumpish anatomy. The clown's gaping mouth can be seen as part of a system of meanings: there is no bodily closure for the clown just as there is no narrative closure. Through images of incompleteness or non-containment, the language of laughter signifies something akin to what Turner calls *communitas*. Bakhtin is equally suggestive about the actor's use of his eyes. To allow the eyes to bulge is to render them protuberances, grotesque objects. To use them as the main bodily signifiers, as in neo-classical drama, would be to suggest that a closed individual character is locked behind them.[39]

Bakhtin's remarks on obscenity prompt me to go beyond him. While obscenity in Rabelais or *Mankind* is predominantly anal, the obscenity of the Elizabethan clown is genital. The clown's link with the regenerative earth weakens in the Elizabethan period, his sexual aspect strengthens. Within the official Elizabethan culture, the mythologizing of pre-marital romantic love obviously relates to a new ascription of value to education and leisure, to the nuclear family (as against the guild or dynastic unit), to personal choice (in religion, occupation, domicile) and to the personal choice of marriage partner in particular (now that an economically desirable partner might compete with a dynastically desirable partner). The sexual obscenity of the clown is bound up with this new mythology. In Bakhtin's language, the clown's extruding phallus (Kemp's staff, truncheon or broom-handle) signals that the individual cannot be rendered enclosed and complete by the state of marriage. In post-Bakhtinian language, we may prefer to say that the clown deconstructs a sexual mythology which other parts of the play work powerfully to construct.

My excursus into bear-baiting in this chapter was stimulated by a now classic semiological essay on cockfighting by the American anthropologist Clifford Geertz. In 'Deep Play: Notes on the Balinese

William Kemp and Harry Hunks

Cockfight', Geertz evokes the Benthamite term 'deep play' to point up his observation that the gambling associated with the Balinese sport lacks a rational objective in terms either of money or of status. Geertz's conclusions will serve to mark my own point of arrival:

Like any art form – for that, finally, is what we are dealing with – the cockfight renders ordinary, everyday experience comprehensible by presenting it in terms of acts and objects which have had their practical consequences removed . . . What it does is what, for other peoples with other temperaments and other conventions, *Lear* and *Crime and Punishment* do; it catches up these themes – death, masculinity, rage, pride, loss, beneficence, chance – . . . It puts a construction on them, makes them, to those historically positioned to appreciate the construction, meaningful – visible, tangible, graspable – 'real' in an ideational sense. An image, fiction, a model, a metaphor, the cockfight is a means of expression; its function is neither to assuage social passions nor to heighten them (though in its playing-with-fire way it does a bit of both), but, in a medium of feathers, blood, crowds, and money, to display them.[40]

The purpose and condition of human life, in Geertz's terms, is not sexuality, aggression, wealth or power so much as the imposition of meaning upon life. The effect of cockfights, like the effect of inversionary carnival rituals, is not – as Burke and Turner would have it – to reinforce but rather to describe status distinctions. The Balinese cockfight – like the Elizabethan clown, I wish to add –

provides a metasocial commentary upon the whole matter of assorting human beings into fixed hierarchical ranks and then organizing the major part of collective experience around that assortment.[41]

Turner distinguishes cognitive and emotional aspects of ritual, in order to argue for a theory of psychic release. Geertz refuses that distinction, arguing that emotion is used for cognitive ends. The Balinese learns through the fight 'what his culture's ethos and his private sensibility . . . look like when spelled out externally in a collective text'.[42]

The assertion that the performance is a 'collective text' is a helpful starting point. The written text is the product of an author, and subsequently the property of a company. The performance is a text of a different order, but one which also, despite problems of accessibility, requires a close reading. Only through a close reading can its plurality of meanings become exposed. Within this collective text, the clown is a complex signifier. We can first (subject to the available evidence) analyse the signifiers of which the clown is compounded:

177

his staff, his use of his eyes, his Anglicized name in the script, his (apparent) freedom to improvise, and so on. We can then move on to look at the individual actor as a signifier.

The audience invested Kemp with character just as they invested blind Harry Hunks with character. Barthes' *Mythologies* demonstrates the value of neologisms in semiological analysis:[43] and 'plebeianness' might be the best term to coin for Kemp-as-sign. Once 'plain', 'honest' Will was recognized as a sign, the sign could be manipulated to generate new descriptions of society, new meanings. Beneath Pyramus's beard, plebeianness is shown to be incompatible with a certain level of erotic and tragic experience. Beneath Falstaff's doublet, in a knight's role, the sign of plebeianness is used to generate new and contradictory pictures of the social order. Jonson used the sign in a new way again. He challenged the identification of clown with licensed misrule by casting Kemp as Cob, the embodiment of Lent. The old distinction between divinely sanctioned rule and divinely sanctioned misrule became inoperative. Different again, as Cock, Kemp-as-sign was used to connote stability in a destabilized society.

Gentility was an important concept in Elizabethan thought and social organization. Plebeianness was important as a sign of all that gentility was not. A highly developed theoretical discourse allowed Elizabethans to articulate the ethical/social ideal of gentility. Theatrical signs provided the best available language in which an alternative ideal could be conceived and articulated. Broadly speaking, the debate about gentility gave way to a debate about power in seventeenth-century theatre. If it came to seem an irrelevance to describe the world in terms of clowns on the one hand, gentlemen on the other, part of the explanation may be that the clown-as-sign was too potent.

In the drama of post 1600, the assortment of human beings into a hierarchical order was no longer displayed as the organizing principle governing most human experience. Robert Armin was, most obviously, a visual signifier whose primary signified was mental deformity. The assortment of human beings into two groups of unique individuals, one group with well-endowed, well-motivated personalities, the other group with deformed personalities, became the basis of a new theatrical language used by men to describe their existence.

The idea that the actor communicates through deploying a system

of signs, a system which the audience must be skilled enough to read, is relevant to contemporary debates about acting. Against the Stanislavskian emphasis on the truthful mimesis of reality, Brecht held up the example of the ancient sign-systems of Chinese theatre. The debate thrives. In 1984 John Barton of the Royal Shakespeare Company advised players of Shakespearean roles to follow Hamlet's advice and to 'imitate nature'.[44] He takes Hamlet's advice to be not a set of neo-classical precepts but a truth about good acting. He asks actors to balance 'heightened' against 'naturalistic' elements in the text.[45] This quest for the mean replicates Hamlet's advice that actors should not overstep the modesty of nature. The actor's central problem is seen as one of handling a text rather than handling an audience. A different and obviously Brechtian approach was urged in 1984 in a book by Steve Gooch. Gooch proffers a manifesto based upon his work in fringe and community theatre, and upon his rejection of the production processes of mainstream theatre.

For an actor, then, to look at his audience as he would normally at people in the same room with him, to speak from the whole of his person to the whole of theirs, would be to restore the dignity and humanity driven out of theatre by packaging, directorial 'concept', naturalistic 'consistency' in texts and the 'hothouse' school of acting . . .
    A new aesthetic approach which enabled actors to conduct this kind of 'conversation between equals', to look their audience in the eye even when clowning or when their characters are gripped by anger, fear or insanity, is a potential held by theatre alone.[46]

Elizabethan clown actors knew how to create a double persona – Kemp/Bottom, Armin/Touchstone, Singer/Assinico – and they could therefore speak as themselves – 'Kemp', 'Armin', 'Singer' – and could 'look their audience in the eye'. Like the Brechtian actor, the clown would project a point of view about the role which he presented. There was no attempt to recreate a consistent 'real' world in Elizabethan theatre, no assumption that the actor's task involved re-experiencing the emotions of the character, no proposal that the audience were invisible *voyeurs*. The clown performed *with*, and not *to*, an audience constructed as equals. My reading of the Elizabethan clown cannot so easily be aligned with Barton's approach. Hamlet's view of theatre cannot be taken as Shakespeare's, and Shakespeare's cannot be taken as Kemp's. To 'imitate nature' is not, nor ever has been, an objective goal. The idea that the actor can project meanings which are contrapuntal to the words, neither extracted from the

words nor inherent in them, is difficult to reconcile with Barton's personal and institutional commitment to the primacy of the Shakespearean text.

Since this is a book centred on one particular actor, I should like to end by quoting the best description that I know of a great *farceur*: Kierkegaard's description of Friedrich Beckmann at the Königstäter Theatre in Berlin in 1841.

Kierkegaard first acknowledges that 'every attempt at an aesthetic definition which might claim universal validity founders upon the farce, which is by no means capable of producing a uniformity of mood in the more cultured part of the audience'. This is not theatre for the 'real theatrical public' which 'wants (or at least imagines it wants) to be ennobled or educated at the theatre', which 'wants to have had (or at least to imagine that it has had) a rare aesthetic enjoyment'. Kierkegaard enjoys his own emancipation from 'the aesthetic obligation to laugh, admire, be touched, etc.' What he enjoys, as a spectator of farce, is 'to be himself in a comically productive relation to the theatrical performance'.[47]

Kierkegaard describes the existential leap of comic actors who can 'plunge into the abyss of laughter and then let its volcanic force cast them up upon the stage'. He admires the way Beckmann used his 'indomitable common sense' to produce a state of frenzy. I should like to think that Kierkegaard's tribute to Beckmann could be applied equally well to Kemp. Beckmann was famed in the roles of Bottom and Falstaff. Specifically, I believe that an Elizabethan spectator would likewise have registered Kemp's skill as being in the first instance physical, that Kemp, like Beckmann at thirty-eight, could the better play a youth because of his age, that a role of Kemp's was also seen as a temporary incognito, and that Kemp's dance was seen as the natural climax of his act.

In the artistic theatre properly so called one seldom sees an actor who can really walk and stand . . . but what Beckmann is capable of I have never before beheld. He can not only walk but he can *come walking*. This ability to 'come walking' is a very different thing, and by this stroke of genius Beckmann improvises the scenic environment. He can not only represent a wandering apprentice lad, he can come walking like him, and that in such a way that one sees the whole thing: through the dust of the highway one espies a smiling village, hears its subdued din, sees the footpath which winds yonder down to the pond where it turns off at the smithy . . . However this young apprentice is no characterization; for that the figure is too hastily sketched in its truly masterly contours, it is an incognito in which dwells the

mad demon of laughter, which soon disengages itself and carries the whole thing off with unbridled mirth. In this respect Beckmann's dancing is incomparable. He has sung his couplet, now the dance begins . . . The madness of laughter within him can no longer be contained either in mimicry or in *réplique* – only to take himself like Münchausen by the nape of the neck and abandon himself to crazy caprioles is consonant with his mood.[48]

Armin's motley

Leslie Hotson's *Shakespeare's Motley* (1952) is a dazzling blend of scholarly research and scholarly sleight of hand. Hotson sought to demonstrate: (a) that the Elizabethan fool's 'motley' was not a patterned cloth but a tweed of variegated threads; (b) that this 'motley' – as distinct from 'pied' – coat was always a full-length coat; and (c) that this costume was the regular wear of Shakespeare's fools. None of these propositions can be sustained.

MOTLEY

The whole point of a fool's costume is, of course, that it should instantly be recognizable. E. W. Ives has drawn attention to a portrait of Lord Muncaster's fool of *c.* 1660 in which a check pattern of blue and yellow on white seems to have been produced on the loom.[1] This tallies with Dekker's assertion that one may weave on a 'motley-loom' something 'like a beggar's cloak ... full of stolen patches, and yet never a patch like one another'.[2] Etymologically, the term 'motley' refers to colour rather than to a type of wool. 'Velvet motley' is found in the early Tudor period, and Joseph's coat of many colours naturally became a 'motley' coat in Caxton's version.[3] In *The Three Ladies of London* (1584) a face 'painted motley' is also said to be 'parti-coloured'.[4] Breton in 1600 refers to a rural actor in 'a painted motley coat'[5] – implying that it was not the weaver who made the coat 'motley'. Hotson himself quotes Anton's reference to 'chequered motley, vert et argent' in 1613.[6] A fool's motley, then, was a coat of many colours. We may accept as representative Jonson's testimony when he provides for La Fool a coat (of arms) of chequered yellow, blue, red, and other colours.[7]

The 'motley' or 'pied' costume was conventionally worn with the cockscomb and bauble, and constituted an emblem of folly. *Qua* emblem, the costume was often worn, as we saw in Chapter 1, by the

Vice/fool in a dramatic or quasi-dramatic context. The costume is often illustrated: it is worn, for instance, by Harman's rabbit-fools in *The Ground-Work of Coney-Catching* (1597). Breton's literary invocation of the guise is typical:

> I would I were an innocent, a fool
> That...
> Wear'd a pied coat, a cock's comb and a bell,
> And think it did become me passing well.[8]

The problem begins when we turn to the costume actually worn by domestic fools in the late sixteenth century. The language of emblems was a universal one, and few masters were willing to associate themselves too closely with an emblem of folly that would reflect on themselves.

Nowhere in sixteenth-century Europe are real court jesters pictured as wearing the motley and cockscomb outfit.[9] Thomas More's fool wears a conventional tawny livery, with More's badge in his hat.[10] Household accounts and the miniature in Henry VIII's psalter[11] show that Henry's fool, William Somers, had no distinguishing uniform in normal court life – although he did wear a painted coat in a Lord of Misrule game,[12] a 'fool's coat' in Armin's account of him,[13] and there was a distinguishing coat for the actor who played him on the stage of the Rose.[14] Like John i' the Hospital, who also wore a standard livery rather than a fool costume,[15] Somers was marked as a fool mainly by the supply of handkerchiefs which he needed to mop his saliva.[16] Provincial gentry, out of the public eye, were able to be more eccentric in their tastes. A Yorkshire gentleman in 1613 gave his fool 'a long coat, a fantastical cap, and such like attire the better to solace and make sport for' his master.[17] Armin's Jack Oates rejects the theoretically appropriate attire:

> Motley his wearing, yellow or else green,
> A coloured coat on him was seldom seen.
> No fool's cap with a bauble and a bell...

He preferred a straw hat, dyed red and blue, and offset this glory with a quieter coat, yellow or green on a neutral background.[18]

Let us examine next the appendages of the 'motley' costume: the cockscomb and the bauble. The cockscomb, in English practice, was usually honed down from a full cock's head to a pointed phallic hat. Richard Day's *Book of Christian Prayers* (1578), which illustrates

many contemporary costumes, shows both forms: a morris fool wears a simple pointed cap tipped with a bell, and a female fool in the dress of a gentlewoman has both a cock's head and ass's ears on her cap. Both carry bladders on a stick.[19] The traditional *marotte* – the fool's head on a stick – appears in innumerable continental illustrations, but seems to make no appearance in sixteenth-century England. The fool in the Betley window carries one, but this is a historical recreation of a supposed pre-Reformation morris.[20] A fool in the morris might carry a ladle.[21] Lord Muncaster's fool carried a cane, as his staff of office, and Hotson discovered that the historical Jack Oates was issued with a 'painted cane'.[22] The term 'bauble' seems to be very loosely defined. In *Antonio's Revenge*, the fool's bauble seems to comprise simply 'a little toy of a walnut shell and soap to make bubbles'.[23]

When we turn to the Shakespearean theatre, we see that both the emblematic tradition, mediated through the festival – particularly the morris dance – and through the interlude, and the real life tradition, mediated through the researched impersonations of Robert Armin, were available to the dramatist.

The long coat

The 'motley' or 'pied' costume was worn short in the sixteenth century. Geoffrey Whitney reproduces a woodcut (Fig. 6) showing a fool in long hood, skirted jerkin and hose, and terms the costume 'motley' in 1586. Dekker's Babulo in 1599, because he was born an innocent, wears a motley jerkin.[24] Deloney likewise envisages William Somers in a motley jerkin and motley hose.[25] Lord North in 1577 issued his fool with enough motley for a pair of gaskins, hose, coat and netherstocks.[26] A short jerkin rather than a long coat was the norm.

Hotson describes the custom of dressing idiots in the garb of children, a plain ground-length side-coat. Though this image was made available through the German woodcuts in *The Ship of Fools*, the English emblematic tradition ignores this costume through the sixteenth century. Nashe first brought the costume into a play, though not into a playhouse, when he dressed Will Somers in the borrowed long coat of a natural fool.[27] Nashe plays on the custom again when he portrays Gabriel Harvey as a natural fool in a long coat.[28] This costume was a plain one, and Hotson distorts the

evidence when he maintains that Jack Oates's costume concealed the knees: the thighs were visible enough.[29]

The guarded coat

The 'guarded' version of the idiot's plain long side-coat became a recognized stage garment only in the early seventeenth century. In a normal costume, a 'guard' – a band of cloth parallel with the hem – was usually an indication that the wearer was in livery.[30] Serving-men by this means, and in accordance with sumptuary law, could wear a fabric commensurate with their master's station rather than their own. In *The Merchant of Venice*, as we have seen, Launcelet is distinguished by the elaborateness of the guarding on his standard livery coat, and there is no evidence that he wears a long fool's coat. There is an early allusion to a long, guarded coat in *Soliman and Perseda* when the artificial fool is ironically promised as his reward the costume of an honoured 'natural': 'a guarded suit from top to toe'.[31] There is no evidence for such a costume appearing on stage, however, before *The Malcontent* in 1604. It rapidly became a conventional stage garment. Justice Overdo wears a 'guarded coat' when he impersonates mad Arthur of Bradley.[32] Will Somers wears a long guarded gown in Delaram's engraving of *c.* 1620. In *A Pleasant History of the Life and Death of Will Summers* (1637), Somers and Wolsey's fool are shown wearing unwaisted long coats with much bolder guarding; bells on the elbows and different types of fool's cap now complete the costume.[33]

The long motley coat

Bobadilla was sentenced to wear a *large* motley coat in 1598,[34] but I find no reference to a *long* motley coat before the prologue to *Henry VIII*, which Hotson rightly construes as an apology for the absence of Armin as Somers.[35] According to Shakespeare/Fletcher, the audience will be disappointed if it expects to see a fool:

> In a long motley coat, guarded with yellow
>
> (*Prologue*, l. 16)

The writer has sown confusion by conflating, in an ironic disparagement of popular taste, two distinct fool outfits – the short motley garment, and the plain side-coat marked as courtly livery by guard-

ing around the hems. (The particular significance of 'yellow' escapes me.) The costume is impossible, and has no parallel in extant iconography. The boldness of motley would obscure the more discreet yellow figuring. Two emblematic systems would be conflated, to imply that court livery was the garb of folly.

At some point the long motley coat, unguarded, was introduced onto the stage. A fool in a long chequered coat appears on the title-page of *A Maidenhead Well Lost* (1634), and the same garment, but waisted, appears in the painting of Lord Muncaster's fool. We can place no confidence in the fact that Armin describes the unsocialized Lean Leonard, who wore a long frieze coat in *Fool upon Fool*, as 'motley warm' in *Nest of Ninnies*. Armin had lost the original set of verses when preparing substitutes in 1608,[36] and he seems not to have known Leonard at first hand. The phrase is evidence only of Armin's preconceptions in 1608.

Armin's stage costume

Hotson's third proposition, that Armin had some kind of uniform stage costume, is based on a false premise. The conventions of Elizabethan theatre, unlike those of *commedia dell'arte* or *Noh*, for instance, were always in a state of flux. The vitality of the Elizabethan theatre lay in its refusal ever to accept a *status quo*. In respect of the fool character, writers and actors were expected to provide ever-new variants in order to sustain interest. These variations were effected, in the first instance, visually.

We are in a position now to examine such clues to costume as the texts provide. We shall look at the four roles where the text yields worthwhile evidence.

As You Like It

The relevant points are as follows:

1 Since Rosalind and Celia are in disguise, the 'Clowne *alias* Touchstone' must be in disguise too.
2 Only Jaques perceives that Touchstone is wearing 'motley'. The rustics see him as a 'master' or courtier.
3 Jaques mentions Touchstone's motley eight times. He also calls him 'fool' eight times in the space of eight lines (II.vii.12–19).

4   Jaques reports that Touchstone draws a dial from his *poke* (II.vii.20).

This is not the emblematic costume, the motley hose and jerkin, for rustics would be expected to identify such a traditional garment, and the garment is not *obviously* motley, or Jaques would be tedious to the audience. Hotson glosses 'poke' as a large bag, and interprets it tendentiously as the idiot's all-enveloping side-coat.[37] A 'poke', however, is the most precise available term for a bagged sleeve in a gown. The *OED* traces this meaning back to 1402. Now a bagged sleeve with a bell on the elbow is a well-established fool's garment. Dekker refers to a motley coat 'with four elbows' as part of Will Somers's wardrobe,[38] and almost all illustrations of fools reproduce this feature. I conclude, therefore, that Touchstone must wear a coat that is motley in colour, is marked as a fool's coat by hanging elbows, and yet in certain respects is of a wholly unfamiliar design. Hotson's speculation that Touchstone wore a *long* motley coat is therefore wholly consistent with the evidence of the text. The idiot's long coat had not previously been seen on the London stage, and an idiosyncratic motley version of this would justify Jaques's constant harping upon Touchstone's appearance. The long coat is not proven, however. The woven, chequered type of motley is not associated with fools in the sixteenth century, and this may equally well be the novelty that prevents all but Jaques from deciphering Touchstone's identity.

Twelfth Night

1   Feste wears 'gaskins' or wide breeches (I.v.24).
2   Feste puns that if his dishonesty is mended, he is but 'patched' (I.v.43).
3   With his mention of a monk's cowl, Feste alludes to his parti-coloured fool's cap: *'cucullus non facit monacham:* that's as much as to say, as I wear not motley in my brain' (I.v.54).
4   Feste states that he did 'impeticos' Sir Andrew's gratuity (II.iii.27).

Lord North's fool wore gaskins of motley in 1577.[39] Queen Elizabeth's Italian fool, more decorously, wore gaskins 'trimmed with lace of various colours'.[40] It is reasonable to assume, therefore, that Feste's gaskins appeared to be 'patched' or motley-coloured. Gas-

kins were in fashion in the 1570s, and Feste's costume thus associates him with the two knights who live, in spirit, in a bygone world. Feste's headgear is equally traditional. The point of his jest is that he does wear motley on top of his head – blue and yellow were typical colours for a fool's cap.[41] It is necessary to add, *pace* Hotson, that the term 'hood' (i.e. *cucullus*) is a synonym for 'cap' in this context.[42]

There is an obvious problem when we try to relate this old-fashioned Elizabethan outfit to a supposed long coat. Gaskins are hardly likely to be worn under a long coat, and there can be no point in jesting upon the consequences of their falling. The source of the confusion is Dr Johnson's interpretation of 'impeticos' as a reference to the fool's petticoat. A 'petticoat', in normal Elizabethan usage, is not a side-coat or gown, but a skirt hanging from the waist, and the term is nowhere else associated with fools. Now gaskins, in the regular style, hung loose to the knee, and Nashe made the obvious connexion between gaskins and skirts when he wrote derisively of Spaniards wearing 'a wide pair of gaskins ["gascoynes"] which ungathered would make a couple of women's riding kirtles'.[43] Feste invokes the term 'petticoat' for his ample and unfashionable gaskin breeches.

The Malcontent

1   At the start of Passarello's first scene, Malevole comments on the fool's guarding:

    Mal.   You are in good case since you came to court, fool. What, guarded, guarded!

    Pas.   Yes, faith, even as footmen or bawds wear velvet, not for an ornament of honour, but for a badge of drudgery (I.viii.7–10)

2   At the end of the scene, Malevole alludes to the guarding again:

    Pas.   You'll know me again, Malevole.

    Mal.   Oh, aye, by that velvet.

    Pas.   Aye, as a pettifogger by his buckram bag. (I.viii.57–9)

3   Bilioso (Passarello's master) promises that when ambassador to Florence he will, amongst other great expenses, dress his fool in velvet. He will wear his own velvet embroidered 'because I'll differ from the fool somewhat' (III.i.57).

4   When the pair return from Florence, Bilioso displays new

stockings and perfume. Passarello claims to have borrowed money, and drinks a pledge like 'gentlemen' or 'knights'. As Passarello then makes his final exit, Malevole asks the bawd: 'how dost thou think o' this transformation of state now?' (v.ii.40).

Passarello refers to himself as a 'serving-man' (III.i.148) and the guarding betokens this. There is nothing inherently remarkable about a guarded coat for a footman, as Passarello remarks. Malevole jests on 'that velvet', but an audience at a distance cannot discern whether the guarding is in fact of velvet. The remarkable feature of the initial costume must be that a fool's long side-coat has been converted to a livery coat. The coat would have to be unwaisted to be truly strange and worth comment. When Passarello makes visual comparisons between himself and a bawd in a dress, or a lawyer ('pettifogger') in a gown, he refers to his own long coat. A fool's long guarded coat was a novelty on stage in 1604.

Upon their return from Florence, Passarello's new finery emulates Bilioso's. Passarello's new 'velvet' outfit will be some kind of parody of contemporary foreign fashion. It must make him look as dumpy as possible in order to reinforce the visual contrast between servant and master. Bilioso is 'the leanest ... actor in the whole pageant', a 'father of maypoles', and he displays his 'calf in a long stocking' (I.viii.53; I.iv.44; v.i.1) The bawd responds to the question about Passarello's transformation: 'some must be fat, some must be lean; some must be fools, and some must be lords' (v.ii.44). Physique rather than costume now tells master and servant apart.

The fool's velvet relates more or less directly to the new situation at court. All sumptuary legislation was repealed at the start of the reign,[44] and James's court was associated with conspicuous consumption. I offer a further speculation. I have suggested that Armin already had impersonated the fools John Stone and Charles Chester. It is possible that Armin is here taking off Archie Armstrong, the new fool at court. Much later, an engraving represents Archie in a long, black guarded coat,[45] and an observer in 1629 states that Archie's coat was made of velvet.[46] We lack evidence for Archie's earlier dress.

Passarello's guarded coat attracted immediate notice. Writing a few months later, Chapman had D'Olive offer a 'guarded coat' to a diminutive half-wit page boy, probably in side-coats already.[47] Day

in 1605/6 jests that it is necessary to be a 'plain fool' – 'The only wear, for the guarded fool is out of request'.[48] The guarded costume was by now recognized as a new conventional dress for a stage fool.

King Lear

1 The fool repeatedly offers Lear his cockscomb (I.iv.93–103).
2 The fool refers to himself as 'The one in motley here' (I.iv.143).
3 The fool points to himself and Lear, saying: 'here's grace and a cod-piece, that's a wise man and a fool' (III.ii.40).

The ancient setting and the feudal character of Lear's regime render the emblematic or traditional parti-coloured costume appropriate. Lear's fool belongs to a vanished world, and not to the social reality of 1605.

There is no evidence that the fool's cap included a representational cock's head or ass's ears. There is better evidence for what lay beneath. Fools often had their heads shaved to prevent lice.[49] Lear's fool associates his own 'head-piece' – ambiguously cap or hair – with the problem of lousing (III.ii.25–30). This gives point to the jest:

give me an egg, and I'll give thee two crowns ... thou had'st little wit in thy bald crown when thou gav'st thy golden one away. If I speak like myself in this let him be whipped that first finds it so.   (I.iv.152–62)

The fool contrasts his own literal baldness with the metaphorical baldness of Lear, who is white-haired (III.ii.24). He proves that he speaks *like* himself, the often whipped fool, by removing his cockscomb to reveal his baldness. Having found this excuse to remove his fool's cap, however, he is enabled to proffer it once again to 'bald' Lear as a substitute crown.

While the cockscomb is a substitute crown, the fool's bauble is traditionally a substitute sceptre. There is no iconographic evidence to suggest that a fool's costume ever incorporated a prominent codpiece. Rather, the fool puts his bauble between his legs in order to mime:

> The cod-piece that will house
> Before the head has any ...   (III.ii.27–8)

There is more opportunity for phallic mime when the fool threatens at the audience:

> She that's a maid now, and laughs at my departure,
> Shall not be a maid long, unless things be cut shorter.
>
> (I.v.48–9)

Hotson discerned the pun which the rhyme requires – on the French *deporter* – a 'bauble'.[50] The pun confirms that the regular French type of bauble, the *marotte* or fool's head on a stick, was used in Lear.[51] The 'cod-piece' is personalized as 'he' at III.ii.29. Armin's description of Sir Timothy Truncheon as 'ever my part-taking friend'[52] shows that the actor was familiar with using a personalized bauble. Another passage can thus be explained. When the fool asks: 'Dost thou know the difference, my boy, between a bitter fool and a sweet one?', the obvious 'boy' for him to address is his *marotte*. Lear answers on behalf of the *marotte*. The lines which follow:

> That Lord that counselled thee
>   To give away thy land,
> Come place him here by me,
>   Do thou for him stand:
> The sweet and bitter fool
>   Will presently appear;
> The one in motley here,
>   The other found out there.   (I.iv.137–44)

play most easily if the 'thou' in question is the *marotte* who can swivel his gaze from the sweet fool in motley (Armin) to the bitter fool (Lear). The routine was cut from the Folio text. If the Folio text represents a version revised after 1611, we might deduce that Armin's successor was not able or willing to use a *marotte*.[53] Gary Taylor, however, argues that censorship explains the cut, and that the scene pointed too clearly to the influence of James's fool, Archie Armstrong, over James.[54] Whatever the explanation, we should note that the fool's *marotte* was not found in sixteenth-century English fooling, and was therefore a sign of antiquity, a sign that Lear's concepts of fatherhood and kingship are outmoded.

Notes

For Shakespeare's plays, line references are to the New Arden edition. For Jonson's plays, line references unless otherwise stated are to *Ben Jonson*, ed. C. H. Herford, P. and E. Simpson (1925–52). For other plays, see the edition cited. I have given the place of publication only for books published outside the United Kingdom. References to Nungezer are to the standard reference work on Elizabethan and Stuart actors, Edwin Nungezer, *A Dictionary of Actors . . . before 1642* (New Haven, Conn., 1929).

Preface

1 See, however, my discussion of Brome's evidence in Chapter 3.
2 *Apology for Poetry*, ed. H. A. Needham (1931), pp. 30, 54.

1 The Vice

1 In *English Moral Interludes*, ed. Glynne Wickham (1976), ll. 452–607. A. W. Pollard in the EETS edition of *The Macro Plays* first made the suggestion that Mischief and Titivillus are doubled; but since he considered the play 'about as degrading a composition as can well be conceived', it is not surprising that later editors failed to explore the logic of his idea.
2 Bernard Spivack, *Shakespeare and the Allegory of Evil* (1958), pp. 147–9, 176–7; cf. Glynne Wickham, *Early English Stages*, I (1963).
3 F. H. Mares, 'The origin of the figure called "the Vice" in Tudor drama', *Huntington Library Quarterly* 22 (1958) 11–29; J. A. B. Somerset, '"Fair is foul and foul is fair": Vice-comedy's development and theatrical effects' in *The Elizabethan Theatre* 5 (Ontario and London, 1975), ed. G. R. Hibbard, pp. 54–75.
4 *Shakespeare and the Allegory of Evil*, pp. 135–7.
5 David Wiles, *The Early Plays of Robin Hood* (1981), p. 5.
6 J. C. Cox, *The Churchwardens' Accounts* (1913), p. 291.
7 George Puttenham, *The Arte of English Poesie*, ed. G. D. Willcock and A. Walker (1936), pp. 27, 84; E. K. Chambers, *Medieval Stage*, II (1903), p. 343; *Malone Society Collections* 7 (1965) 209; W. Watson, *Decacordon* (1602), p. 156.
8 Edward Webb, *Travailes* (1590), ed. E. Arber (1868), p. 31; A. Feuillerat, ed., *Documents Relating to the Revels at Court in the time of King Edward VI and Queen Mary* (Louvain, 1914), p. 194.
9 Feuillerat, *Revels Documents*, p. 73.

10 *Malone Society Collections* 2, ii (1923) 207; N. J. O'Conor, *Godes Peace and the Queenes* (1934), pp. 108–26.
11 Thomas Preston, *Cambises* (publ. 1569, perf. *c.* 1560), ed. J. Q. Adams, in *Chief Pre-Shakespearean Dramas* (Boston, 1924), ll. 698–9.
12 Ibid. ll. 739–45.
13 See Spivack, *Shakespeare and the Allegory of Evil*, p. 184.
14 For the relationship between fools and a 'guarded coat', see my Appendix.
15 John Redford, *Wit and Science*, Malone Society edn (1951), pp. 23–5; W. Wager, ed., *The Longer Thou Livest The More Fool Thou Art* (1568), Sig. G2.

2 Tarlton: the first 'clown'

1 A. Wettach ('Grock'), *Life's a Lark*, trans. M. Pemberton (1931), pp. 226–7.
2 The second of the three parts was entered in the Stationers' Register in 1600. The first extant edition is dated 1613.
3 *Almond for a Parrat* (1590); *Apology for Actors* (1612) – Nungezer, pp. 216, 222.
4 John Davies, *Wits Bedlam* (1617) – Nungezer, p. 362.
5 *The Famous Victories of Henry V . . . as it was played by the Queen's Majesty's players* (1598); cf. *Tarlton's Jests.*
6 Nungezer, p. 352.
7 E. K. Chambers, *The Elizabethan Stage*, IV (1923), p. 274.
8 Ibid. II, p. 88, IV, p. 286.
9 *Early English Stages*, II, 2 (1972), pp. 99–100.
10 Nungezer, pp. 348, 352. A ballad entitled 'Tarlton's jig of a horse-load of fools' is a forgery by Collier.
11 Edmund Bohun, *Character of Queen Elizabeth* (1693) – Nungezer, p. 350.
12 Wettach ('Grock'), *Life's a Lark*, p. 241.
13 Induction to *Bartholomew Fair.*
14 *Truth of our Times* (1638) – Nungezer, p. 363.
15 *Return from Parnassus* (*c.* 1599); Nashe, *Pierce Penniless* (1592); Peacham, *Thalia's Banquet* (1620) – Nungezer, pp. 357, 358, 362.
16 *Truth of our Times* – Nungezer, p. 363.
17 T. Wright, *Passions of the Mind in General* (1601); S. Rowlands, *Letting of Humour's Blood* (1600); *The Partiall Law* – Nungezer, pp. 359, 360, 362; Greene and Lodge, *Looking Glass for London*, cited by Roma Gill in 'Such conceits as clownage keeps in pay', in *The Fool and the Trickster*, ed. P. V. A. Williams (1979).
18 *Malone Society Collections* 2, iii (1931), 266–8.
19 I have also come across records of his appearance at Canterbury, (?)Dover, Gloucester, Leicester, Lydd, Lyme, New Romney, Norwich: see *Malone Society Collections* 2, ii and 7; J. T. Murray, *English*

Dramatic Companies (1910); W. Kelly, *Notices of the Drama in Leicester* (1865); and *OED* under 'jester'.

20 *Laneham's Letter*, ed. F. J. Furnivall (1907), p. 41.

21 *Songs & Ballads . . . from a manuscript in the Ashmolean Museum*, ed. Thomas Wright (1860), p. 157.

22 A. Feuillerat, ed., *Documents Relating to the Revels at Court in the time of King Edward VI and Queen Mary* (Louvain, 1914), p. 73.

23 David Wiles, *The Early Plays of Robin Hood* (1981), pp. 28, 39–42.

24 *Wit's Misery* (1596): Lodge, *Works*, IV (1883), p. 84.

25 *Calendar of State Papers, Domestic* – Nungezer, p. 351.

26 Wiles, *Early Plays of Robin Hood*, pp. 12–14.

27 W. Vaughan, *Golden Fleece* (1626); *Greene's Newes both from Heaven and Hell* (1593) – Nungezer, pp. 357, 363.

28 Thame churchwardens' accounts: Bodleian library; Northill churchwardens' accounts: *Beds. Hist. Rec. Soc.* 33 (1953) 7; N. J. O'Conor, *Godes Peace and the Queenes* (1934), p. 115; Ponet: cited in S. Billington, *A Social History of the Fool* (1984), p. 40; Mares, 'The origin of the figure called "the Vice" in Tudor drama', p. 24; Feuillerat, *Revels Documents*, p. 119.

29 *Knight of the Burning Pestle*, New Mermaids edition. Interlude iv.33, 53.

30 *The Three Ladies of London* (printed 1584); *The Three Lords and Three Ladies of London* (printed 1590). In the second play, 'Simplicity' is a ballad singer, and sells a picture of Richard Tarlton. Wilson's text gives only the title of the ballad, 'Peggy and Willy': the ballad is about Tarlton, and is printed in *Shirburn Ballads*, ed. A. Clark (1907), p. 352.

3 Kemp: a biography

1 R. J., *The Most Pleasant History of Tom-a-Lincoln, the Red-Rose Knight*, ed. R. S. M. Hirsch (Columbia, S.C., 1978). Part I was entered in the Stationers' Register in Dec. 1599.

2 E. K. Chambers, *The Elizabethan Stage*, II (1923), p. 160; William Warner, *Albion's England* (1589), p. 108.

3 *An Apology for Actors* (1612) – Chambers, *Elizabethan Stage*, IV, p. 252.

4 *Dictionary of National Biography*, under Mary Fitton; Roy Strong, *The Cult of Elizabeth* (1977), pp. 23–30; in a dedication to all the Maids of Honour, in Antony Gibson, *A Woman's Worth* (1599), Anne Russell appears first in order of precedence.

5 *Malone Society Collections* 2, iii (1931) 271.

6 R. C. Bald, 'Leicester's men in the Low Countries', *Review of English Studies* 19 (1943) 396; R. C. Strong and J. A. Van Dorsten, *Leicester's Triumph* (1964), p. 84.

There is no clear evidence that William Kemp was the 'Mr Kemp called Don Gulihelmo' resident at Dunkirk on 12 Nov. 1585: see H. S. D. Mithal, 'Mr Kemp called Don Gulielmo', *Notes & Queries* 205 (1960) 6–8.

7 Bald, 'Leicester's men'; Robert Dudley, Earl of Leicester, *Correspondence*, ed. J. Bruce (1844), p. 246.
The entry in Leicester's account book for 2 Jan. 1586 reads:
Your l. gave William Kempe the player therty shillinges the same night in your bed chamber out of the ten poundes which I gave your l. for play with Coult Moris & my l. of Essex at doble hand lodam which thertye shillinges your l. saie was in exchange of a rose noble which was geven him by Count Hollocke.

8 Sidney, *Works*, ed. A. Feuillerat, III (1923), p. 167: there can be no doubt now that Sidney's 'William my Lord of Lester jesting plaier' was Kemp (Chambers *et al.* transcribe 'Will' following an obviously incorrect reading by Bruce); Sidney, *Apology for Poetry*, ed. H. A. Needham (1931), p. 54.

9 Stowe, *Annales* (1615), p. 716; Strong, *Cult of Elizabeth*, pp. 134–46; miniaure by Hilliard reproduced in ibid., p. 68.

10 Bald, 'Leicester's men'; Leicester, *Correspondence*, p. 258.

11 Leicester, *Correspondence*, p. 260; *Shakespeare Survey* 22 (1969) 121; Alfred Cohn, *Shakespeare in Germany* (1865), p. xxxv.

12 C. R. Baskervill, *The Elizabethan Jig* (Chicago, 1929), pp. 226–7. There are no firm grounds for Baskervill's suggestion that Kemp introduced his jigs to the continent in 1585–6.

13 Nashe's dedication to *Almond for a Parrat* (1590) is fantasy. Although Arlecchino purported to be a Bergamask, no player of the part really came from Bergamo.

14 Nashe, *Strange Newes* (1592): *Works*, ed. R. B. McKerrow, I (1910), pp. 286–7.

15 This is noted in the patent of May 1593: Chambers, *Elizabethan Stage*, II, p. 123.
Kemp's name is first definitely recorded in the list of Strange's Men licensed to play in the provinces in May 1593. *A Knack to Know a Knave* was published in 1594. Shakespeare's *Titus Andronicus* is possibly a reworking of the '*Titus and Vespasia*' produced by Strange's Men in April 1591: the title page refers to Derby's (i.e. Strange's) company.

16 J. B. Leishman, ed., *The Three Parnassus Plays* (1949), p. 339.

17 The Chamberlain's company was clearly providing an element of self-parody. Glynne Wickham identifies Quince the Carpenter as the carpenter James Burbage – *Early English Stages*, II, part 2 (1972), p. 183.

18 Guilpin, *Skialetheia* (1598), Satire v.

19 *Antipodes* (1640) – ed. A. Haaker (1967), p. 40.

20 Herbert Berry, 'The Playhouse in the Boar's Head Inn, Whitechapel', *The Elizabethan Theatre* 1 (Toronto, 1969), ed. D. Galloway, pp. 45–73.

21 *Every Man Out of His Humour* IV.viii.145; Chambers, *Elizabethan Stage*, II, p. 365.

22 *The Travails of the Three English Brothers* (1607). Smith's diary confirms that the meeting was in Rome – Nungezer, p. 219. For Arlecchino, cf. T. Martinelli, *Compositions de rhetorique de Mr Don Arlequin*

(Paris, 1601); Delia Gambelli, 'Arlecchino: dalla "preistoria" a Bian-
colelli', *Biblioteca Teatrale* 1 (1971).

23 Weelkes, *Airs* (1608) – Nungezer, p. 221.
24 Nungezer, p. 219.
25 *Roxburghe Ballads*, 1 (1873), p. 78.
26 Nungezer, p. 215.
27 The troupe had visited Amsterdam, '?Redberg', Cologne and Burgstein-
furt. This must also have been the troupe that visited Groningen on 13
Oct. 1601 – *English Studies* 41 (1960) 72. For the use of 'John', see C. R.
Baskervill, *The Elizabethan Jig and Related Song Drama* (Chicago,
1929), pp. 93, 127–8. Cf. Chambers, *Elizabethan Stage*, II, p. 326.
28 Baskervill, *Elizabethan Jig*, pp. 219–20.
29 Alfred Cohn, *Shakespeare in Germany* (1865), p. cxxxiv.
30 Nungezer, pp. 37, 122, 263.
31 Chambers, *Elizabethan Stage*, IV, pp. 329–35.
32 Ibid. II, pp. 226, 230, IV, p. 335.
33 An educated guess has it that the turnover was approaching double that
of the Chamberlain's Men: L. G. Salingar, 'Les Comédiens et leur public
en Angleterre (1520–1640)', in Jean Jacquot, ed., *Dramaturgie et Société*,
II (Paris, 1968), pp. 545–6.
34 See L. B. Wright's admirable analysis of the plays of Heywood, 'the most
significant of the stage spokesmen of burgher ethics and ideals': *Middle-
class Culture in Elizabethan England* (Chapel Hill, 1935), pp. 636–51.
35 The identification seems reasonable. Though the extant text of 1606
contains Jacobean allusions, the appearance of 'Nobody' in costume in
an entertainment on 27 June 1603 suggests that the play was older – see
Jonson, *Works*, ed. Herford and Simpson (1925–52), VII, p. 128. Critics
have not hitherto pointed to a more compelling piece of evidence. Four
lances were purchased at the same time as Kemp's costume; and the
climax of the play (in the English text only) is a set-piece combat between
two pairs of knights, complete with drum and colours, alarums and
excursions – *Nobody and Somebody* (1606), sig. G4v. Earlier in the play,
the same four knights also go hunting together.
   The text of *Jemand & Niemand* was published in *Englische Comedien
und Tragedien* (1620) and is extant in manuscript. The clown Robert
Reynolds, alias Pickleherring, took the part: Nungezer, p. 295.
36 *Henslowe's Diary*, ed. R. A. Foakes and R. T. Rickert (1961), p. 215.
37 Chambers, *Elizabethan Stage*, II, p. 230.
38 *Henslowe's Diary*, ed. Foakes and Rickert, p. 196
39 Nungezer, pp. 64, 282, 287, 309, 328; L. Hotson, *Shakespeare's Motley*
(1952), pp. 109–10.

4 Kemp's jigs

1 Nashe, *Works*, ed. R. B. McKerrow, 1 (1910), p. 83; C. R. Baskervill,
The Elizabethan Jig and Related Song Drama (Chicago, 1929), pp.
354–64; David Wiles, *The Early Plays of Robin Hood* (1981), pp.
21–30.

2 *Elizabethan Jig*, p. 6.
3 Ibid. pp. 364–5.
4 Marston, *Scourge of Villainy* (1598), Satire xi.
5 John Northbrooke, *Treatise against Dicing, Dancing, Plays & Interludes* (1577).
6 See A. J. Cook, 'Bargains of incontinency', *Shakespeare Studies* 10 (1977) 271–90.
7 Guilpin, *Skialetheia*: Baskervill, *Elizabethan Jig*, p. 112.
8 *A Ballad in Praise of London 'Prentices, and what they did at the Cockpit Playhouse, Shrove Tuesday, 1617* – Charles Mackay, ed., *Songs of the London Prentices and Trades* (Percy Soc., 1841), p. 97.
9 Letter by A. Galli in *Review of English Studies* 1 (1925) 186.
10 *Fair Maid of the Inn* (1626): Baskervill, *Elizabethan Jig*, p. 115.
11 *Strange Horse Race* (1613): Baskervill, *Elizabethan Jig*, p. 112.
12 E. K. Chambers, *Elizabethan Stage*, IV (1923), p. 297.
13 Ibid. IV, pp. 340–1; on forced entries, see A. J. Cook, *Privileged Playgoers of Shakespeare's London* (Princeton, 1981), pp. 220, 242.
14 L. G. Salingar illustrates the point with an analysis of rents – 'Les Comédiens et leur public en Angleterre (1520–1640)', in Jean Jacquot, ed., *Dramaturgie et Société*, II (Paris, 1968), p. 549.
15 E. K. Chambers, *Elizabethan Stage*, II, pp. 503 ff.
16 The 'fool' in *The Wooing of Nan* carries a 'bauble' – see Baskervill, *Elizabethan Jig*, p. 436. Only the provenance of this jig – Dulwich College – certifies that it is a stage jig rather than a folk play. It may be a deliberate pastiche. The fool in the *Jig between a Paritor and a Fool* appended to *Canterbury his Change of Diet* (1641) is a royal jester, and wears a fool's cap with bells on the tip and ears. The jig seems to be a parody rather than a piece written for performance.
17 *Anatomy of Abuses*, ed. F. J. Furnivall (1877/9), p. 148.
18 Printed by Baskervill (*Elizabethan Jig*) as texts no. 25, 26, 20, 21, under the titles:
   – *Roland genandt. Ein Fewr new Liedl der der Engellendisch Tantz genandtl zugebrauchen auff allerley Instrumentenl &c. Gar kurzweilig zusingen vnd zu Dantzen: In seiner eignen Melodey.*
   – *Zwey Schone newe Liederl genanndt der Rolandtl von der Männer vnd Weyber vntrew. – Das erste. Von den Männernl &c.*
   – *A proper new ballett, intituled Rowlands god sonne, To the tune of loth to departe.*
   – *Singing Simpkin* (from R. Cox, *Actaeon and Diana*, printed c. 1656).
19 I.H., *This World's Folly* (1615): Baskervill, *Elizabethan Jig*, p. 112 n.1.
20 Baskervill, *Elizabethan Jig*, p. 112 n.1.
21 *Attowell's Jig* or *Frauncis New Jigge, betweene Frauncis a Gentleman, and Richard a Farmer* (registered 1595): Baskervill text no. 22; untitled jig: *Malone Society Collections* 9 (1977) 24–9; *Das ander Engeländisch Possenspiel von Pückelherings Dill dill dill . . . Gantz lustig mit fünff Personen zu agirn*: Baskervill text no. 28; *The Black Man* (from Kirkman *Wits* (1673)): Baskervill text no. 23; *Fool's Fortune* in Star Chamber Records: C. J. Sisson, *Lost Plays of Shakespeare's Age* (1936).

22 Nungezer, pp. 281–2; cf. Chapter 3 above.
23 *Il teatro delle favole rappresentative* (Venice, 1611) – translated as *Scenarios of the Commedia dell'Arte*, trans. and ed. by H. F. Salerno (New York, 1967). Scala was a leading actor-director during the Shakespearean period, and his collection reflects the work of the leading professional companies.
24 William A. Ringler, 'The number of actors in Shakespeare's early plays', in G. E. Bentley, ed., *The Seventeenth-Century Stage* (Chicago, 1968), pp. 110–34.
25 *Henslowe Papers*, ed. W. W. Greg (1907).
26 The latter argument is set out in the Revels edition of *Antonio's Revenge*, ed. W. R. Gair (1978), pp. 15–16; Harold Jenkins sets out the counter view in the New Arden edition of *Hamlet* (1982).
27 For the wearing of feathers, see for example the title-plate to Kemp's *Nine Days' Wonder* (Fig. 3); Wiles, *Early Plays of Robin Hood*, p. 15; *Old Meg of Herefordshire* (1609). For feathers as a fool's emblem, see L. Hotson, *Shakespeare's Motley* (1952), p. 5 n.1 – citing Greene's *Friar Bacon and Friar Bungay*. A peacock's feather might also adorn a fool's cap – see Hotson, p. 78 n.1.
28 For this reading of 'pajock', see Harold Jenkins's note *ad loc.* in the New Arden edition (1982).
29 Nungezer, pp. 351, 354.

5 'The clown' in playhouse terminology

1 T. W. Baldwin, *The Organization and Personnel of the Shakespearean Company* (Princeton, 1927), p. 244.
2 Herford and Simpson, *Ben Jonson*, IX (1950), p. 280 cite Holinshed's *Chronicles* (1577). The Latin etymology gives rise to an extended pun upon *colonus* as 'farmer'/'colonist' in Jonson's *Tale of a Tub* I.iii.31–46.
3 John Northbrooke, *Treatise against Dicing, Dancing, Plays & Interludes*, in Shakespeare Society, *Early Treatises on the Stage* (1843), p. xvi.
4 *Apology for Poetry*, ed. H. A. Needham (1931), pp. 54–5; Frances A. Yates, *Astraea* (1975), pp. 88–98; Nungezer, p. 352; and see p. xii.
5 Sigs. I2v., K4v.
6 A comprehensive check-list is provided in Thomas L. Berger and William C. Bradford, *An Index of Characters in English Printed Drama to the Restoration* (Englewood, Colorado, 1975). Chapman terms a wealthy agelast 'an old clown' in *May Day* (performed *c.* 1609) – but this figure is not *the* clown, and the word appears only once. In Armin's *Two Maids of More-clacke* (published 1609), the direction 'Enter Tutch the clowne' indicates that this was a part written in the first instance to be played by the author – sig. A2v.
7 Edited by J. C. Bulman and J. M. Nosworthy for the Malone Society (1980).
8 *Works*, ed. Herford and Simpson (1925–52), III, p. 108.
9 C. J. Sisson, *Lost Plays of Shakespeare's Age* (1936), p. 144.
10 *Gull's Hornbook* (1609): Nungezer, p. 328.

11 *Taylor's Feast* (1638): Nungezer, p. 328.
12 W. Haughton, *Englishmen for my Money* (1616); A. Munday (with Chettle), *Downfall of Robert, Earl of Huntingdon* (1601).
13 *Henslowe's Diary*, ed. R. A. Foakes and R. T. Rickert (1961), p. 318.
14 *Fool upon Fool* (1600), sig. D4v; *Quips upon Questions* (1600), sigs. A1, E1.
15 Cooke, *Greene's 'Tu Quoque'* (1614), sig. G2v.
16 Nungezer, p. 298: Part One of Heywood's play attributes the part of Clem to Robins, Part Two lists 'Clem the clown'; in Shirley's *Wedding* (1629), Rawbone opens the epilogue with the words 'Gentlemen, pray be favourable to wake a fool dormant amongst ye.'
17 Nungezer, pp. 83–4.
18 Edited by W. W. Greg and H. Jenkins for the Malone Society (1961). Scott McMillin, 'The Book of Sir Thomas More: a theatrical view', *Modern Philology* 68 (1970–1) 10–24, notes on p. 14 that the role of the clown was written into the manuscript for the benefit of a specific actor.
19 *The Escape of Jupiter* (c. 1622) – ed. Malone Society (1978); *The Captives* (1624) – ed. Malone Society (1953).
20 *Catiline* (1611): dedication.
21 David Bevington, *From Mankind To Marlowe* (Harvard, 1962), pp. 265–73.
22 Jonson, *Works*, ed. Herford and Simpson, III, p. 108; *Taming of A Shrew* (1584), induction; G. E. Bentley, *The Seventeenth-Century Stage* (Chicago, 1968), pp. 32–3.
23 E. K. Chambers, *Elizabethan Stage*, II (1923), p. 421; Turner, *Dish of Lenten Stuff* (c. 1615): Nungezer, p. 319.
24 *The Actors' Remonstrance* (1643).
25 *Henslowe's Diary*, ed. Foakes and Rickert, p. 318.
26 *King Lear* I.iv.95–108; cf. my appendix.
27 An example from Derby's Men's repertoire is *Trial of Chivalry* (published 1605). In the period before 1594, it is rarely possible to allocate specific plays to specific companies.
28 Ed. Malone Society (1923), l. 377.
29 'The Clownes all Exit.' – III.i.105; 'Exit Clow.' – v.i.205.
30 R. Greene, *Orlando Furioso*, ed. Malone Society (1907), ll. 897, 1028.
31 *Every Man Out of His Humour*, 'The Characters of the Persons'; *Every Man In His Humour*, II.iii.13, IV.ii.1.
32 S. Rowlands, *Works*, ed. Edmund Gosse (1880), I, p. 63. The book had appeared by 1 June 1599, when it was burnt by the Bishop of London – see Rowlands, *Uncollected Poems*, ed. F. O. Waage (Gainesville, Florida, 1970), p. xi. Rowlands probably alludes in this passage to a lost play from the Chamberlain's repertoire: *Cloth Breeches and Velvet Hose* (Stationers' Register: 1600).

6 The roles of Kemp 'the clown'

1 *Two Gentlemen of Verona* (1969), pp. xxi–xxxv.

2 See below, p. 100; see also Robert Weimann, 'Society and the individual in Shakespeare's conception of character', *Shakespeare Survey* 34 (1981) 23–32.

3 E.g. most recently by A. R. Humphreys in the New Arden edition (1981), p. 79.

4 B. Maxwell, *Studies in the Shakespeare Apocrypha* (New York, 1956), pp. 72–108. The early date is given in F. E. Schelling, *Elizabethan Drama*, I (1908), p. 286; it is acccepted in L. B. Wright, *Middle-Class Culture in Elizabethan England* (Chapel Hill, 1935), p. 624; the later date is suggested in Irving Ribner, *The English History Play* (Princeton, 1957), p. 205, and is accepted in A. Harbage and S. Schoenbaum, *Annals of English Drama 975–1700* (1964).

5 For the play's influence, see the edition by A. E. H. Swaen (Louvain, 1912), p. xlii; also C. R. Baskervill, 'Source and analogues of *How a Man May Choose a Good Wife from a Bad*', *PMLA* 24 (1909) 511–30.

6 See my discussion of *Romeo and Juliet* below, pp. 83–94). Pipkin is also given a list of names to invite to the feast. At the feast, he schemes to obtain tit-bits.

7 In Shakespeare, the word 'humour' (and its compounds) appears only ten times after the end of the reign: compare thirteen times in *Henry V* and twenty-six times in *Merry Wives*.

8 Essex's intrusion into the royal bedchamber upon his return from Ireland is reflected in the King's decision to deprive the Marshal of the key to the royal bedchamber. Essex was Master of the Queen's Horse, and the Marshal sacrifices his horse so that the King's can be shod. There is an allusion to Elizabeth/Cynthia when the Marshal claims it is impossible that 'the lustre of a petty star / Should with the moon compare'. Essex's role as the Queen's supposed lover is reflected in the Marshal's unwillingness to marry the princess because this would give him 'a mistress, not a wife'.

9 *Pace* A. M. Clark, *Thomas Heywood* (1931), p. 30, I find no evidence that the state of the text is proof of revision. A careless printer must be responsible for the dramatis personae.

10 It has been argued that the reporter was commissioned by the actors: W. L. Halstead, 'A note on the text of *The Famous History of Sir Thomas Wyatt*', *Modern Language Notes* 54 (1939) 585–9; for the conventional view, see Dekker, *Dramatic Works*, ed. F. Bowers (1953–61), I, pp. 399–404; and Ribner, *The English History Play*, pp. 215–18.

11 'Playwrights at work: Henslowe's, not Shakespeare's, *Book of Sir Thomas More*', *English Literary Renaissance* 10 (1980) 439–79.

12 *Sir Thomas More* is linked to *Thomas Lord Cromwell* in source and subject matter. I allocate the first draft of both to the mid 1590s.

13 Chillington, 'Playwrights at work', pp. 471–2.

14 Revels edition, ed. R. W. Van Fossen (1961), pp. lxiv–lxix.

15 Ibid. scene iv. line 106.

7 The genesis of the text

1 See P. W. K. Stone's discussion of the genesis of the *Lear* Quarto in *The Textual History of King Lear* (1980), p. 35. Stone's theory is not generally accepted: Stanley Wells summarizes current views in *The Division of the Kingdoms: Shakespeare's Two Versions of KING LEAR*, ed. G. Taylor and M. Warren (1983), pp. 12–13.
2 New Arden edition, ed. B. Gibbons, p. 1.
3 New Arden edition (1930), p. 27. G. Blakemore Evans in the *New Cambridge Shakespeare* edition (1984), pp. 1–6, advocates May 1596 on the basis of a recent study of Nashe's influence upon the writing.
4 G. Melchiori, 'Peter, Balthasar, and Shakespeare's art of doubling', *Modern Language Review* 78 (1983) 777–92.
5 See the note to I.ii.39 in the New Arden edition.
6 On the title-page of Q1, the play is said to have been 'often (with great applause) plaid publiquely, by the right Honourable the L. of *Hunsdon* his Seruants'.
7 *Old Fortunatus* (1599) I.i.329 – *Dramatic Works*, ed. F. Bowers (1953).
8 *The New Shakespeare* edition, ed. J. Dover Wilson and G. I. Duthie (1955), p. 209; 'Shakespeare's art of doubling', p. 782; see below, p. 164.
9 H. Granville Barker, *Prefaces to Shakespeare*, IV (1963), p. 64 – originally published in 1930; New Penguin edition (1967), p. 266.
10 New Arden edition (1980), pp. 14, 283–4.
11 Melchiori, 'Shakespeare's art of doubling', p. 788, proposes Benvolio as the obvious double for Balthasar.
12 Ibid. p. 784.
13 New Arden edition (1980), pp. 15–16.
14 *Romeus and Juliet*, l. 2697: G. Bullough, ed., *Narrative and Dramatic Sources of Shakespeare*, I (1957).
15 I.iii.80. References to *Every Man In His Humour* are to the Quarto version in the Regents parallel text edition, ed. J. W. Lever (1972).
16 See Robert Weimann, 'Laughing with the audience: 'The Two Gentlemen of Verona' and the popular tradition of comedy', *Shakespeare Survey* 22 (1971) 35–4.
17 *Discoveries* (1641), pp. 128–9.
18 See Jonas A. Barish, *Ben Jonson and the Language of Prose Comedy* (Cambridge, Mass., 1960), p. 132.

8 The conventions governing Kemp's scripted roles

1 See Elizabeth Burns, *Theatricality – a study of Convention in the Theatre and in Social Life* (1972), p. 110. I draw upon Burns's broad argument that theatrical conventions 'authenticate' social conventions.
2 *Every Man In His Humour* III.v.34.
3 I draw in this paragraph upon the argument of Jiří Veltruský in 'Basic features of dramatic dialogue' and 'Dramatic text as a component of

theatre', *Semiotics of Art: The Prague School Contribution*, ed. L. Matejka and I. R. Titunik (Cambridge, Mass., and London, 1976).

4 *Shakespeare and the Popular Tradition in the Theater* (Baltimore and London, 1978), p. 213.

5 Ibid. pp. 225–8, citing *Timon of Athens* I.ii, *Troilus and Cressida* v.ii.

6 Raymond Williams has some useful notes on modes of address in Elizabethan drama in *Writing in Society* (1984), pp. 31–64.

7 *The Merchant of Venice* II.ii.46.

8 *Two Gentlemen of Verona* II.iii.13; C. R. Baskervill, *Elizabethan Jig* (Chicago, 1929), p. 449; *Every Man In His Humour*, I.iii.57; *Woman Killed With Kindness* (Revels edition) IV.106.

9 *Macbeth* II.iii.9; *Measure for Measure* IV.iii.12.

10 Original dates of publication and editions cited as follows: William Haughton, *Englishmen for my Money* (1616), Stationers' Reg. Aug. 1601 – in *A Select Collection of Old English Plays*, ed. R. Dodsley and W. C. Hazlitt (1874–6), x; Thomas Heywood, *The Four Prentices of London* (1615); Henry Chettle and John Day, *The Blind Beggar of Bednall Green* (1659); Anthony Munday, *The Downfall of Robert, Earl of Huntingdon* (1600) and *The Death of Robert, Earl of Huntingdon* (1600) – in Dodsley and Hazlitt, VIII; *I Tamar Cam*, in *Henslowe Papers*, ed. W. W. Greg (1907); George Chapman, *The Blind Beggar of Alexandria* (1598); Thomas Dekker, *Old Fortunatus* (1600) – in Dekker, *Dramatic Works*, ed. F. Bowers (1953), I; Thomas Dekker, *The Shoemaker's Holiday* (1600) – in *Dramatic Works*, I; Thomas Dekker, Henry Chettle and William Haughton, *Patient Grissel* (1603) Stationers' Reg. March 1600 – in Dekker, *Dramatic Works*, I.

I have excluded *Sir John Oldcastle*, *An Humorous Day's Mirth*, and *Two Angry Women of Abingdon* from this list because in each of these it is not clear which of two roles belongs to the clown.

11 See my discussion of the passage at the end of Chapter 5.

12 Nungezer, p. 328.

13 *Downfall*, ed. Dodsley and Hazlitt, p. 153; *Bednall Green*, Sig. E2v; *Fortunatus* IV.ii.10.

14 *Thomas Lord Cromwell*, Sig. D.

15 *Four Prentices*, Sigs. D4, H2v, H3; *Englishmen*, p. 513; *Fortunatus* II.ii.328; *Downfall*, pp. 192, 200; *Bednall Green*, Sigs. G4, E2; *Shoemaker's Holiday* III.ii.3, 14, v.iv.55.

16 *How a Man May Choose a Good Wife from a Bad* – Dodsley and Hazlitt, IX, p. 57.

17 *Every Man In His Humour* III.iii.12.

18 *Woman Killed with Kindness*, Revels edition xii.30.

19 *Much Ado About Nothing* III.v.38–40; *How a Man May Choose*, ed. Dodsley and Hazlitt, p. 43; *Love's Labour's Lost*, v.i.124, I.i.240–6.

20 E.g. *Fortunatus* I.ii.18–19.

21 Nungezer, p. 327.

22 *Englishmen for my Money*, ed. Dodsley and Hazlitt, p. 504.

23 *Thomas Lord Cromwell* (1602), Sigs. B3v–B4.

24 See my discussion in Chapter 3.

25 Bernstein, *Class, Codes and Control* (1973), p. 94.
26 *Shakespeare's Festive Comedy* (Princeton, 1959); Northrop Frye, *Anatomy of Criticism* (Princeton, 1957), 'The argument of comedy', in *Shakespeare: Modern Essays in Criticism*, ed. L. F. Dean (New York, 1967), 'Old and New Comedy', in *Shakespeare Survey* 22 (1971); Neil Rhodes, *Elizabethan Grotesque* (1980).
27 *An Almond for a Parrat* (1590).
28 *Two Gentlemen of Verona* II.v.23. Cf. II.iii.19.
   Launce confirms the Cambridge students' charge that 'to lay thy leg over a staff' was part of the clown's stock in trade: *Three Parnassus Plays*, ed. J. B. Leishman (1949), p. 129.
   For the staff as sign of office carried by the Lord of Misrule, see for example Beaumont, *Knight of the Burning Pestle*, New Mermaids edition (1969) Int.iv.33; and the Cambridge ceremony of 1638 cited in S. Billington, *A Social History of the Fool* (1984), p. 41. See my appendix for reference to the Muncaster portrait of Tom Skelton, where the legend on the painting lists the fool's many burlesque offices, and for a record of a domestic fool with 'a painted cane'.
29 Eric Partridge, *Shakespeare's Bawdy* (1955), pp. 88, 138, 70, 113; Pego is given as 'penis' in Grose, *Dictionary of the Vulgar Tongue* (1796).
30 *Midsummer Night's Dream* IV.i.3, IV.i.51. Compare the rose garland worn by the potter in *The Play of Robin Hood, Very Proper to be Played in May Games* (1562).
31 *Thomas Lord Cromwell* (1602), Sig. EV, II.iii.87.
32 *Much Ado About Nothing* IV.ii.
33 *The Royal King and the Loyal Subject*, in *Dramatic Works*, ed. R. H. Shepherd (1874), pp. 58, 70.
34 *Sir Thomas Wyatt* II.iii, in Dekker, *Dramatic Works*, I.
35 See William A. Ringler, Jr, 'The number of actors in Shakespeare's early plays', in *The Seventeenth-Century Stage*, ed. G. E. Bentley (Chicago, 1968), p. 133.
36 *The Royal King and the Loyal Subject*, ed. Shepherd, p. 70.
37 Henry Porter, *The Two Angry Women of Abingdon*, publ. 1599 and performed by 1598, in Dodsley and Hazlitt, VII, p. 360.
38 Berry, *Shakespeare's Comic Rites* (1984), p. 137.

9 Falstaff

1 Dover Wilson, *The Fortunes of Falstaff* (1943), pp. 124–5.
2 Leslie Hotson's suggestion is accepted in William Green, *Shakespeare's Merry Wives of Windsor* (Princeton, 1962) *passim*; in the New Arden edition of *Merry Wives*, ed. H. J. Oliver (1971), p. xlv ff.; in the New Arden 2 *Henry IV*, ed. A. R. Humphreys (1966), p. xvii; in the Oxford edition of *Henry V*, ed. G. Taylor (1982), p. 66; in the New Penguin 2 *Henry IV*, ed. P. H. Davison (1977), p. 14. G. R. Hibbard in the New Penguin *Merry Wives* (1973), p. 50, holds out for a date of *c.* 1600, but concedes the existence of a source text of 1597.
3 New Arden edition, p. xxvii; New Penguin edition, p. 213.

4 The suggestion that Kemp was the pirate was first made by H. D. Gray in 'The roles of William Kemp', *Modern Language Review* 25 (1930) 261–73. The New Arden editor (p. xxvii n. 2) suggests an understudy, but I know of no evidence for a system of understudying. The player of the Host – Duke or Beeston, I presume – must have stayed to play Nym or Pistol in *Henry V*, since some of their dialogue creeps into the *Merry Wives* Quarto.

5 Note to the Cambridge edition (1953), p. 157.

6 Cf. J. A. Bryant, 'Shakespeare's Falstaff and the mantle of Dick Tarlton', *Studies in Philology* 51 (1954) 149–62.

7 On the stage history, see A. C. Sprague, *Shakespeare and the Actors* (Cambridge, Mass., 1944), p. 90.

8 See the servant illustrated on Hogenburg's map (1572).

9 See the induction to *Bartholomew Fair*, l. 14; also references collected in Joseph Strutt, *Sports and Pastimes of the People of England* (1838), pp. 261–2, and in the New Arden edition of *Henry IV Part One*, note to I.iii.227.

10 The London Museum has a sixteenth-century example from Finsbury: see M. R. Holmes, *Arms and Armour in Tudor and Stuart London* (1970), pp. 3, 9, 20.

11 *Survey of London* (1603), p. 96; *Sir Thomas More*, ed. Malone Society (1961), l. 468.

12 Cited in the *OED* under 'waster'. The *OED* also cites other synonyms: 'staff or waster' (1533), 'a sword or any other waster' (1561), 'wasters or truncheons' (1570).

13 For Launcelet see *Merchant of Venice* II.ii.65; cf. Chapter 8 n.28 above.

14 *Mundus et Infans*, ll. 539, 633, in *Three Late Medieval Morality Plays*, ed. G. A. Lester (1981).

15 Jonson, *The Devil is an Ass* I.i.85, *Staple of News*, 2nd Int., pp. 11–13; *Twelfth Night* IV.iii.128; *Henry V* IV.iv.74; Fulwell, *Like Will To Like* (1587), Sig. E2v.

16 Cf. James Black, '*Henry IV*: a world of figures here', in *Shakespeare: the Theatrical Dimension*, ed. P. C. McGuire and D. A. Samuelson (New York, 1979), pp. 165–83.

17 I am grateful to Michael Smith for this observation.

18 As did Charles Kemble in 1829: see A. C. Sprague, *Shakespeare's Histories: Plays for the Stage* (1964), p. 71.

19 *Henry V* IV.vii.127. Cf. Philip Stubbes's classic account of 'these doublets with great bellies, hanging down beneath their pudenda, and stuffed with four, five, six pound of bombast at the least' – *Anatomy of Abuses*, cited in C. W. and P. Cunnington, *Handbook of English Costume in the Sixteenth Century* (1970), p. 90.

20 *Tudor Royal Proclamations*, ed. P. H. Hughes and J. F. Larkin (New Haven, 1969), no. 726.

21 M. C. Linthicum, *Costume in the Drama of Shakespeare and his Contemporaries* (1936), pp. 227, 225.

22 I.ii.5, 31; II.iv.223, 446; I.ii.132; II.iv.108; V.iv.58.

23 *Jacke-a-Lent*, in *Works* (1630), p. 114.

24 La guerra di Carnevale e di Quaresima (1554), in *Il teatro italiano*, I, part i; *Dalle origini al Quattrocento*, ed. E. Faccioli (Turin, 1975), pp. 271–90. I am grateful to Professor Michael Anderson for giving me a copy of his unpublished translation, and for drawing my attention to a description of Carnival as a stout, round and red-faced man doing battle with Lent in Bologna, Shrove-tide 1506: Faccioli, *Dalle origini*, I, part ii, pp. 708–9.

On Brueghel's painting, see the discussion by C. Gaignebet, 'Sur un tableau de Brueghel', *Annales: Économies, Sociétés, Civilisations* 27 (1972) 313–45.

25 J. R. Planché remembered the effect as 'more painful than amusing': *Recollections and Reflections*, in G. Salgādo, ed., *Eyewitnesses of Shakespeare* (1975), p. 180.

26 *Every Man In His Humour* (Folio text) Prologue, ll. 9–11.

27 v.iv.95 and cf. III.ii.142, v.iv.72. For the staging see H. Hartman, 'Prince Hal's "shew of zeale" ', *PMLA* 46 (1931) 720–3.

28 'The Prince's dog', in *King Henry IV: Casebook*, ed. G. K. Hunter (1970), p. 195.

29 'Notes on Comedy', in *Comedy: Meaning and Form*, ed. R. Corrigan (New York, 1965), p. 190; *Some Shakespearean Themes* (1966), p. 47.

30 *The Fortunes of Falstaff* (1943), p. 122.

31 New Penguin edition, p. 34.

32 Ibid. p. 32.

33 Note to 2.III.ii.24.

34 Falstaff poses as jig-maker when he threatens to have 'ballads made on you all, and sung to filthy tunes': 1.II.ii.43 – and cf. 2.IV.iii.47. Like Kemp on his way to Norwich, Falstaff challenges competitors to 'caper with me' – 2.I.ii.192. He evokes the dancer's drum at 1.III.iii.205.

35 Macilente concludes the epilogue to *Every Man Out of His Humour* (in the public theatre version) by inviting the audience to 'make lean Macilente as fat as sir John Falstaff'. I construe this as an apology for a vanished Falstaff, a Falstaff who might have been expected to perform an epilogue. For Falstaff as epilogue, see Martin Holmes, *Shakespeare and His Players* (1972), p. 47.

36 Note to 2.I.ii.116; for a more helpful approach, see Caroline Spurgeon, *Shakespeare's Imagery* (1965), pp. 377–80.

37 Vickers, *The Artistry of Shakespeare's Prose* (1968), p. 129.

38 See H. J. Oliver's discussion in the New Arden *Merry Wives* (1971), pp. liv–lv.

39 The 'Hostess' is termed 'mistris quickly' by the Prince at III.iii.90 in the Quarto. If this were conceived as an orthodox proper name, the initial letter would surely be in upper case.

Falstaff's companions are 'Haruey, Rossill, and Gadshill' at *1 Henry IV* I.ii.182. The Folio text of *2 Henry IV* substitutes 'Bardolfe' for 'sir Iohn Russel' in the stage direction at the head of II.ii. See the New Arden *2 Henry IV*, p. xv.

40 See J. L. Hinely, 'Comic scapegoats and the Falstaff of *The Merry Wives of Windsor*', *Shakespeare Studies* 15 (1982) 37–54.

41 *Merry Wives* New Arden edition, p. liii.
42 *Henslowe's Diary*, ed. R. A. Foakes and R. T. Rickert (1961), p. 214.

10 Robert Armin

1 Facts and references are gathered in Nungezer, pp. 15–20.
2 Nashe, *Works*, ed. R. B. McKerrow (1904–10), I, p. 280; G. Harvey, *Pierce's Supererogation* (1593): Nungezer, p. 17. Armin's anti-Martinist views are evidenced in his dedicatory epistle to *A Brief Resolution of a Right Religion*, by C. S. (1590).
3 Sigs. H2v; A2v.
4 Armin's dedicatory epistle to G. Dugdale, *A True Discourse of the Practices of Elizabeth Caldwell* (1604), certifies that he was in the service of William Brydges, who became Lord Chandos in 1594. This confirms the evidence of *Fool upon Fool*.
5 J. T. Murray, *English Dramatic Companies*, II (1910), p. 32; *Malone Society Collections* 2, part 3 (1931), pp. 274–5.
6 *Wag.*   Vilaine, call me Maister *Wagner*, and let thy left eye be diametarily fixt upon my right heele, with *quasi vestigias nostras insistere.*

  Clo.   God forgive me, he speaks Dutch fustian . . .
                (*Doctor Faustus*: 'A' Text (1604), in
                Marlowe, *Works*, ed. F. Bowers, II (1981),
                p. 231)

  Tutch. You must have your left eie Diamiter wise,
         Fixt on my right heele, and all the offices,
         A servant owes in dutie to his Master, performe
         As naturally as if the fortie shilling time
         Were come, lest I leave talking welch, and crack your pate
         in English.   (*Two Maids of More-clacke* (1609) Sig. F)

The 'B' text of *Faustus* has the *right* eye fixed on the *left* heel.

7 E. K. Chambers, *The Elizabethan Stage*, IV (1923), pp. 330–1.
8 *Tarlton's Jests* (1611), Sig. C2v: the book was registered in August 1600.
9 *Tarlton's Jests* (1611), Sig. C2v:

In Armin's version, the quip runs:

            A wonder how, me thinkes it is unfit,
            To see an Iron Gridiron turne a Spit.
            No, no, mee thinks it is more unfit,
            To see a blockhead asse have any wit.   (Sig. B2)

In the Tarlton version, a gallant offers:

            Me thinkes it is a thing unfit
            To see a Gridiron turne the spit.

And Tarlton quips:

            Me thinkes it is a thing unfit,
            To see an Asse have any wit.   (Sig. C4)

For the continuation of the tradition of flinging themes in the early seventeenth century, see J. Taylor, *Fennor's Defence*, cited in Nungezer, pp. 223–4, and P. Davison, *Popular Appeal in English Drama to 1850* (1982), pp. 39–40.

10 Armin pictures himself:

> Writing these Embles on an idle time,
> Within my windowe where my house doth stand
> Looking about, and studying for a Rime . . .   (Sig. c)

11 The name 'Pinck' occurs in Armin's dedication to Lady Mary Chandos which prefaces Dugdale, *A True Discourse of the Practices of Elizabeth Caldwell* (1604). 'Pinked' fabric is fabric with tiny ornamental holes.

12 Leslie Hotson, *Shakespeare's Motley* (New York, 1952), p. 77.

13 Ibid. p. 15; C. S. Felver, *Robert Armin, Shakespeare's Fool* (Kent, Ohio, 1961), p. 101.

14 The Elizabethan references are listed in J. P. Feather's introduction in the Johnson Reprint Corporation edition of the *Collected Works* (New York and London, 1972). Liddie in the Garland edition of *Two Maids* (New York and London, 1979), p. 16, raises the possibility that these may be intended to give period flavour: but the references are not pointed enough for this explanation to be credible.

15 Chambers *The Elizabethan Stage*, III, p. 210; Felver, *Robert Armin, Shakespeare's Fool*, p. 73; J. P. Feather, 'Robert Armin and the Chamberlain's Men', *Notes & Queries* 217 (1972) 448–50. Liddie in the Garland edition does not dissent.

16 Leslie Hotson discovered the will: see *Shakespeare's Motley*, pp. 108–9.

17 I accept the attribution made by Muriel Bradbrook in *Shakespeare the Craftsman* (1969), pp. 71–2, and by J. P. Feather in the Johnson Reprint Corporation edition of Armin's *Collected Works*. *Pace* the objections of H. F. Lippincott in *The Library* 30 (1975) 330–3, I note that no other 'R.A.' (Robert Allott, Robert Anton) is known to have written for the theatre. This is a play for the public playhouse, requiring a Clown, musicians, a descent from the heavens, a trap-door in the stage, two doors and a curtained discovery space, a passing over the stage. Robert Armin was armigerous by 1615 (Hotson, *Shakespeare's Motley*, p. 110), so could claim to be 'Gent.' The literary and historicist aspirations of the text explain the linguistic differences. D. J. Lake in *Notes and Queries* 222 (1977) argues that the prevalence of 'whilst' (for 'while') and absence of 'ye' (for 'you') betokens a different author. An analysis of the language which Armin wrote for himself to deliver in the theatre would yield very different results. Here is a specimen of Armin/Morion's elliptical and logic-defying prose – a description of masquers and harpists arriving:

> Oh, my Lord, my father is comming to your Grace, with such a many of Damsons and shee shittle-cockes: They smell of nothing in the world but Rozin and Coblers waxe; such a many lights in their heeles, & lungs in their hands, above all cry, yfaith.   (Sig. c2v.)

18 Armin is one 'who hath been writ downe for an Asse in his time, & pleades . . . not-withstanding his Constableship . . .'; *The Italian Tailor and his Boy* (1609), Sig. A3.

19 *Scourge of Folly:* Nungezer, p. 20.

20 See Marston, *The Malcontent*, Revels edition, ed. G. K. Hunter (1975), p. xlix. The Passarello additions are usually attributed to Webster.

21 Garland edition, xi.109.

22 For a discussion of Armin and Stone, see Guy Butler, 'Shakespeare and the two jesters', *Hebrew University Studies in Literature and the Arts* 11 (1983) 161–204. Butler cites a reference to Stone's 'So great a head' from John Cooke, *Epigrammes* (1604). Cf. *Twelfth Night* I.v.83; also *Volpone* II.i.65. Butler (p. 191) points out that Tutch's ballad in *Two Maids* has the refrain 'O stone, stone ne ra, stone ne ra, stone' and reads this as an allusion to John Stone.

23 See Jonson, *Works*, ed. Herford and Simpson (1925–52), IX, pp. 405–6, where Aubrey is cited. Dekker certifies the pun in his *News from Gravesend* (1604) when he cites as tavern fools 'meere Stones, and Chesters, Fooles, Fooles and Jesters' – *Dekker's Plague Pamphlets*, ed. Wilson (1925), p. 68 – cited by Butler, 'Shakespeare and the two jesters', p. 193. Cooke's epigram (see above, n.22) refers to Stone as a 'jester' – and we must avoid being confused by our modern usage which takes a 'jester' to be a 'court jester'.

24 Cf. Neil Rhodes's valuable discussion of Carlo's role in *Elizabethan Grotesque* (1980), p. 138.

25 *Every Man Out of His Humour* V.v.40; *Troilus and Cressida* V.i.v. I cite the New Arden's reading. Q and F read 'Thou crusty batch of nature', which may be a metaphor from baking. The point is the same: a 'batch' would be a composite with no individual shape.

26 *Nest of Ninnies* (1608), Sig. G.

27 *Character of the persons*; II.iii.103, V.vi.53.

28 I.iv.109. Cf. also *The Malcontent* III.i.145–9, where Passarello compares himself to a dog.

29 Butler, 'Shakespeare and the two jesters', p. 183, also reads Armin's phrase 'this poore Petite of transformation' in the dedicatory epistle to *The Italian Tailor and his Boy* as a punning reference to Armin's stature.

30 *Every Man Out of His Humour* I.ii.223–6; *Scourge of Folly* (1610): Nungezer, p. 20; *Troilus and Cressida* V.i.65.

31 *Twelfth Night* IV.ii.61; *All's Well That Ends Well* IV.v.47.

32 Enid Welsford, *The Fool* (1935), pp. 56–60.

33 *Magnificence*, ed. P. Neuss (1980), l. 523: 'So large a man and so little of stature'. This cannot be a boy because the actor is bearded – l. 355. For a parallel of *c.* 1505, see Hawes's description of a dwarf fool in a pied coat in *Pastime of Pleasure*, cited in Welsford, p. 123.

34 P. L. Duchartre, *The Italian Comedy* (New York, 1966), pp. 218, 138. The plates are of the seventeenth and eighteenth centuries, respectively.

35 C. C. Stopes, *Shakespeare's Environment* (1914), pp. 272–5; cf. Welsford, *The Fool*, pp. 148, 136.

36 Whitney appended his own or translated verses to older woodcuts. The cut of the fool in motley is taken from Sambucus, *Emblemata* (Antwerp, 1566).

37 *Every Man Out of His Humour, Character of the persons; Volpone* III.iii.13.

38 *All's Well That Ends Well* II.ii; *As You Like It* V.iv.

39 *A Fair Maid of Bristow* (1605), Sig. B4v.

40 George Wilkins, *Miseries of Enforced Marriage* (1607), in *Old Plays* (1874), ed. Dodsley and Hazlitt, IX, pp. 471, 497.

41 See my discussion of *Merry Wives* at the end of Chapter 9. I therefore propose 'Pistol' as pirate along with Kemp.

42 II.i.40, 40, 45, 73, 29; cf. 'dogs' at III.ii.21.

43 The Oxford edition, ed. Gary Taylor (1982), p. 63.

44 *Julius Caesar* I.iii.15ff.

45 I.iii.19; II.i.106–11 – for the architectural relevance, see John Orrell, 'Sunlight at the Globe', *Theatre Notebook* 38 (1984) 69–76.

46 *Coriolanus* I.i.88; II.i.42ff.

47 *Coriolanus* II.i.104; II.i.68; IV.vi.132. We know too little about the costume conventions for Roman plays. Dekker implies that the cap was a mark of low status when he refers to the tradition that Roman freedmen were called 'to the cap': M. C. Linthicum, *Costume in the Drama of Shakespeare and his Contemporaries* (1936), p. 217. Enobarbus's cap probably marks him as a common soldier – like Fluellen, Williams and Pistol. Timon's senatorial friends wear cap and gown: III.vi.104–12. This probably establishes them as citizens. 'Flat caps as proper are to City Gowns' writes Dekker, as to 'Kings their Crowns': Linthicum, *Costume*, p. 225.

48 *Cymbeline* I.i.26; II.i.26, 13; II.i.46.

49 See my appendix on 'Armin's motley'.

50 I.i.200; I.i.269; II.ii.54; II.ii.89.

51 IV.iii.253; IV.iii.276; IV.iii.368 – with further 'dog' references at IV.iii.202, 358; IV.iii.359.

52 III.ii.122; for Trinculo's costume, see II.ii.62; III.ii.30; IV.i.224, 230 and V.i.297.

53 New Arden edition, ed. J. H. P. Pafford (1966), pp. xviii–xix. Crane was also responsible for the description of Launce and Speed as 'clownish fools'.

54. IV.iii.88. As an instance of the fool's customary whipping, Butler, 'Shakespeare and the two jesters', cites the whipping of John Stone at Bridewell in 1605 for insulting the Lord Admiral.

55 New Arden edition, p. xxii.

56 IV.iv.750; IV.iii.103; V.ii.164ff.

57 *The London Prodigal*, ed. C. F. T. Brooke in *The Shakespeare Apocrypha* (1918). II.i.134–7; V.i.174.

58 *The Malcontent* I.viii.22.

59 The extant music is printed and discussed in the New Arden edition of *Cymbeline*, ed. J. M. Nosworthy (1969), pp. 212–13. Armin in *Nest of Ninnies* writes in the dedicatory epistle: 'I may live to make you amends

if not no more but this, such a one died in your debt, and thats a Countertenor many a one sings.'

Armin's best-known song, 'When that I was and a little tiny boy' (*Twelfth Night* v.i.388) – repeated in *Lear* III.ii.74 as 'He that has and a little tiny wit' – becomes all the more pointed when we bear Armin's voice in mind as well as his size.

60 *Cymbeline* IV.ii.105.
61 *Two Maids of More-clacke*, Garland edition, xii. 52–7; *Cymbeline* IV.i.2–9. I have modernized the spelling, but retained the original punctuation.

11 William Kemp and Harry Hunks

1 *Coleridge on Shakespeare*, ed. T. Hawkes (1969), p. 215.
2 From the book of the series: Ronald Harwood, *All the World's a Stage* (1984), p. 15.
3 Oscar Brownstein, 'Why didn't Burbage lease the Beargarden?' in *The First Public Playhouse*, ed. Herbert Berry (Montreal, 1979), p. 88.
4 Song from *Wits and Drollery*, in E. K. Chambers, *The Elizabethan Stage*, II (1923), p. 870 n.2.
5 G. L. Hosking, *The Life and Times of Edward Alleyn* (1952), p. 123.
6 Chambers, *Elizabethan Stage* , p. 471.
7 There survives a list of victims when a stand collapsed in 1583: Chambers, *Elizabethan Stage*, IV, p. 229; Davies, *Epigram 47*, in *Poems*, ed. R. Krueger (1975), p. 150.
8 Chambers, *Elizabethan Stage*, II, pp. 455–6.
9 A. de Laguna, *Materia Medica* (1570), translated in René Graziani, 'Sir Thomas Wyatt at a cockfight', *Review of English Studies* N.S. 27 (1976) 299–303.
10 *Bull, Bear and Horse* (1638): ed. Spenser Society (1876), p. 59.
11 George Wilson, *Commendation of Cocks and Cockfighting* (1607), cited in G. R. Scott, *The History of Cockfighting* (1957), p. 82.
12 *Bull, Bear and Horse*, pp. 16–17.
13 Cited in G. L. Hosking, *The Life and Times of Edward Alleyn* (1952), pp. 128–9.
14 See the extant playbill printed in Chambers, *Elizabethan Stage*, II, p. 458. Cf. the account by the Duke of Najera's secretary, in ibid. II, p. 454. In Taylor's volume, Jackanapes' horse appears 'lastly'. When Evelyn visited the Bear Garden in 1670, 'all ended with the Ape on horseback' – *Diary*, ed. E. S. de Beer (1955), III, p. 549.
15 Munday, *Downfall of Robert, Earl of Huntingdon*, in *Old Plays*, ed. Dodsley and Hazlitt, VIII (1874), 124. The Duke of Najera refers to a pony: Chambers, *Elizabethan Stage*, II, p. 454.
16 *Bull, Bear and Horse*, pp. 55–6.
17 *Robert Laneham's Letter*, ed. F. J. Furnivall (1907), pp. 16–17.
18 The list is included in a lease, reprinted in C. L. Kingswood, 'Paris Garden and the Bear Baiting', *Archaeologia* 70 (1920) 175.
19 Kingswood reprints Taylor's list in ibid. p. 166.

20 Jonson, *Epicoene* III.i.50; John Davies, *Epigram* 43, in *Poems*, ed. Krueger, p. 149.
21 The most interesting names are those of Faunte's bulls in 1600: 'Bevis' and 'Star of the West' betray an obvious association with chivalric romance. Letter cited in Hosking, *Life and Times of Edward Alleyn*, p. 128.
22 Dekker, *Work for Armourers* (1609), cited in Chambers, *Elizabethan Stage*, II, p. 457; Nashe, *Unfortunate Traveller* (1594), in *Works*, ed. R. B. McKerrow (1904–10), II, p. 310.
23 John Briley, 'Of stake and stage', *Shakespeare Survey* 8 (1955) 107.
24 Chambers, *Elizabethan Stage*, IV, p. 35.
25 *Winter's Tale* IV.iv.338; cf. Jonson, *Oberon*, p. 282.
26 v.i.144–56; cf. *3 Henry VI* v.vii.10–11.
27 2.v.i.54; 3.v.ii.17–19; 3.i.170 s.d.; 3.II.i.152.
28 G. Salgado, *Eyewitnesses of Shakespeare* (1975), p. 30; Chambers, *Elizabethan Stage*, IV, p. 249.
29 Stubbes, *Anatomie of Abuses* (1583), cited in Chambers, *Elizabethan Stage*, IV, p. 225.
30 See Oscar Brownstein, 'The popularity of baiting in England before 1600', *Educational Theatre Journal* 21 (1969) 237–50; cf. Glynne Wickham, *Early English Stages* (1959–81), II, part ii, p. 55.
31 *Early English Stages*, II, p. 45; Scott, *History of Cockfighting*, p. 93.
32 *Popular Culture in Early Modern Europe*, pp. 187, 202.
33 Welsford, *The Fool*, pp. 202, 327.
34 Turner, *The Ritual Process* (Chicago, 1969), p. 96.
35 Ibid. p. 110. For a treatment of the clown owing much to Turner's ideas, and to this passage in particular, see Edward Berry, *Shakespeare's Comic Rites* (1984), pp. 118 ff. Berry associates the clown/fool with the liminal stage in rites of passage, specifically with the transition of youth into adulthood and marriage.
36 *Ritual Process*, pp. 200–3.
37 Bakhtin, *Rabelais and His World*, trans. H. Iswolsky (Cambridge, Mass., 1968), pp. 8–9.
38 Ibid. pp. 22–3.
39 Ibid. pp. 316.
40 Geertz, *The Interpretation of Cultures* (1975), pp. 443–4.
41 Ibid. p. 448.
42 Ibid. p. 449.
43 *Mythologies*, trans. A. Lavers (1973), pp. 120–1.
44 John Barton, *Playing Shakespeare* (1984), p. 6.
45 Ibid. pp. 25ff., 70ff.
46 Gooch, *All Together Now: An Alternative View of Theatre and the Community* (1984), p. 79.
47 Søren Kierkegaard, *Repetition*, trans. W. Lowrie (New York, 1964), pp. 61–4.
48 Ibid. pp. 68–9.

Appendix: Armin's motley

1 'Tom Skelton – a seventeenth-century jester', *Shakespeare Survey* 13 (1960), 90–105.
2 *The Wonderful Year* (1603), Sig. A3v.
3 Norwich Sacr. Roll (1505), Caxton's Bible (1483) – cited in OED.
4 R. Wilson, *The Three Ladies of London* (1584), Sig. A2v.
5 *Pasquil's Mad-cap*, in *Works*, ed. A. B. Grosart (1966), p. 11.
6 *Moriomachia* (1613), Sig. B4 – cited in L. Hotson, *Shakespeare's Motley* (New York, 1952), p. 35.
7 *Epicoene* I.iv.41–3; and cf. *Every Man Out of His Humour* III.ii.29.
8 *I Would, I Would Not* (1614), p. 13.
9 E. Tietze-Conrat, *Dwarfs and Jesters in Art* (1957), p. 27; A. Belkin, 'Here's my coxcomb: some notes on the fool's dress', *Asspah*, Section C, 1 (1984), pp. 40–54.
10 Rowland Lockey's miniature of 1595–1600 in the Victoria and Albert Museum is based on an engraving by Holbein, reproduced in Enid Welsford, *The Fool* (1935), opposite p. 165. (The paperback reprint omits the illustrations.)
11 Hotson, *Shakespeare's Motley*, pp. 82–3.
12 A. Feuillerat, ed., *Documents Relating to the Revels at Court in the Time of Edward VI and Queen Mary* (Louvain, 1914), p. 49.
13 *Fool upon Fool* (1600), Sig. E3.
14 *Henslowe's Diary*, ed. R. A. Foakes and R. T. Rickert (1961), p. 318.
15 Cf. Fig. 5. Hotson (*Shakespeare's Motley*, p. 54) identifies the costume correctly. He is wrong, however, to deduce that there is something inherently child-like about the coat.
16 C. C. Stopes, *Shakespeare's Environment* (1918), p. 263.
17 Hotson, *Shakespeare's Motley*, p. 98.
18 *Fool upon Fool* (1600), Sig. A3–A3v. Hotson rests his case, that motley was a tweed of variegated threads, on this passage – *Shakespeare's Motley*, p. 8.
19 *Book of Christian Prayers*, or 'Queen Elizabeth's Prayer Book' (1578), 92v., 100v.
20 E. J. Nichol, 'Some notes on the history of the Betley window', *Journal of the English Folk Dance and Song Society* 7 (1952) 59–67. Francis Douce reproduces a selection of continental *marottes* in *Illustrations of Shakespeare* (1807).
21 Nashe, *Works*, ed. R. B. McKerrow (1904–10), I, p. 83.
22 Hotson, *Shakespeare's Motley*, p. 8 n. 1.
23 Marston, *Antonio's Revenge* (performed 1600/1), Revels edition, ed. W. R. Gair, IV.i.s.d.
24 *Patient Grissel* I.ii.304; cf. III.i.114 – in Dekker, *Dramatic Works*, I, ed. F. Bowers (1953).
25 *Jack of Newbury*: in *Works*, ed. F. O. Mann (1912), p. 40.
26 M. C. Linthicum, *Costume in the Drama of Shakespeare and his Contemporaries* (1936), p. 82.
27 In *Summers' Last Will and Testament* Summers jests: 'As sure as this

coat is too short for me': in Nashe, *Works*, ed. McKerrow, III, p. 294.

28 Nashe, *Works*, ed. McKerrow, III. p. 17.

29 *Shakespeare's Motley*, p. 8; *Fool upon Fool* (1600), Sig. A3v.

30 Linthicum, *Costume in the Drama*, 151; cf. *Measure for Measure* III.i.94–6, where it is said to be the function of a 'livery . . . to invest and cover in . . . guards', and *Albumazar*, in *Old Plays*, ed. Dodsley and Hazlitt, XI, p. 366, where 'guarded footmen' are mentioned.

31 Kyd, *Works*, ed. F. S. Boas (1901), II.i.243.

32 *Bartholomew Fair* II.vi.16.

33 The earliest extant edition is of 1676.

34 *Every Man In His Humour*, Quarto text, v.iii.360.

35 *Shakespeare's Motley*, pp. 77.

36 H. F. Lippincott, in *The Library* 30 (1975) 330–3, citing his edition of *Fool upon Fool* (Ann Arbor, 1972).

37 *Shakespeare's Motley*, p. 51.

38 *Gull's Hornbook*, in Dekker, *Non-Dramatic Works*, ed. A. B. Grosart, II (New York, 1963), p. 202.

39 Linthicum, *Costume in the Drama*, p. 208.

40 C. C. Stopes, *Shakespeare's Environment* (1918), p. 271.

41 *Wisdom of Doctor Doddypoll* (1600), Sig. F3.

42 *Shakespeare's Motley*, p. 5. Breton uses 'hood' to complete a rhyme in lieu of 'cap' in *Pasquil's Fools-cap* (1600), stanza 7; cf. also Lindsay, *Satire of the Three Estates*, ed. J. Kinsley (1954), pp. 194–5, where cap, hat and hood are synonymous.

43 *Unfortunate Traveller:* in Nashe, *Works*, ed. McKerrow, III, p. 300.

44 *Statutes of the Realm* I Jac.I.c.25.

45 See Enid Welsford, *The Fool* (1935), opposite p. 172. Jonson confirms the long coat in *Staple of News* III.ii.132. The illustrations to *A Pleasant History of . . . Will Summers* may owe something to Archie, since the text ends with a reference to 'late Archie'.

46 *A Relation of some Abuses*, cited in Hotson, *Shakespeare's Motley*, p. 64.

47 *Monsieur D'Olive* IV.ii.46 – in Chapman, *Comedies*, ed. A. Holaday (Urbana, Ill., 1970).

48 Day, *Isle of Gulls* (1606), Sig. H3v.

49 Mary's fool Jane had her head shaved: see Stopes, *Shakespeare's Environment*, p. 260; a natural fool with a shaven head, cockscomb, bell and *marotte* appears in Bodleian Library, Douce Portfolio 142, no. 284. In *c.* 1604 Marston introduced a bald fool into *The Fawn*: Dondolo, attendant fool to the Duke of Urbino.

50 Hotson, *The First Night of Twelfth Night* (1961), p. 169.

51 A French engraving collected in the Douce Portfolio 142, no. 468, entitled *Théâtre de la vie humaine* and dated to *c.* 1630, illustrates the classic gesture performed with the *marotte*.

52 In his preface to *Quips Upon Questions* (1600).

53 P. W. K. Stone, *The Textual History of King Lear* (1980), pp. 234, 126 and *passim*.

54 *The Division of the Kingdoms: Shakespeare's Two Versions of KING LEAR*, ed. G. Taylor and M. Warren (1983), p. 105.

Select bibliography

Place of publication is given only for books published outside the United Kingdom.

Fools and clowns: specialist materials

Arden, Heather. *Fool's Plays: A Study of Satire in the 'Sottie'*. 1980

Armin, Robert. *Collected Works*, ed. J. P. Feather. New York and London, 1972

    The History of the Two Maids of More-Clacke [1609], ed. A. S. Liddie. New York and London, 1979

Bald, R. C. 'Leicester's men in the Low Countries', *Review of English Studies* 19 (1943) 395–7

Baldwin, T. W. *The Organization and Personnel of the Shakespearean Company*. Princeton, 1927

Baskervill, C. R. *The Elizabethan Jig and Related Song Drama*. Chicago, 1929

Belkin, A. ' "Here's my coxcomb": some notes on the fool's dress', *Assaph*, Section C (Theatre Studies) no. 1 (1984) 40–54

Berry, Edward. *Shakespeare's Comic Rites*. 1984

Billington, Sandra. *A Social History of the Fool*. 1984

Black, James. '*Henry IV*: a world of figures here', in *Shakespeare: The Theatrical Dimension*, ed. Philip C. McGuire and David A. Samuelson, pp. 165–83. New York, 1979

Bradbrook, M. C. *Shakespeare the Craftsman*. 1969

Brissenden, Alan. *Shakespeare and the Dance*. 1981

Bryant, J. A. 'Shakespeare's Falstaff and the mantle of Dick Tarlton', *Studies in Philology* 51 (1954) 149–62

Busby, O. M. *Studies in the Development of the Fool in Elizabethan Drama*. 1923

Butler, Guy. 'Shakespeare and the two jesters', *Hebrew University Studies in Literature and the Arts* 11 (1983) 161–204

Cohn, Alfred. *Shakespeare in Germany*. 1865

Doran, John. *The History of Court Fools*. 1858

Douce, Francis. *Illustrations of Shakespeare*. 1807

    Portfolio of Prints [Bodleian Library], sections 133, 137, 142

Evans, G. L. 'Shakespeare's fools: the shadow and the substance of drama', *Stratford-Upon-Avon Studies* 14 (1972) 142–59

Feather, J. P. 'Robert Armin and the Chamberlain's Men', *Notes and Queries* 217 (1972) 448–50

Select bibliography

Felver, C. S. *Robert Armin, Shakespeare's Fool*. Kent, Ohio, 1961

Feuillerat, A., ed. *Documents Relating to the Revels at Court in the Time of King Edward VI and Queen Mary*. Louvain, 1914

Goldsmith, Robert H. *Wise Fools in Shakespeare*. 1955

Gray, A. K. 'Robert Armine, the Foole', *PMLA* 42 (1927) 673–85

Gray, H. D. 'The roles of William Kemp', *Modern Language Review* (1930) 261–73

Happé, Peter. '"The Vice" and the popular theatre, 1547–80', in *Poetry and Drama*, ed. A. Coleman and A. Hammond, pp. 13–31. 1981

Hazlitt, W. C., ed. *Shakespeare Jest Books*. 1864

Hinely, J. L. 'Comic scapegoats, and the Falstaff of *The Merry Wives of Windsor*', *Shakespeare Studies* 15 (1982) 37–54

Holmes, Martin. *Shakespeare and his Players* (1972)

Hotson, L. *Shakespeare's Motley* (1952)

Ives, E. W. 'Tom Skelton – a seventeenth-century jester', *Shakespeare Survey* 13 (1960) 90–105

Kelly, William. *Notices of the Drama in Leicester*. 1865

Kemp, William. *Kemps Nine Daies Wonder: Performed in a Daunce from London to Norwich*. 1600

Kerrigan, John. 'Revision, adaptation, and the fool in *King Lear*', in *The Division of the Kingdom: Shakespeare's Two Versions of KING LEAR*, ed. G. Taylor and M. Warren, pp. 195–245. 1983

Lippincott, H. F., ed. *Robert Armin's 'Fool upon Fool'*. Ann Arbor, 1972

Lowe, Barbara. 'Early records of the morris in England', *Journal of the Folk Dance and Song Society* 8 (1957) 61–80

Mares, F. H. 'The origin of the figure called "the Vice" in Tudor drama', *Huntington Library Quarterly* 22 (1958) 11–29

Melchiori, G. 'Peter, Balthasar, and Shakespeare's art of doubling', *Modern Language Review* 78 (1983) 777–92

Mithal, H. S. D. 'Mr Kemp called Don Gulielmo', *Notes and Queries* 205 (1960) 6–8

Newton, S. M. *Renaissance Theatre Costume*. 1975

Nungezer, E. *A Dictionary of Actors*. New Haven, 1929

O'Conor, N. J. *Godes Peace and the Queenes*. 1934

Scala, Flaminio. *Scenarios of the Commedia dell'Arte*, trans. and ed. H. F. Salerno. New York, 1967

Sisson, C. J. *Lost Plays of Shakespeare's Age*. 1936

Somerset, J. A. B. '"Fair is foul and foul is fair": Vice-comedy's development and theatrical effects', in *The Elizabethan Theatre* 5, ed. G. R. Hibbard, pp. 54–75. Ontario and London, 1975

Stopes, C. C. *Shakespeare's Environment*. 1914

Stubbes, P. *Anatomy of Abuses*, ed. F. J. Furnivall. 1877–82

[Summers, Will]. *A Pleasant History of the Life and Death of W. S.* 1676

Swain, Barbara. *Fools and Folly during the Middle Ages and the Renaissance*. New York, 1932

Tarlton, Richard. *Tarlton's Jests* [1638], ed. J. O. Halliwell. 1884

Tietze-Conrat, E. *Dwarfs and Jesters in Art*. 1956

Welsford, Enid. *The Fool: His Social and Literary History*. 1935

Select bibliography

Wiles, David. *The Early Plays of Robin Hood.* 1981
Willeford, William. *The Fool and his Sceptre: A Study in Clowns and Jesters and their Audience.* 1969
Williams, P. V. A., ed. *The Fool and the Trickster.* 1979
Wilson, John Dover. *The Fortunes of Falstaff.* 1943

General historical and theoretical works

Bakhtin, Mikhail. *Rabelais and his world*, trans. H. Iswolsky. Cambridge, Mass., 1968
Barber, C. L. *Shakespeare's Festive Comedy: A Study of Dramatic Form and its Relation to Social Custom.* Princeton, 1959
Barish, Jonas A. *Ben Jonson and the Language of Prose Comedy.* Cambridge, Mass., 1960
Barthes, Roland. *Critical Essays*, trans. R. Howard. Evanston, 1972
Mythologies, trans. A. Lavers. 1973
Barton, John. *Playing Shakespeare.* 1984
Bentley, G. E. *The Jacobean and Caroline Stage.* 7 vols. 1941–68
Bentley, G. E., ed. *The Seventeenth-Century Stage.* Chicago, 1968
Berger, T. L. and W. C. Bradford. *An Index of Characters in English Printed Drama to the Restoration.* Englewood, Colorado, 1975
Bernstein, Basil. *Classes, Codes and Control.* 1971
Bethell, S. L. *Shakespeare and the Popular Dramatic Tradition.* 1944
Bevington, David. *From 'Mankind' to Marlowe: Growth of Structure in the Popular Drama of Tudor England.* Cambridge, Mass., 1962
Bradbrook, M. C. *The Rise of the Common Player: A Study of Actor and Society in Shakespeare's England.* 1962
Brown, J. R. *Shakespeare's Plays in Performance.* 1966
Burke, Peter. *Popular Culture in Early Modern Europe.* 1978
Burns, Elizabeth. *Theatricality: A Study of Convention in the Theatre and in Social Life.* 1972
Chambers, E. K. *The Mediaeval Stage.* 2 vols. 1903
The Elizabethan Stage. 4 vols. 1923
Chillington, C. A. 'Playwrights at Work: Henslowe's, not Shakespeare's, Book of *Sir Thomas More*', *English Literary Renaissance* 10 (1980) 439–79
Coleridge, S. T. *Coleridge on Shakespeare*, ed. T. Hawkes. 1969
Cook, A. J. *Privileged Playgoers of Shakespeare's London.* Princeton, 1981
Corrigan, R., ed. *Comedy: Meaning and Form.* New York, 1965
Cunnington, C. W., and P. Cunnington. *Handbook of English Costume in the Sixteenth Century.* 1970
Davis, N. Z. *Society and Culture in Early Modern France.* 1975
Davison, Paul. *Popular Appeal in English Drama to 1850.* 1982
Deak, Frantisek. 'Structuralism in theatre: the Prague School contribution', *The Drama Review* 20 (T 72) (1976) 83–94
Duchartre, P. L. *The Italian Comedy.* New York, 1966

Select bibliography

Duvignaud, Jean. *Sociologie du théâtre: essai sur les ombres collectives.* Paris, 1965

Farnham, W. E. *The Shakespearean Grotesque.* 1971

Frye, Northrop. *Anatomy of Criticism.* Princeton, 1957

Geertz, Clifford. *The Interpretation of Cultures.* 1975

Goldstein, J. M., and P. E. McGhee. *The Psychology of Humor.* New York and London, 1972

Gooch, Steve. *All Together Now: An Alternative View of Theatre and the Community.* 1984

Goodlad, J. S. R. *A Sociology of Popular Drama.* 1971

Gurr, Andrew. *The Shakespearean Stage: 1574–1642.* 1970

Harbage, A. and S. Schoenbaum, eds. *Annals of English Drama 975–1700.* 1964

Holmes, Martin. *Shakespeare's Public.* 1960

Janicka, Irena. *The Popular Theatrical Tradition and Ben Jonson.* Lodz, 1972

Jonson, B. *Timber, or Discoveries.* 1641

Kierkegaard, Søren. *Repetitions: an Essay in Experimental Psychology,* trans. W. Lowrie. New York, 1964

Lamb, C. *The Last Essays of Elia.* 1929

Linthicum, M. C. *Costume in the Drama of Shakespeare and his Contemporaries.* 1936

Matejka, L. and I. R. Titunik. *Semiotics of Art: The Prague School Contribution.* Boston, 1976

Mayer, D. and K. Richards. *Western Popular Theatre.* 1977

Puttenham, George. *The Arte of English Poesie,* ed. G. D. Willcock and A. Walker. 1936

Rhodes, Neil. *Elizabethan Grotesque.* 1980

Salingar, L. G. 'Les Comédiens et leur public en Angleterre (1520–1640)', in *Dramaturgie et Société,* ed. Jean Jacquot. Paris, 1968

Shakespeare and the Tradition of Comedy. 1974

Sidney, Sir Philip. *Apology for Poetry,* ed. H. A. Needham. 1931

Spivack, B. *Shakespeare and the Allegory of Evil.* 1958

Sprague, A. C. *Shakespeare's Histories: Plays for the Stage.* 1964

Shakespeare and the Actors. Cambridge, Mass., 1944

Stone, P. W. K. *The Textual History of King Lear.* 1980

Thomas, Keith. 'The place of laughter in Tudor and Stuart England', *The Times Literary Supplement* 21 Jan. 1977, pp. 77–81.

Turner, Victor W. *The Ritual Process.* Chicago, 1969

Vickers, Brian. *The Artistry of Shakespeare's Prose.* 1968

Weimann, Robert. *Shakespeare and the Popular Tradition in the Theatre: Studies in the Social Dimension of Dramatic Form and Function.* Baltimore and London, 1978

'Society and the individual in Shakespeare's conception of character', *Shakespeare Survey* 34 (1981) 23–32

Wettach, A. ['Grock']. *Life's a Lark,* trans. M. Pemberton. 1931

Wickham, Glynne. *Early English Stages.* 3 vols. 1963–81

Select bibliography

Williams, Raymond. *Marxism and Literature.* 1977
  Culture. 1981
  Writing in Society. 1984
Wright, L. B. *Middle-Class Culture in Elizabethan England.* Chapel Hill,
  1935

Index

Index

Index

Index

Lyly, John 85

Macbeth 89, 151, 161, 164
Magnificence 3f, 150
Maidenhead Well Lost, A 186
Malcontent, The 145f, 148, 162, 185, 188ff
Mankind 1ff, 21, 176
Marlowe, Christopher 43
marotte 184, 191; see also fool: fool's bauble
may-game 4, 21f, 63, 81, 112
Measure for Measure 150, 161f
Merchant of Venice, The 7ff, 53, 75, 102, 111ff, 122, 185
merriment 33f
Merry Wives of Windsor, The 117, 132ff, 151
Midsummer Night's Dream, A 7, 54f, 70f, 74f, 112f, 178, 180
mime 50, 84, 95, 109
mimesis (and dramatic illusion) ixf, 10, 93, 96, 122, 126f, 131f, 136, 142, 154f, 157f, 179
mimicry 138, 147, 158
minstrel 19f, 69
Miseries of Enforced Marriage, The 151
misrule see Lord of Misrule
monologue 8, 60, 67, 101, 107ff, 119, 130ff, 160f
Monsieur D'Olive 189
morris dance 5, 22, 24ff, 44f, 48, 111, 162f, 184
motley 54, 59, 149f, 155, 182ff; see also fool: fool's coat
Mucedorus 68, 170
Much Ado About Nothing 55, 75f, 104f, 112f, 115, 144
Munday, Antony 64, 67, 80
Mundus et Infans 3, 122
mystery plays ix, 5, 99

Nashe, Thomas 34, 89, 111, 136, 170, 184
neo-classicism ixf, 4, 8, 40, 43, 62f, 75, 96, 154f, 157, 165
Nobody and Somebody 40, 77

Oberon 170
Old Fortunatus 88, 103ff, 114
Orlando Furioso 70
Othello 151, 162, 171

Pallant, Robert 38, 117
Patient Grissell 104ff, 111, 184
phallic emblems 84, 86, 111, 122, 133f, 176, 190f
Phillips, Augustine 41, 53
'Pickleherring' 52, 196n.35
plot structure 63, 73, 101ff, 129, 161ff; see also closure
Prince Charles's company 143
Promos and Cassandra 62
puritanism 171

Queen's Men (Queen Elizabeth) 11, 22, 104, 106; for Queen Anne's company, see Worcester's Men

Red Bull playhouse 40, 51, 66f, 69
Renegado, The 67
reported texts 70, 79, 83, 117
Richard II 39, 57, 151
Robins, William 67
role, relation of actor to 2, 9, 16, 29, 59, 70, 88, 98, 113, 126ff, 152, 158, 165, 173, 179
Romeo and Juliet 39, 77, 83ff, 104f, 113
Rose playhouse 39, 183
Rowland 38, 48ff, 104, 120
Rowland's Godson 50f
Rowlands, Samuel 71, 104
Royal King and Loyal Subject, The 40, 78f, 105f, 111ff, 178

scribe 67, 73, 156
serving-man: role taken by clown viii, 3, 7, 10, 81, 84ff, 121, 151, 185
Seven Deadly Sins, The 33
Shakespeare, William: aesthetic aspirations ix, 57; working methods 84ff; character construction 70f, 74f, 92f; stage directions and speech-prefixes

222

Index

67ff, 74ff, 90ff, 118, 145; not
Hand 'D' 80; relations with
Kemp 25, 34ff, 146; relations
with Armin 136, 140
Shoemaker's Holiday, The 104ff,
111ff
Sidney, Philip x, 31, 62, 129
signs x, 8, 122f, 125f, 153, 170,
172, 175f, 177f, 191
Singer, John 11, 41, 64, 71, 103ff
Singing Simpkin 51f, 102, 104, 120
Sir John Oldcastle 40, 134f,
202n.10
Sir Thomas More 67, 80f, 112
Sir Thomas Wyatt 39, 79f, 113
Soliman and Perseda 185
Somers, William 21, 140, 183ff,
187
stage: use of downstage position
102, 106, 131, 174
stage directions *see* Shakespeare:
stage directions
Strange's Men 33f
Summer Lord *see* Lord of Misrule

Tamar Cam 64, 103, 113
Taming of a Shrew, The 69
Taming of the Shrew, The 74
Tarlton, Richard viii, 11ff, 57, 62,
71, 102, 119, 129, 138f, 151
Tarlton's Jests 11ff, 138, 144
Tempest, The 155, 159, 161f
themes, giving of by the audience
14, 16, 138f, 155
Thomas Lord Cromwell 76f, 104ff,
107ff, 112
Three Ladies of London, The 3, 22,
182
Timon 63
Timon of Athens 102, 155
Titus Andronicus 34, 74, 151

tragedy *see* genre
Trial of Treasure 68
Troilus and Cressida 102, 145,
147f
Turner, Victor 173ff
Twelfth Night 56, 145, 147f, 156,
162
Two Angry Women of Abingdon
114, 202n.10
Two Gentlemen of Verona, The 54,
73f, 102, 104f, 111ff, 148
Two Maids of More-clacke, The
137, 140ff, 160, 183

Valiant Welshman, The 143, 150
verisimilitude *see* mimesis, neo-
classicism
Vice 1ff, 22ff, 102, 158; Vice's
dagger 86, 122
Volpone 150, 155, 161

Webster, John 80
Wedding, The 67
Weimann, Robert 102, 165
Welsford, Enid 173
Whetstone, George 62
Whitefriars' playhouse 142f
Wickham, Glynne 3, 15
Wilson, John Dover 89, 117, 127
Wilson, Robert 22
Winter's Tale 156f, 170
Wit and Science 9
Wits, The 121
Woman Killed with Kindness, A
39ff, 81f, 102f, 105, 106f, 112
Worcester's Men (subsequently
Queen's Men) 38ff, 66, 69, 79,
117, 134

Youth 3